T0195938

CHRONICLES OF
South Africa

A Psychohistorical Analytic Assessment
of a Traumatized Nation

MOIKWATLHAI BENJAMIN SEITISHO

authorHOUSE®

AuthorHouse™ UK
1663 Liberty Drive
Bloomington, IN 47403 USA
www.authorhouse.co.uk
Phone: 0800 047 8203 (Domestic TFN)
*   +44 1908 723714 (International)*

Published by AuthorHouse 07/31/2019

ISBN: 978-1-7283-9097-0 (sc)
ISBN: 978-1-7283-9096-3 (e)

The Road to Freedom, is via the Cross …
—Thandazani Ma-Afrika!

For people to RECONCILE, the truth has to
be TOLD, spoken and shared …
—Moikwatlhai Benjamin Seitisho

For my paternal and maternal grandparents,
South Africans of all hues; trauma, not hatred,
turned the tide against you from being true agents
of a healing transformation.

Also dedicated to the memory of
Dr Frederik Van Zyl Slabbert (2 March 1940–14 May 2010),
Leader of the Progressive Federal Party 1979–1986,
A Stellenbosch University product that denounced apartheid.
Dr Slabbert, you are enshrined in the heart and spirit of the
new South Africa you tirelessly and selflessly fought for.

Tribute to Mother
Mrs. Elizabeth Majoalane Seitisho
10 October 1924–18 July 2015

TRIBUTE TO MY MOTHER

Dear mother: I will forever call to mind our days of youth. Through our teens and through our adolescence… stupid years of youth! Which, in retrospect, you wisely and motherly guided and counseled – and now I know just how much you cared and how deeply indebted I am to you.

I will forever cherish your affections which remain indelibly engraved in my heart and my soul… When I faltered you were always by my side; when I fell down you lovingly picked me up.

How can I forget the inspiring telegram you sent us when Fort Hare University flared up during the June 16 1976 Soweto Riots?

Your guiding wisdom, encouragement and counsel in one statement will forever ring in my mind. Like Biblical Ruth you stood firm by your beliefs. You hung tenaciously to what you believed to be true; above all you respected the TRUTH and you taught me to stand by it.

It is this that defines your character and personality. You taught me to put the interests of others above mine; which is the essence of leadership. I always share what you taught me with the youth as you firmly taught us as children in the John Wesleyan Methodist Catechism Class that "Modimo ke Moya – Modimo o hohle" (God is Wind – God is everywhere). Your FAITH made me STRONG and instilled in me a sense of Godliness and doing to others as I would them do unto me.

I am eternally grateful for your life. People like you stay forever enshrined in our hearts. They stay there all the time...

Dear mother, let me lovingly wrap you in my warm and tender love...

I LOVE YOU MOTHER – I ALWAYS HAVE...

Your loving son Moikwatlhai Benjamin Joseph Webb Seitisho

Contents

Preface

If you want to build a nation, look at what those who destroyed did to undo it for an all-inclusive development. Dr Malan was a prophet of Afrikaner national growth, and Dr Verwoerd was a brilliant psychologist recognized by American universities but a bad apple for South Africa. His vision was a good one but should be made all-inclusive to build a new South African nation. But we should all foreswear the ANC's and EFF's corruption and despise their racial hatred by resisting irresponsible land redistribution at every turn. It will harm those it purports to save and make us food for vultures. Broad-Based Black Economic Empowerment is a form of reverse racism that favours very few connected blacks who are fronts for those in power, to bleed the national treasury dry. We now have to pay it back in petrol price hikes. Is this governance? Men of conscience will always emerge and speak out to put South Africa on a path of righteousness under one flag, one nation, and one God. Reliving a painful past is counterproductive. It must be used to chart a way towards a true, constructive, and pragmatic reconciliation directed by the human conscience.

A nation without a conscience is a dead nation. As you go through this book, do so with an open mind and let your conscience speak to you as you listen to that silent but vocal voice of reason to face the truth without flinching.

This book chronicles some major events in South Africa and may repeat some to show how they shaped our history as a people. Simply defining history as a story of the human race's past, the book seeks to analyse a history that is by no means rosy. With the tragedy of the holocaust in mind, the human past is a record of a friction triggered by economics which influenced racial attitudes, psychosocial stereotypes, and racial prejudices.

Some events, like the 1976 Soweto riots, attracted international attention and sympathy, and out of them evolved a generation of black people that developed racial hatred. Some, like Tsietsi Mashinini, were ejected out of the country, and the offshoots of a politicized youth developed from Steve Biko's Black Consciousness Movement. Today their fatherly leaders are Musibudi Mangena and Thami Ka Plaatje of the Azanian People's Organization (AZAPO) generation. Some went into the diaspora in the United States, Canada, and the United Kingdom. Those who remained inside the country developed a black national consciousness that stood them alone in the wilderness of interracial friction that bled South Africa literally and figuratively. The death sentence claimed black lives, the most depressing instance being that of Solomon Mahlangu, who defied the apartheid state with the words that reverberated throughout the Black Consciousness Movement. He faced the gallows saying his blood would water the tree of liberty. He became an instant hero that gave the struggle for liberation a fierce momentum, with Chris Hani at the helm. A school in Tanzania immortalized Solomon Mahlangu's nationalist heroism.

The South African past evolved out of the need for economic activity that resulted in the creation of a halfway station established to facilitate trade between the west and the east. The result was a Dutch settlement in 1652 whose aim was focused on expanding this mission. When the Napoleonic wars broke out, they introduced Britain in South Africa. The British shaped our history, and missionary activity introduced the Bible into the sociocultural life of South African black tribes. This holy book had a major influence in changing the Africans' lifestyles and life view. It introduced Christian principles and a new value system. It challenged some Africans' traditional practices, such as marriage. The Bible, small as it is, shook the British conscience into questioning some of its practices and the way it related to African tribes. Dr David Livingstone, a modern St Luke medical doctor evangelist, gave Christianity a new nuance in Africa. He braved the barbarous African tribes and became a thorn in the flesh of British colonial policy and pricked its conscience. He preached and taught the gospel to African tribes and changed them to Christ, affecting British colonial policy and practice tremendously in the process. He became a walking conscience that gave colonialism new spectacles in its dealings with African tribes. His benevolence ultimately resulted in the emancipation of slaves.

However, the British presence in South Africa was to affect developments positively. Out of biblical teachings, the concept of freedom was born, and men and women were freed from the debasing practice of slavery. The Dutch, who had evolved into a new African race called Afrikaners or Afrikanders, did not take kindly to the freedom of their slaves that put their subjects on a racially equal footing with them. It had an adverse effect on their socioeconomic practices. The result was the Great Trek of 1834–1837 in groups under various leaders. This event produced Afrikaner leaders whose names lived long after them in towns, streets, and buildings names. Andries Pretorius Street from the N1 in Bloemfontein was a shining example of such memorials but was changed to Raymond Mhlaba Street by the government after the 1994 revolution. Other memorials in towns across the country are still in place in towns like Wepner named after Louw Wepner and Hobhouse after Emile Hobhouse who nursed Afrikaners during the horrific Anglo Boer War of 1899.

The Great Trek, regarded as a central event in the history of South Africa, gave the Afrikaners a national identity that developed and evolved into "die mense" (the people) along the lines of the biblical children of Israel in Egypt. The South African national anthem, a patriotic nationalist expression, emanates from this central event. The frontier wars between the British and the Amaxhosa over land and the Great Trek as well, resulted in bloody conflicts with native tribes in the hinterland.

The Afrikaners had left the Cape colony in a huff, moving away from the British government's liberal dictatorship so they could govern themselves to maintain proper relations between masters (Afrikaners) and servants (African people), free of British interference. This in itself was a new concept of Afrikaner freedom which evolved into racial segregation, with land acquisition being central. Out of this, apartheid policy was born in 1948 when an academic leadership took over. This new academic perspective used a philosophy born out of Stellenbosch University to evolve new racial policies introduced by Dr Malan after winning the elections using apartheid in electioneering to bring an awareness of the threat Africans posed to Afrikaner minority interests. To develop these interests, the Afrikaners denied other races theirs and subjugated them under racial legislation that denied them political rights and debased their humanity. Their quest for land resulted in the taking of African tribes' land, and present-day Lesotho lost vast tracts of land as a result. Fearing a total loss of independence and Afrikaner subjugation, King Moshoeshoe led Lesotho towards becoming a British protectorate. An Afrikaner politics shaped along racial lines evolved, and at the centre was the hunger and struggle for land.

This struggle was to escalate and introduce policies that were to shape the history of South Africa. Land became a central factor and today has become a thorny issue threatening interracial relations. Africans today feel that the freedom that gave Afrikaners land by fair or foul means, depending on one's racial perceptions, delivered only political freedom, whilst still resulting in economic enslavement. Freedom is now defined by economic activity in which the black youth, under rather questionable leaderships, seek land ownership. The 2019 general elections in South Africa have thrust land into the forefront of political debates, and by and large, it is a major contentious issue which should be closely and sensitively watched.

South Africa is the last hope for Africans continentally, and this is reflected in the African peoples' diaspora down south to real freedom denied in their countries of origin. It is also the last hope of South Africans of all hues because, indeed, there is no further expansion they can run to and require a reasonable negotiated settlement to resolve something that could become racially explosive. South Africa has also become home to several international humans who also form part of the equation.

This new struggle for land by South Africans has resulted in this book. It is a struggle that justifies the economic freedom the Afrikaners attained from the brutish British yoke which they in turn imposed on Africans in their native land—South Africa. It is a cyclic historical incident that needs redress in a sensitive, sympathetic way. Conversely, it has the potential to flare out of total control if not sensitized by government.

The centrality of the Mfecane in African history is also a result of the struggle for land acquisition. When the African diaspora took place from the African Great Lakes, it resulted in a settlement in Natal that flared into skirmishes, clashes, and conflicts over land. Shaka Zulu emerged as a leader that literally spearheaded these explosive intermittent wars. When these tribes in Natal grew in number, land became an important commodity, and other tribes had to flee Shaka's wrath as he emerged strong and mighty. It is out of this event that heroes of the period emerged—and villains as well. Whilst Mzilikazi emerged as a villain, Moshoeshoe emerged as a hero that saved the Basotho from Shaka's wrath through diplomatic means, as he believed that if one is not strong, he should be wise. He is a leader known for very wise statements, such as "Even if a dog is yours, when you tread on it, it will bite you", meaning that his peaceful nature did not make him timid. He was a man of peace, but not at any price. The Basotho pride themselves on the fact that that their stronghold, Thaba Bosiu (a mountain stronghold), was never mounted in war. Mzilikazi also fled Shaka's wrath, attacking other tribes in his wake. He settled in what is Zimbabwe today, where his followers are known as the Ndebele.

The struggle for land and its acquisition resulted in present-day settlements in Southern Africa, which dispossessed the Khoisan, who are the true owners of this land. They were pastoralists who did not have a fixed place of abode and remained in search of greener pastures for their flocks. These groups were outnumbered and dispossessed of their land by the marauding tribes that occupied land in a horseshoe-shaped pattern throughout Southern Africa. Modern events that followed after the arrival of the white man took this struggle for land forward, and gave it a new definition, meaning and direction.

This book analytically chronicles this past in a constructive way in the face of an issue that may either break or make South Africans as a nation. Land is a vital resource for development and structural growth because no man can develop from space. Plants cannot grow from space. They need the soil, and therefore land, for nurturing and growth.

Our mainstay is agriculture. South African farmers who have left our shores have been recognized in their new-found lands for their good nose for agriculture. They have helped stabilize food production and security in their new countries. They have carried forward a practice that has always been based on a close relationship that exists between economic development and the size of the share of agriculture in national income and employment creation. Agricultural economists believe that the fewer the farmers and farm workers in comparison with those engaged in other sectors of our economy, and the smaller the share of agriculture in national income (gross domestic product), the more advanced the economy is likely to be.

This analysis was made in the 1980s but holds true today. A simple example is the number of taxis in the taxi industry today and the daily takings earned by taxi owners. This industry used to make its owners wealthy, but today their income is at its lowest, as we see most local taxis going around with very few passengers. The industry is also plagued by unregistered pirate taxis. This simple example explains the bigger land issue picture to throw light on what could happen if we were to suddenly have 100,000 farmers, which would make farms much smaller and affect production adversely. We presently have about 55,000 farmers, and these are succeeding in keeping granaries full and food prices reasonable despite fuel increases. It thus makes sense that emerging farmers need at least 3,000 hectares to be productively serviced by the Vrystaat Koporasie Beperking (VKB) in Maluti-a-Phofung Local Municipality.

This means the land issue in our country should be stealthily and very carefully addressed, and that it should not be addressed through emotions and greed. Land policies should keep the theory of farm production in mind to ensure that the land issue is addressed peacefully and sensitively. Love for the soil alone does not determine success in agricultural practice, as love for children does in teaching. In agriculture people must know what they are doing to keep land scientifically maintained for maximum production to keep silos and granaries full for the nation to be well fed. We must also keep in mind that after an irresponsible implementation of a now discredited land policy in Zimbabwe, South Africa is the sole breadbasket of Southern Africa. Our trucks go beyond our borders to feed fellow Africans.

It is for this reason and this reason alone that this book sensitively reacts to land expropriation without compensation in South Africa. Letters to various media houses on the subject have been written to address this matter. This work chronicles past and current incidents for an intervention that may help us apply our minds unemotionally on the land issue. The hard hitting material is by a writer that has taught history over the years, noting that history is a broad subject. It is not only a development of past human frictions but is also a story of cultural, social, and political developments, of course shaped by economics. Having looked through aspects of economic history in South Africa and how they affected political developments, I have found that economic activity through the discovery of diamonds and gold precipitated the outbreak of the Anglo-Boer War of 1899–1902. This subject will be dealt with in much more detail later.

Everything that has happened in the world is a result of human economic activity. The changes of governments have been effected by economic issues. The United States of America grew to become what it is out of a united human effort of making her a citadel of democracy. President Franklin Delano Roosevelt felt the need to dream a New Deal that saved capitalism from socialism in a clash of an international ideological conflict that divided the world into two hostile camps, the East and the West. England, a known island country having on its lap Ireland, which it seems to lovingly toss up and down like a baby, became a power to reckon with because of economic activity. She ruled the waves and controlled the world remotely—so much so that her language has become a major international instrument of communication. Unifications and revolutions were steered by economic activity, and this has transcended time to present-day South Africa and Namibia, with lessons to draw from Zimbabwe. Her overreactions to the Lancaster House Settlement debacle have destroyed a once thriving economy. History, so to speak, is a result of economic issues, and land is the major causal factor of historical conflicts. Our leaders in present-day South Africa must take a leaf from history to avoid hostile confrontations. If you want to test the United States, interfere with her oil suppliers that feed the thirsty industries that are sustaining her economy and her people.

Ideas herein expressed are the author's own. They are shaped by an analytic application of how the history he taught has power and influence on the current raging land policy debates on land expropriation without compensation. Debate on this issue and its interpretation and ultimate implementation should be informed by well-considered facts and not populist rhetoric that will destroy what has taken years of hard scientific work to build. The current agricultural yields revealed in the public domain should inform politicians and emerging farmers that the land issue must be sensitized. Errors cannot be tolerated. We cannot afford errors of any size or nature, and the major error we should avoid as we do a plague is embracing populist views. They will plunge the postrevolution state and nation down an economic precipice and, possibly, into hot conflict.

After the Zimbabwean experience, there can be no room for errors caused by populist rhetoric and a misdirected so-called revolutionary nationalist patriotism. Considerate, well-thought-out nationalism should be our guiding light for the sake of the love of our land. Patriots should be driven by a spirit of nationalism to jealously guard against the destruction of a legacy bequeathed by our forebears, both black and white. It would be an error of alarming proportions for the people of South Africa, and indeed neighbouring countries after the ominous destruction of the Zimbabwean economy, not to heed a national conscience of setting aside political differences. We need to preserve our common legacy for our common posterity. We cannot afford to err over this. We must, as a people seeking solutions to our challenges, relate arguments herein made with what appears in the media in all its forms, to apply our minds without prejudice. Prejudiced views based on idealism must give way to practical pragmatic views that will save man from himself and, I dare say, his stupid pride. Pride is always followed by a fall and is a result of the South African economy today as the rand reacts to markets shaken by political developments. Each time the land issue is tackled, markets react inappropriately. Let us watch this with a rising sense of realism and not idealism. It is idealistic to claim the land using parliamentary majority representations, but it is not a pragmatic realism to claim and take land by numbers in Parliament simply to undo the 1913 Land Act. We need to feed the newly defined politically charged ethnographic concept of "die mense" (people) of South Africa. We must not let the dark, ominous clouds of our racial past destroy what it took the Land Bank one hundred years plus to develop.

As Dr Martin Luther King Jr. once stoically and philosophically advised, we should not allow emotions to drown us together as fools. If we allow populist rhetoric to reign supreme in our minds, it will become raging floods that will drown us. In the absence of Noah's ark, we only have one another to run towards and remake this beautiful land as people of South Africa with a common heritage—one beautiful, rich land. Let us not be irresponsible enough to let bigotry destroy our common Canaan, which is oozing with milk and honey.

Dealt with carefully, the land issue will help address poverty and its alleviation. Suffice to add that it is needless to say a reckless application of land policy will have sad and very negative side effects on economic development. We must always keep in mind that agricultural output can be maximized only if farmers are few and farmworkers are also few; to add to this, farmers must have a scientific knowledge of what they are doing. In agricultural practice, there shall always be landowners and land workers. Those who own the land should be those who have the skill to keep it productive for food security. Those who work it shall be those who live by menial labour—not because they are debased but because of their limited scientific skills. Giving a person land for the sake of land distribution is counterrevolutionary. However, giving him land because he has the scientific skill to keep it productive and to service his loans to help others grow their skills and farm production is pro-revolutionary.

You are invited to take a journey through this book, applying your mind to make your own impressions, free of stereotypes, attitudes, and racial prejudice, not to mention emotional racial pride and, I dare repeat, "stupid pride" as expressed in revolutionary rhetoric. Be a realist and journey through this book and make your own informed impressions for better informed analytic judgments as you read through the media or listen and view via electronic media. The past hundred years plus of agricultural output since the Land Bank was established can produce the next hundred years plus of emerging farmers nurtured by experienced and knowledgeable South African farmers with a proven track record to impart agricultural skills practices to service Land Bank loans that should be used to develop emerging farmers. The emerging farmer should allow himself the luxury of being accompanied in the pursuit of commercial farming by experienced men who have been engaged in the practice of agriculture for over one hundred years. Should I venture into farming, this would be my guiding light.

Together we must stand, because divided we shall fall.

Prologue

The title of this book is derived from the well-known book of Chronicles in the Bible. The Chronicles are a repetition of the books of 1 and 2 Kings, with the writer talking about what the kings of Israel did to know and experience the wrath of God. To chronicle is to write about events in the order in which they happened and to explain how those events influenced a course of history. Major South African events had an impact in shaping the history of South Africans, including the establishment of a halfway station by the Dutch, the banishing of slavery, the Great Trek, and incidents inside the country resulting in the British policy of encirclement, leaving the shadow of the British lion overshadowing Afrikaners' self-governance at every turn. This policy discouraged direct foreign links with them, which would threaten British interests.

Major South African events are the arrival of the Dutch for a halfway station at the Cape in 1652, the arrival of the British for strategic reasons when the Napoleonic Wars broke out, the Great Trek of 1834–1837, the establishment of the Boer Republics and their relations with Africans, missionary activity, the discovery of gemstones, the South African War (1899–1902), events leading to and the establishment of the Union of South Africa in 1910 resulting from the South Africa Act, the formation of the South African Native National Congress (later renamed the African National Congress) in 1912, the Land Act of 1913, and developments of friction between Afrikaner nationalism and British imperialism, resulting in Smuts and Botha being seen as Britain's puppet. Also important are the developments towards a singular pursuance of the policy of apartheid that planted a desire for freedom among educated African nationals along the lines of the intelligentsia that opened ordinary citizens' eyes in France, precipitating the French Revolution, during which the Bastille was stormed.

Some of these incidents are herein chronicled to address the need for a reconciling nation to find substantiated practical reason to do so. It is a fact that, despite its policy, the Afrikaner government left a thriving economy and a developing infrastructure. For one hundred years the Land Bank was instrumental in turning the development of the Afrikaner nation around and made farming a tertiary industry contributing not only to food security but also to a gross domestic product that was invested in the development of South Africa. This is something that Harold Macmillan did not fail to mention in the South African Parliament in his "Winds of Change" speech during a tour of Africa.

The Afrikaners left a developing education system and a thriving developing economy, and when Nelson Mandela took over in 1994, an attempt was made to maintain this rhythm, but too many people were left outside the main economic stream that the media became vocal about. The media noted that there was change in South Africa, but this favoured a selected few. One such change was the now discredited Broad-Based Black Economic Empowerment policy that favoured the few black South Africans who failed to contribute to the economic mainstream by creating employment. Such families employed their own children and family members, and it is this that stymied economic growth. Such families became filthy rich and reduced their tax liability by buying fleets of imported vehicles, helicopters, and private jets that can normally be afforded only by international football stars like Ronaldo, Messi, and many other such gifted wizards.

What raises the people's ire is that twenty-five years after Nelson Mandela's release from prison on 11 February 1990, the majority of South Africans are still poor. Even Nelson Mandela's vision of a free, democratic South Africa in which all have equal opportunities for development and self-expression is now challenged as a sham. Apartheid is no more. Millions of South Africans get their basic water needs satisfied for free, whilst others still drink from rivers with animals. The number of households with electricity has sharply shot up, resulting in a load that is affecting economic growth and therefore job creation. The banking system has expanded to embrace the black middle class. However, most of these improvements are cosmetic. The wealth that is created is not circulating among those once marginalized, and this causes debilitating poverty.

In 2006 the shelved South African land issue has to be taken off the shelves and tabled for discussion after the failed willing-seller, willing-buyer principle, which has slowed down land reform and taken it off the rails.

Thoughts about the expropriation of land were bandied about by President Thabo Mbeki during his term in office and in a state of the nation address in February 2010, when he strongly criticized the discredited willing-seller, willing-buyer principle and turned towards expropriation of land, 84 per cent of which was still in white hands—55,000 farmers, to be exact!

Frustrations with the Lancaster House Settlement on land expropriation in Zimbabwe resulted in very tragic dire consequences of squeezing and throttling the Zimbabwean economy. Zimbabwe has now provided a mirror of land reform in both South Africa and Namibia. This means treading very lightly on the matter of land reform is necessary, because a reckless policy implementation will have the direst consequences of destroying an economy capable of feeding, as Egypt did with lands surrounding it during the seven very lean years, after the seven very fat years. South Africa today is the Egypt of those years, and any error in addressing poverty, starvation, and malnutrition will be regretted when vultures feed on collapsing and dying human flesh. This has happened in most African countries and elsewhere in the world, but it can be avoided if we can open our eyes and minds to the lessons history is giving us.

In our municipality, Maluti-a-Phofung, an agricultural cooperative giant exists that has found answers to the debate on land development and land issues. As politicians talk, through its practices, especially the Biliemielie event, this cooperative, the Vrystaat Koporasie Beperking, is letting action be the answer by addressing change for all who care for the land. This addresses what the media has been questioning over the years— that there is change in South Africa, but for whom? No doubt none want change for the worse, but all want change for the better; hence the need not to undo what it took the Land Bank one hundred years to build. This is reflected in the success story the Vrystaat Koporasie Beperking (VKB) has built over the same period; it is still going strong for the love of the land in its Vision 2020 emerging farmers' business policy project. This in turn is reflected in the greening of previously unproductive land in the hands of emerging farmers between Qwaqwa and Kestel and Reitz in the Free State, which had been on an unproductive slide before VKB's interventions. Our major problems in South African policies are talks that do not translate into action as the VKB does. If we can address this, answers can be found and implemented to address the land issue in a constructive, sensitive way.

State of the nation addresses have been made to note things we can see, but these have not translated into anything, and they have all become myths. State of the provinces addresses have also been made, as have state of the municipality addresses. These addresses should have resulted in action in areas in which the state of the nation and state of the province addresses did not result in implementation or action. Municipal budgets did not take into account the state of the nation and state of the province addresses, but should they have done so, land could have been scientifically and productively used. It is this error that future government administrations must address for continuity. Municipal councillors and mayors must be the eyes and ears of provincial administrations to inform national government policies. Emerging academics in their masters and PhD studies are addressing problems faced by people in municipalities, and it is these people that must inform municipalities to inform the nine provinces and the national government.

Constitutionally, South African presidents have a five-year term which can be extended into another and final term, and for this constitutional practice to bring about progressive change, outgoing administrations must inform incoming ones in relay fashion to win the race of development. Since 1994, South Africa has seen one African National Congress administration undoing the other in a trial-and-error way that has succeeded only in destroying the economy. South African presidents until now have not been able to perpetuate previous presidents' programmes, similar to the way the Obama administration carried over the Bush Jr administration's conflict when Obama dispatched US soldiers to continue a war in Afghanistan he promised to end. In South Africa there has been a failed continuation of policy from one president to the next, and trial-and-error experimentation has had a very negative effect on economic development. The land issue today is centrally positioned to address the failed economic rehabilitation of the South African economy after apartheid. Care and diligent effort must guide the process, because we cannot afford to fail; we cannot afford to negligently and greedily undo what has been blamed on apartheid since 1994, even in instances in which the current post-apartheid government must finger itself for corrections. We must remember that denials leave a wound festering, but agreement is followed by addressing the causal factors, which can bring about a new lease on life. Reconciling the nation is the only viable solution to the land debacle, and such reconciliation must be genuine but realistic. The South African past is built on a negative racism, and this must be addressed to produce a nation that can bury the hatchet and work together. This is the only solution, and there is no other!

As a nation, we must all firmly stand against a chaotic reclaiming of land, and this should be our guiding light, with any party not respecting this being dealt with in the strongest of terms to save the nation from itself. We must look at our ecotourism and imagine an Africa without its prized fauna and flora—an Africa that is capable of poaching its own land, driven by greed and inability to plan, lack of unemotional discussion, and a firm implementation of land policy. Africa must deal with corruption culprits equally firmly and, if need be, even lose an election based on the right decisions, because elections are won and lost on good policies and healthy, well-defined election manifesto statements. However, a good and realistic manifesto can win hearts. If based on populist rhetoric, it will definitely result in the grinding of teeth in a perpetually failing economy.

Let this be food for thought as discussions on land expropriation without compensation rage on going into the 2019 elections cycle and beyond, based on political sobriety and not an intoxicating wine of populist rhetoric. Sobriety will lead voters to decry measures and decisions taken; intoxication by rhetoric will lead to a hangover of frustrations and regret. After a drinking spree, natural alcohol is dispersed with soft drinks, but the alcohol of derogatory populist statements aimed at appealing to the masses to garner votes will take years to get rid of. Universities will produce unemployable graduates. Our youth, especially, should be careful not to be swept off their feet and engulfed by obviously false promises that promote the selective and now racist Broad-Based Black Economic Empowerment policy. South Africa belongs to all who live in it. The fatherly statesman Nelson Rholihlahla Mandela advised that if the African National Congress fails the people, then the people should do to it what they did to the apartheid government. Maybe that hour has come. The mistakes of trial and error since 1994 should now be effectively addressed by a hung Parliament in a coalition government to save South Africa from herself. History over the twenty-five years since 1994 has proved that the ANC cannot govern alone with political honesty and integrity.

What takes five years to destroy may take years to change before it can be pointed in the right direction for correction. We need to plan capacity building through a coalition government rather than a one-party government—especially one led by the ANC. After twenty-five years, there is nothing to show but a debilitating, corruption-riddled economic stagnation that is taking the country and its people nowhere and has earned it junk status with the International Monetary Fund.

Capacity planning refers to building human capital, which requires skills. Such skills can be acquired only through educative teaching and learning. This is the only way of making certain that the nation develops. Looking at the apartheid development strategy based on nation building, we see that schools were built, and so were universities. The apartheid government used the science of teaching to inculcate skills, and children were subjected to intellectual tests that helped channel them towards certain sciences. Development under apartheid was aimed at skills development, and it paid dividends and resulted in the development of human capital. There is currently a need to focus on this strategy of developing human capital to help create self-sustaining South Africa–oriented economic development programmes. South Africans must learn that not everything done and practised by apartheid governance was bad. Its only bad streak was racism. If the same development strategy can be turned around to address national challenges, it can be the answer we are looking for. Every cent the apartheid government generated and budgeted for development went into national and not personal coffers. Theft from the national treasury to fund the strengthening of apartheid was dealt with in the strongest, most severe terms, and the B. J. Vorster example is the best that can be cited.

Today's South African leaders can take a leaf from developments in Rwanda, where capacity building is bearing fruit. Her turning around of her misery after a debilitating civil war of unprecedented proportions makes Rwanda a wonder to behold. As South Africans, we have our own civil ways, albeit on a smaller scale. However, these had a racist and tribal character like those of Rwanda. Rwanda has to be seen to be believed. Diasporan Rwandans in Canada who were negatively critical of Paul Kagame during his visit to Toronto must be hanging their heads in shame as the African Union implements and makes use of this leader's gifts. South Africans must also consider this lesson to build a postapartheid society. Looking at Johannesburg today and comparing it to Kigali will leave one wondering whether, if Rwanda does it, starting with cleanliness, we cannot do it as well.

Letters to various newspapers and magazines, show how appreciative people are of what they see in Rwanda and what they see in the Gambia, for example. The manner in which Yahya Jammeh in Gambia dealt with the colonial legacy when he left the British Commonwealth is reminiscent of the way Verwoerd did it as well, but they were on the back foot of policies that destroyed their governments. Such letters, as we read them, should help us wear new spectacles when reviewing our own histories in our quest to build human capital. The South African condition should be one of those letters we should regretfully call to mind. Yes, there is a good side to any leader. Churchill is one such leader; why did the English flush him out of office in an election after the Second World War? Leaders are for a moment, and Churchill was certainly the right man when democracy was threatened by dictatorship. His masterful statements kept the war away from the English stage after Chamberlain's policy of appeasement via peace with honour.

Africans have the weakness of crediting leaders on matters that, in retrospect, can be seen to have harmed their own economies. They also have a tendency to hero worship. As the lesson in Zimbabwe shows, a man was kept in power, building an economy that with one stroke of a pen was destroyed because of hero worship! The fact of the matter is that if you cannot be a follower, you can never be a leader, because if you cannot follow, you cannot endure constructive criticism. You then keep leading when you should be a follower, and you end up leading people, even yourself, into destruction, as did Hitler and, years later, Muammar Gaddafi. From the pages of history, we must be able to separate good apples from bad ones. A leader's deportment speaks louder than his words. When a leader is misleading, his entire person and position sells him out. When a leader is candid, he is most believable, but when what he says is too good to be true and does not reflect realistic challenges, then he should not be heeded. There were some leaders when we went into the 2019 general elections that had lost income and resorted to forming new political parties for employment as members of Parliament (MPs) and yet some were genuinely concerned about the ANC's political direction and sought to challenge it.

Those who lost income as MPs, they stood to earn comfortably what they had lost, and people should see through and not be hoodwinked by such so-called leaders. Looking at African states, one soon realizes that they all have a common streak of being left by leaders worse off than they were before they came into power, and this stagnate African development. The Gambia is currently struggling to wriggle out of a quicksand of extreme poverty because of the kind of leaders who believe that if you are a follower, you can never be a leader. The fact is that a good leader is a good follower, just as a good listener makes a good speaker.

It is matters such as these that we need to take note of when we seek new directions, whilst calling to mind that Verwoerd also left the Commonwealth and directed his country towards the policy mayhem we are left to deal with to this date. Lessons out of history books must inform today's policies before pride goes before a fall, because what we want is a better future for our progeny to earn their respect and, above all, their love, as well as their love for our common fatherland.

We must keep in mind that language is a most respected cultural tool that people pride themselves with. We need, however, to appreciate and accept that we require a common language of communication whilst respecting our own. I have often pondered over the years since 1994 what language is capable of unifying the people of South Africa, and I have come up with one solution. Whilst maintaining our languages and speaking them at any given opportunity when we are together, standard English should be maintained within the four walls of a classroom. All languages, however, should be allowed expression outside classrooms. This method of expression will open up corridors of development with the outside world. This will also promote ties of maintaining peace among people, rather than encouraging people to live as islands, replaying the failure of the construction of the Tower of Babel. We should imagine such a possibility and not let pride get the better of us, because a communicating world is a safe world. Our languages in all schools and tertiary institutions must be given prominence, and *ons moet mekaar onse tale gebruik vir ontwikeling* (we must use our languages for development). This will help remove our stereotypes, attitudes, and prejudices with a view to find one another and promote reconciliation in South Africa. I once observed two friends at the University of the Free State, one white and the other black, conversing in two languages. The white student was addressing the other in Afrikaans, and the other was sharing communication in English. This is something that has stayed with me, because I have also heard an isiXhosa-speaking person in conversation with a Sesotho-speaking person, and comfortably so. However, a common language of teaching to develop human capital is best left among those who stay and learn together without compromising Standard English.

As Africans of various hues, we must also be wary of the negative images of the outside world. Being always portrayed by the Western media as starving Africans should not bode well with us. This is a challenge that should bring us together and help us to develop our countries as Africans. Our portrayal as starving is a negativity we should shy away from. This again takes us back to the land issue and the need for us to develop spectacles of working together to avoid it. It should also nurture our pride to avoid the portrayal in every possible way. American music stars conducted by Quincy Jones sang a fundraising song for poverty alleviation for Africa, and so did Bob Geldof in 1985. What does this do to our image?

It is such day-to-day comments in our communities and articles in the media that should conscientize African leaders into making the right choices and opting for scientific land development practices that will sustain African agriculture. The choice is in our hands not only as leaders but also in our voting practices. Staying away from the polls because the African National Congress is failing is not correct political and democratic behaviour. What is correct is, as Mandela advised, is doing to the ANC, if it fails us, what we did to the apartheid government—full stop!

But we must avoid emotional expressions of voting and apply realism. Idealism and idolizing leaders will lead to our destruction. In the face of adversity, we become idealistic and questionably heroic! We put an *X* at a regrettably wrong place inside a ballot box wherein only you knows where you have put the *X* that may determine whether you self-destruct or emerge from the dungeons of gloom and self-destruction whilst still a member in good standing. You do not have to vote for your party even when you feel it is failing you at every turn! We want a sustainable state, not a welfare state whose grant only feeds us for a day. We want a working economy that will employ us based on what we have been trained to do for ourselves; we do not wish to live on handouts that do not sustain our hearts' desires in living a good life. Our nationalism and patriotism must inform our needs and wants—our country as our pride and our love for our people! Never have we seen mentally sick people roaming the streets, as the case is now. Never have we had failing municipality and infrastructure, as the case is now! Never have we seen a failing education system, as the case is now! Never have our hospitals been unsafe, though a few are now! Never have we had water provision shortages, as the case is now! The 'nevers' I can recount can fill up the remainder of this chapter!

We can restore our pride and being by putting our X in the right place come next elections. The failure of discipline in our schools plagued by drug addiction and abuse should be discouraged by our X being written in the right place to change our lives for the better.

Our nationalism and patriotism (love for Africa) should inform our votes for the kind of leaders who will take us to Canaan, the Promised Land: the right Moses and the right Joshua, the right Deborah and the right Samaritan woman!

Chapter 1

INTRODUCTION

Social relations in preindustrial South Africa were characterized by various factors. Some of these were the practices of slavery and conquests after the frontier wars decimated populations. Conquered black tribes became a subject people as unskilled black labour forces went under white control. The situation was such that menial labour meant a loss of social status for a white person, and even the poorest of white people considered themselves superior to blacks in South Africa. This, as the Great Trek of 1834 was to prove, defined a clear distinction between white and black, which is another way of saying between master and servant—in that order. This grew over the years into a situation where race defined relations among the people of South Africa and developed into an institutionalized racial policy along Lord Lugard's policy of dividing and ruling in Nigeria. This bred interracial strife, which grew into hardened attitudes, stereotypes, and a racial prejudice that kept the two races territorially apart.

South Africa's ethnic groups also developed senses of negativity among themselves, and this resulted in hostilities among blacks because their townships were designed along ethnic differences. This bred deep-seated interethnic and interracial hostilities over the years 1910 to 1994, with apartheid being institutionalized into policy after 1948. This also bred poverty along racial lines and inequalities which were to have disastrous sociopolitical effects on postapartheid attempts at reconciliation. These should, however, stimulate ways and means of discouraging them at every turn. Attempts at reconciliation have been made, and these proved to be papering over the cracks that are today growing.

South Africans have discovered that Mandela drinking tea with Verwoerd's widow and sharing the Nobel Prize with F. W. De Klerk is not a panacea that can solve the fundamental problems of poverty, racism of the past, and the inequalities drawn along racial lines. To save a young reader a trip to a dictionary to keep sight on the developing introduction, "panacea" refers to something that offers answers to all problems. Indeed, if Mandela, Verwoerd's widow, Betsie Schoombie, and De Klerk thought a publicized cup of tea and an internationally recognized prized honour would placate and pacify the masses, they all three had another think coming. The scars run too deep to make racism a forgettable experience and reconciliation a river to cross, with most caught up in its raging waves, which threaten even those who want to swim across and reach one another in outstretched arms of brotherhood and sisterhood. In retrospect, it is clear that South Africans have no other choice but to save themselves from economic ruin. There is a saying that one should keep his friends close but even his enemies even closer, in the sense of reconciliation—to change mindsets and to embrace one another.

The world surely stands astounded by the gravity of the deep cut apartheid has been and the violent situation that has developed inside the country as it has become a tourist destination focused on visits to Roben Island. It is this "violence"-triggering trauma that conceived this chronicled offering.

The "rosy" rainbow nation, so dubbed by Archbishop Desmond Mpilo Tutu, was to change into a very ugly scenario, reflecting the scars of 1910–1994 which showed that change had come a little too late. Generations of South Africans were ushered by birth into an ideologically evolving South Africa, whose indoctrinating policies developed a deep-seated anger and hatred. This is reflected in Chris Hani's statement of a deeply suppressed annoyance and anger that the armed struggle was suspended without a broad-based consultation in the Eastern Cape rally. Those who were embroiled in the day-to-day physical aspect of the struggle had not been consulted. In this statement, annoyed, Hani noted that his immunity had been lifted at the time the decision was made. From the beginning, reconciliation was tainted by anger—a very shaky foundation indeed that was bound to crack and crumble, as it did. On the surface it appeared to have been addressed, but deep inside it had not been.

People were soon shaken to their roots by the extent of the trauma of transformation in South Africa. There was the legendary blade runner, whose legs were amputated at the knees at eleven months, whose achievements from 2004 to 2012 in Athens, Beijing, London, and Christchurch, catapulted him to the very zenith of international stardom, fame, and recognition. But then so did his boiling temper and addiction to an assortment of ammunition. It sent him to the next level when it exploded. A concealed, suppressed anger was to explode into expressions of trauma in a violent episode that disturbed the nation and the status quo on one Valentine's Day. This incident calls for the truth to be investigated to find a lasting, meaningful solution so the nation might find closure as a future building endeavour. To what extent are South Africans affected by this revolution? How deep-seated is their anger?

Closely viewed, trauma is the result of a damaged mind and is the result of a distressing event. It is a result of overwhelming levels of stress exceeding one's ability to cope or integrate one's emotions with an experience. It may result from a situation of distress or a recurring event or events, which overwhelm those going through the experience and can be precipitated over days, weeks, years, and even decades as the traumatized person struggles to cope with the circumstances that prevailed and are still prevailing. Trauma can lead to depression and a loss of one's mind. It is a mind-numbing experience by virtue of the size of what is happening. Those traumatized express it in different reactions and overreactions. The shot that killed Chris Hani expresses a trauma by someone who left his country because of socialistic views which he saw and heard in Chris Hani. So traumatizing was this that he did the unthinkable, which at the moment he could be regretting. That shot sent South Africa into panic, and that a statement by Mandela cooled tempers and maintained order is still a miracle. F. W. De Klerk and Nelson Mandela, leaders in the limelight of developments, were drawn together, and each relied on the other at that moment of horror to keep the nation under control.

The effects of trauma differ from person to person relating to people's subjective experiences because people react to similar traumatic events differently. Not all people experiencing a potentially traumatic event will become psychologically traumatized. This, however, may result in posttraumatic stress disorder after exposure to a major traumatic event. This discrepant behaviour can be a result of protective factors some people may have in relation to temperamental and environmental factors enabling them to cope. Some fail to cope, as shown in social media and television programmes featuring families who lost loved ones in the 1990–1993 intermittent civil upheavals which were caused by the trauma of political change. Some lost their minds and have infested the country in various parts and are unknown to locals because people in that state of mind travel long distances by foot owing to dementia, and thus they end up displaced. Dementia could also be an expression of the suppression of bad experiences from memory, though it is known to be the result of shrinkage of the brain, as explained by psychiatrists. I know this because my mother was so diagnosed by her psychiatrist.

Trauma is a direct personal experience of an event involving actual or threatened death or serious injury. Threats to one's personal physical integrity, the witnessing of an event involving the above experiences, the learning about an unexpected or violent death, and serious injury experienced by a family member or close associate are all traumatic incidents. The national experience of a revolution that probably was anticipated but that it was believed would never happen threw people into a frantic frenzy and exploded in various forms that the world media, print and electronic, captured for the world to see. What happened in South Africa affected even families, when suddenly, against traditional African practices, women were put on an equal footing with men, and wives with their husbands. The family bond broke at the centre when husbands lost traditional power and control over their wives to maintain traditional and home values. It is an African custom for a father to give a name to a child born of his offspring. But even this power was taken away from fathers, and their children christened their grandchildren. Trauma finds expression in so many ways not easily realizable by the naked eye or mind. It brings about changes that were initially unimaginable.

Memories associated with trauma cannot be directly expressed. Some are preverbal and cannot be recalled, but some are triggered by stimuli from the environment. People's responses to aversive details of traumatic events involve intense fear, helplessness, or horror. Trauma may be caused by feelings of insecurity regarding how a person views the world around him or her, bringing about confusion. This is what political change becomes to those resisting the winds of change. It invokes feelings of insecurity because, to some, the change was not wanted. We are subjects of our environment, and changing what we are used to brings about reactions that reflect trauma and fear regarding the unknown and what it may bring. As people we are comfortable with what we know. We feel safe in a zone we know rather than one we do not know; that is human nature.

I have been fascinated by transformation resulting from revolutions. I have studied and taught the Industrial Revolution and how it nurtured capitalism and bred Marxist socialist economic ideas by Marx and Engels. I have also studied how the French Revolution was brought about by wise men who enlightened peasants and turned them against a repressive government. The Russian Revolution was similar. The unifications of Germany and Italy are also forms of revolutions. These revolutions, especially the French, made me see my subject status in South Africa in the twentieth century as exactly the same as the French peasants' in the eighteenth century. These revolutions planted a desire for freedom from an imposed status of third-class citizenship, meaning that my government taught its subjects subversion. At the time, travelling long distances was accomplished by train, and a comparison between first-, second-, and third-class coaches made blacks realize how low their status was compared to those of other races in what was their fatherland.

Personally I noticed that when in Lesotho I was never confronted by nauseating racial signs on the walls of public amenities. This made me desire to change the racist system that reduces me to a two-legged animal that whites could not share amenities with in my own country.

The late 1980s were full of overtones of change when the economy, under siege by sanctions, could no longer support the apartheid political hegemony. When political change ultimately occurred in 1994, I had been waiting for it for ten long years since 1984, when the P. W. Botha and Samora Machel administrations entered into an accord of nonaggression and good neighbourliness. Watching Samora Machel alongside P. W. Botha on a television screen at my school, having organized a live observation of the accord for my students with my Head of Department, was an incredible experience. It was the first time I observed a South African head of state on an equal footing with a counterpart of a free African country in an academic setting. We were used to P. W. Botha's visits to Qwaqwa, but during those visits his vassals were perpetuating and implementing his policies. The accord with Machel was followed by a ceasefire signed as the Lusaka Agreement, and the gradual disengagement of South African troops from the south of Angola followed.

I formulated an opinion based on the theory that the accord was one of the most significant formal agreements South Africa had entered into with black governments. I saw this as a crack in apartheid's seemingly solid machinery, the inside of which was slowly but surely crumbling. Economic sanctions were like a giant python squeezing the very life out of the apartheid state, killing it slowly, with its very many deep-seated problems adding to its death. This readied me for change. I was genuinely surprised when people, even blacks, were taken by surprise and opposed to the overwhelming revolution we were going through. Perhaps what prepared me for this revolution was a teacher's opinion in my general science class. He said that one can keep a ball suppressed under water but one will soon tire and let it float to the surface. I was then in standard seven (grade nine), and this statement lay embedded somewhere in my mind and grew to more mature interpretations as I grew older and received more informed education.

During the mid-1980s, all seemed well on the outside. Apartheid's policy of balkanizing South Africa seemed well and good with its nine creations: Qwaqwa for the Basotho, Bophuthatswana for Botswana, the Ciskei and the Transkei for the Amaxhosa, Venda for the Bavenda, Kwazulu for the Amazulu, Kangwane, Gazankulu and Lebowa Kgomo. These developed into apartheid creations as places where black South Africans could exercise full political rights unhindered. Two had already become unrecognized banana republics.

Development corporations breathed a lease on life into these homelands, whilst the Land Bank developed and stimulated life into the white economy in tertiary commercial farming, with agriculture scientifically and systematically growing as tertiary industry. The truth is that compared to the blundering, corruption, and disorganization of administration under black majority rule, the white minority government was a well-planned and orchestrated system, oiled with an effective education system. Education was key and was planned according to the needs of the developing minority government's economic needs, based on the "Ons bou onse nasie" (We are building our nation) rhythmic pattern. This gave the apartheid system a firm foundation, with universities and technikons producing personnel needed to promote the economy and academics who became strong, effective leaders of the apartheid state's government machinery.

Stellenbosch, Pretoria, and Potchefstroom Universities excelled as bastions of political education with academic excellence. The undoing of this well-organized and well-planned development became the paralyzing Bantu Education to its recipients, which was to become an albatross around the government's neck, throttling the economy it created, whose growth Macmillan noted in his "Winds of Change" speech. But its policies came round to bite the system, and its economy staggered during the P. W. Botha years.

In mainland South Africa, 87 per cent of the land is white man's land, where blacks have no rights at all. The remaining tiny 13 per cent is shared among the black people of South Africa, proving that land is a prime requirement for development.

It is this that is pushing present-day South Africa to tamper with the constitution for an amendment allowing expropriation without compensation after the failure of the willing-seller, willing-buyer policy. The 1913 Native Land Act, which Sol Plaatje unsuccessfully tackled with all his might, left a sour taste in the mouths of many black nationalists. Solomon Tshekiso Pllatje is glorified as a humble servant of Africa with a minimal education of standard three, but he became part of a delegation of five people in 1914 which included Dr Rubusana and John Dube (president of the ANC), which sailed to England determined to obtain British aid to have the Native Land Act of 1913 overturned. It proved a futile, fruitless exercise, as Lord Harcourt, secretary of state for colonies, lifted not one finger to intervene, stating that General Louis Botha was doing a great job in South Africa and that he was not prepared to intervene in the internal affairs of a free country.

Even John Harris, the secretary of the antislavery Aborigines' Protection Society, who had promised assistance, folded his arms. Plaatje thought their stay would take five months in London, but it took three years. They came back home empty-handed and bitterly disappointed. The British government at the time was appeasing the Afrikaners, as it was just twelve years after the conclusion of the Peace of Vereening, which effectively ended the Anglo-Boer War (later the South African Civil War, 1899–1902) as a result of Lloyd George's intervention for the Afrikaner cause in the British Parliament. Precedence for future discord between the races in South Africa had been set, and this precedence rose and grew with each rising day up to 2019, at which point it has reached a stage of address. However, a political and diplomatic address has to be the order of the day. This has to guide the process of land redistribution and supress the trauma of revolution and let it go out of control as it happened across Beit Bridge. Nationals from that country have strewn them all over South Africa in search of better pastures like nomadic farmers, only this time they have done so for themselves and not for animals.

Plaatje's delegation's disappointment was to be the gripe triggering heated debate in our time on the subject of the restoration of land that was forcefully ripped from the hearts of its rightful owners, taking over where Sol Plaatje and the Dube-led delegation left off. This, for the love of the land, should not be directed by emotional considerations. We must remember the exemplary leadership shown by General Hertzog when he realized the hunger his people were suffering, leading to a compromise. He went into bed with the enemy, General Sumts, for the sake of his people. Malan scorned him, and he saw sense in reaching out to General Smuts for the sake of his people's cause. Such is authentic pragmatic and realistic leadership, which in our times should put the African National Congress and the Democratic Alliance between the same sheets as bedfellows.

Who will forget the bitter end of Sophiatown, which was the centre of black social life and activity, comfort, and entertainment? The insensitive of renaming this place as "Triomf", meaning "triumph", after the melting of black resistance by the wicked hand of the apartheid state made Africans personae non grata in their native land. The pain of black people became the triumph of white people. This is insane, vile, and disgusting, you might say, and I would agree! But such is the nature of power. Pragmatism implies shaking the hand of an enemy with genuine love and affection, and that time for South Africans has arrived!

The Meadowlands matchboxes in Soweto became the new homes of former Sophiatown residents on land they owned. This was carried out not by choice but by a show of force. This calls to mind in black circles the belief that when whites show love, black people will be consumed by hatred. We must, however, heed voices of reason from men like Trevor Huddlestone, Alan Paton, and Dr Van Zyl Slabberts, who did the best they could to save the insane situation. They were friends of the oppressed and, so to speak, the enemies of apartheid South Africa. F. W. De Klerk was a man who put the interests of South Africa before his own. It is men such as these that we should refer to in order to reach sane decisions in a give-and-take situation. Who will forget the woman who reported Hani's slaying to the police? She was of Afrikaner descent, and these are landmarks of a new South Africa that should not blind us from the idea of reconciliation for the love of the land.

The view that when whites are turned to affections, blacks will be turned to hatred is reflected in the Economic Freedom Front's (EFF) uncompromising drive to use the land issue as "payback time". We know as well as the EFF's leadership that its effects will have adverse economic consequences if pursued. The fact is that carrying political baggage does not have any positive spin-offs. It will only exacerbate and escalate the problem.

The EFF's view is manifested in the policies of reactionary political formations which are sadistically hell-bent on making white South African landowners feel alienated from what they have always regarded as their country of birth, which was taken from its rightful owners. This payback time calls to mind chants of "Pay back the money" against the then president Zuma in Parliament, referring to his Nkandla residence's misdirected government funds. This they have dumped like a child dumping a broken toy, and the same will happen when the land being called for expropriation without compensation is destroyed. They will dump it like a broken toy and look for something else to destroy whilst earning a parliamentary salary and the perks that go with it. The rinderpest and drought are not the only agriculture-ruining forces; we also have human rinderpests and droughts, and political formations like the EFF and Black First Land First (BLF) are such human rinderpests and droughts.

AfriForum and land-loving South Africans are feeling the pain of a possible land dispossession, and its CEO, Kriel, is its spokesperson.

Noteworthy is that the EFF did not care a fig for the Nkandla expenditure but just sought to make life unpleasant for then president Jacob Zuma. The apartheid state's national anthem says it all in the view that the Afrikaner regarded South Africa as "die vaderland" (the fatherland), and the pain of loss is too much to bear, as the EFF ululates, making human nature sadistic. The fact is that as history teaches, such misdirected emotions usually come back to haunt the nation. Our example will always be Zimbabwe, where such a policy has become a nightmare to its citizens and government. South Africans of all hues must realize and come to terms with the depths and influence of national anthems as expressions of in-depth patriotic feelings. Our fellow white South Africans are a result of the effects anthems have on people. "Nkosi Sikelel 'iAfrika" invokes feelings of nationalism in black South Africans. In the World Cup, we have seen teams singing their anthems, and this should make us understand one another as South Africans and allow us to feel what others feel after singing an anthem.

The poet Langenhoven, in "Die Stem Van Suid-Afrika" (The Voice of South Africa), instilled in the Afrikaner a deep-seated patriotism and feelings of nationalism. He took South Africa, stoically and patriotically opened Afrikaners' hearts in a political operation, and put South Africa inside their hearts, planting an undying love for the fatherland.

In his ears, especially during his formative years, the Afrikaner heard and still hears the "kreun can ossewa" (the creaking of ox wagons as they were dragged by oxen up and down mountain slopes). The poem has a very strong, lasting, and indoctrinating effect on the Afrikaner's mind. Read its full rendition below, followed by its two English translation versions, and we still have its words in the new all-inclusive postapartheid anthem. Going through the anthem below in a heartfelt recital will make the reader identify with and feel what the Afrikaner is going through, and be drawn towards the Afrikaner in a conciliatory spirit:

Die Stem Van Suid Afrika	–	The Voice of South Africa
(Afrikaans Version)		(English translation)
Uit die blou van ons hemel	–	Sounding out of our blue heavens

Uit die diepte van ons see	–	From our deep seas
Oor ons ewige gebergtes	–	Over our everlasting eternal mountain ranges
Waar die kranse antwoord gee	–	Where echoing cracks resound
Deur ons ververlate vlaktes	–	From our plains where creaking wagons
Met die kreun van osse wa	–	With the creaking and groaning of ox-wagons
Ruis die stem van ons geliefde,	–	Calls the spirit of our beloved country,
Van ons land South Africa.	–	Of the land that gave birth to us, oh South Africa.
Ons sal antwoord op jou roepstem,	–	We will answer to your call,
Ons sal offer wat jy vra:	–	We wil offer what you ask of us:
Ons sal lewe, ons sal sterwe.	–	At thy will we shall live we shall perish or die
Ons vir jou Suid Afrika.	–	O South Africa, dear fatherland.

Today the AfriForum is feeling what blacks felt when their land was forcefully ripped out of their hearts and taken away to be huddled into economically barren homeland creations with a view to create nine deprived black republics with a foetal-like umbilical connection to Pretoria, the seat of government. It is painful not only because of the land's commercial worth but also as a property nestled in their hearts, bequeathed by their forebears.

Black aspirant nationalist political ideals killed nine foetal creations of the apartheid state's seminal racial creations as its squeezing deprived the growing foetuses of much-needed oxygen. Change was inevitable, and the sudden change of political symbols became traumatic and depressing to a people who had planted South Africa in their hearts and made her home through policies that would make the trauma of change painfully unbearable. They may never say it, but believe me, it is painfully unbearable for a nationalist to lose a fatherland. The nationalism that developed and enveloped Africa after the Second World War bears testimony to what the Afrikaners felt when the South West African People's Organisation lost Namibia, and when Africans lost what the Black Consciousness Movement called Azania. It was very painful indeed!

South Africa is a traumatized country whose people are experiencing various levels of stress. Her people are traumatized, and this trauma finds expression in Parliament and public places where amenities are shared. In schools the stressful psychological trauma has reached alarming proportions; learners now resist teacher discipline and react violently against it. Schools have become havens of insecurity because the people were not prepared for change. Television advertisements featuring black and white people, which Dr Andries Treurnicht was opposed to, were not enough to prepare people for change. Nothing prepared the people for this change—nothing at all! An American social science specialist in the field of psychology, Carl Rogers, a humanist American social psychologist and psychotherapist, was appointed by a caring president, F. W. De Klerk. But the Treurnich's opposition of "Ag nee" (oh no) politics negatively affected what could have had far-reaching effects if it had been politically supported. The process of healing and finding closure has to be a scientific process ked by the best in preparing people for change. It should be lauded as a very caring political intervention.

During the first postapartheid democratic elections, I was in Aliwal North, in the Eastern Cape. After the announcement of results with the new president inaugurated, I went into what until the previous day had been a whites-only eatery. After placing an order and being shown to a table by the window, I sat down, being the only black person. I noticed many of my own peering through the window—expecting me to be kicked out, I suppose. They became round-eyed in amazement when I took utensils and began eating peacefully. While having my after-meal drink, I relaxed and read a paper. I was from Qwaqwa and was in a part of South Africa that was not used to having mixed races in a restaurant. Qwaqwa had no racial policies, and I was used to nonracialism, designed by apartheid to serve such nonracial socialisation. But in mainland white South Africa, that was unthinkable. This demonstrates the trauma the people were going through and were experiencing. They sought freedom, but on getting it, they were not adjusting to it.

The white people around me were not as receptive as people should be either, and yet they were not repelled by my "intrusive" presence. Everyone was minding his or her own business and eating. It is a day I will not forget, because thinking back, it reflects the various levels of psychological trauma that the political change herein addressed subjected people to.

It was a soft, silent trauma just a day after the inauguration of a new democratic government, with its first president in postapartheid South Africa having just been sworn in. During the years to come, this was to become explosive as stress levels shot up. Social media displayed violent verbal and physical exchanges between blacks and whites in eateries like Kentucky Fried Chicken.

When Muhammad Ali, as Cassius Clay, became the first black champion of the Olympics, and the United States was traumatized. So was Muhammad Ali. So traumatized was he that a film depicted him going onto a bridge and throwing his Olympic medal into the river after realizing that he may be the champion of the Olympics but that the politics of black and white were still very much in place and that white America still saw his ebony skin. That is putting it mildly to honour a man who was to change very much the face of America. It ate at America's conscience when he challenged being drafted into the US Army to fight in Vietnam. He defied the system, and the trauma resulted in the loss of his title as heavyweight champion of the world, but he mustered the courage to fight right back!

Such is trauma. So traumatized was America that it could not respect a man's right not to be drafted. So traumatized were South Africans that change to them, though be welcomed, still made them behave in ways that reflected the trauma of revolutionary change. We are still traumatized and only time will theraputize us to deal and cope in the new order.

The Land Bank's history, if objectively and scientifically modernized as it has been and given a new mandate, can offer direction to the newly developing postapartheid state's tertiary economy. It needs to be inclusive of emerging farmers without compromising food security, which will surely be the demise of the very people it is trying to help develop into commercial farmers, and this is a process, not an event! Food shortages will hike food prices, and the poor, as in Zimbabwe today, will be the hardest hit should the Land Bank's programme not have government support. The land issue, as the heart of the problem, has to be dealt with very sensitively and delicately to avoid another Zimbabwe, which was once the breadbasket of Southern Africa. Mugabe's ruinous land grabs made its economy a Zimbabwe ruin. These destructive Mugabe-inspired land grabs must be a lesson that emotional rhetoric should have no place in South Africa. It is needless to add that Mugabe was saving his own skin by giving his people a scapegoat for their poverty, and he found an excuse in the Lancaster House's unfinished settlement. This was to give young South African youthful leaders a bad precedence, as Julius Malema enjoyed the limelight shown by Mugabe himself. Scapegoats are limping excuses and safe zones that allow misdirected politicians to mislead the nation. Let us not heed them and be deaf to their divisive, uninspiring messages.

Ever wondered why Malema suddenly dropped his Parliament gimmicks? It is simply because, unlike Thomas Sankara—Africa's own Che Guevara, the Burkinabe revolutionary President of 1983–1987—he does not care for the very people he is using to further his political interests of being employed in Parliament. He is rabble-rousing to earn perks. What is unfortunate is that people are taking the bait, and in the process, like Nero, leaders are fumbling while Rome is on fire. This makes our democracy a sham and renders its constitution a meaningless document whose interpretation has eroded value systems and has compromised democratic practice.

A government is there to create conditions conducive to job creation, but ours is saving ruined state-owned enterprises (SOEs) and does not ensure and secure an environment for these SOEs to self-sustain and generate their own income. The Electricity Supply Commission (ESCOM) and South African Airways (SAA) have become albatrosses around the taxpayer's necks and require bailouts taken from the national treasury, which is the people's pocket. The hashtag #FeesMustFall represents another responsibility of the people, and every budget must think of it as the country sinks into the status of a welfare state. To put this right will take generations in many years to come for the simple reason that state planning is inconsistent with its statements to the nation. Corruption is the major problem, with discord among members of the ruling party being another major problem. If opposition movements can find ways of working together to reduce their numbers to at least three strong parties, the political situation can be addressed and turned around to reorganize economic development. The multiplicity of political parties after a drastic revolutionary change is a worldwide phenomenon experienced not only in South Africa, and these parties can be reduced as they were in countries that experienced such revolutions. There seem to be developing in South Africa "leaders" who are seeking employment by creating political parties for personal gain and employment in Parliament, and not so much to address the political malady that has impoverished many people. This is becoming a new trend.

THE LAND BANK

This is one subject that needs to be truthfully tackled, because it has the capacity to draw blood and be the cause for a political rancour that can engineer populist rhetoric. Peter Mokaba's inflammatory recitation of "kill the farmer kill the boer" must be buried with him, understanding that it was inspired by anger. A call for political sobriety in land-related matters and issues is our gateway to a new economic evolution that the Land Bank can lead us through. Land is a sensitive subject that has resulted in the imprisonment of those who clamoured for it in agitation against Afrikaner governments since 1912. It must therefore be handled with suppressed emotions. Even blaming the ANC by the PAC on the land decisions in the Freedom Charter is politically myopic, because indeed South Africa belongs to all who live and depend on her land yields. Let us try to see beyond our noses.

The year 1912 was quite eventful! It is the year in which the formation of the ANC in Bloemfontein coincided with the formation of the Land Bank to finance white commercial farmers. The background to the Carnegie Commission addressing the poor white problem is traceable from 1890, when whites began to be dispossessed of their land—especially in the Cape and the Transvaal. This poverty gained traction and momentum when racial integration began to emerge in the urban areas. In Grahamstown this racial integration was described as promiscuous, implying that it was unacceptable. In the year 1910, the Afrikaners' republics were united into a union government that began tackling white minority interests, discouraging such racial integration. It thus comes as no surprise to note that in 1912, two years after the formation of the union, a political activity of an economic nature was beginning to take shape when the Land Bank started its financing of white farmers only. This opened an agricultural commercial industry in which white commercial farmers were the sole beneficiaries of well-defined state support against the backdrop of addressing what was to be formally addressed as a scientific inquiry by the Carnegie Commission of 1932, some twenty years later. The Land Bank began applying its mind on providing financial aid and skills development among whites during natural disasters, such as droughts, with a potential to harm commercial farming produce. By this time, battles over land were settled, favouring European settlers and their descendants. This would result in chants of "ma ba yeke umhlaba wethu" (let them leave our land alone) by later black nationalist descendants, and it continues to this day, when even indigenous tribes seek redress over the land issue.

As history shows, the European settlers fought among themselves over land control, fuelling economic growth. In 1910, the Cape, Orange Free State, Transvaal, and Natal came together as provinces in a union born out of the South Africa Act of 1909. During the years 1909–1912, South Africa started developing an agricultural economic sector that favoured white minority interests, which the current youth are calling "white monopoly capital". According to the Land Bank, this tertiary industry in later years extended credit to coloured landowners or those leasing farms. Indian farmers were also offered credit. But according to Land Bank records, there is no evidence of these two newly included racial groups receiving such loans from the Land Bank. However, the servicing of these loans by their white recipients went smoothly. In 2002, "the Land Bank Development Act (2002) replaced the Land Bank Act (1944), paving the way for the completion of the Land Bank's transformation into a developmental agri-finance institution" (*History of the Land Bank: Financing Agriculture for 100 Years*, p. 69). During these years, what the Land Bank accumulated over the years "was eroded due to lack of profits and a high ratio of non-performing loans" (ibid), and this phased out the development fund. This shows that interventions are needed to serve the interests of emerging formerly disadvantaged farmers to capacitate and skill them to service their Land Bank loans so that their development can be facilitated over the years. Agricultural practice is a process that requires patience, and emerging farmers must face this reality. They have to be willing trainees to be nurtured towards commercial farming over the next one hundred years, and they must be divided into harvesting units to realize their potential. Afrikaner farmers developed because of their *eerlikheid* (honesty) to service their Land Bank loans, and this eerlikheid stood them in good stead to arrive where they are today. Agriculture has no magic wand to produce maize, our staple food, in five days; but it does have the scientific skill to fill granaries capable of feeding the nation and exporting surpluses to contribute towards the GDP through productive farming.

Serviced loans in turn fund loans made by previously disadvantaged farmers for the buying of land and equipment, as well as the provision of working capital to up to 60 per cent of the value of their farms. The Land Bank presently has also secured R900 million from a German development bank to service emerging farmers with a view to boost agricultural development. Funds totalling R3.5 billion were also secured from the World Bank, and R50 million from the European Investment Bank. This funding is sustainable, and to keep it so, loans given must be serviced so that the bank can develop agriculture successfully. This implies that produce must equal the ability to service the loans for the wheel of fortune to keep turning. All these developments are aimed at expanding the Land Bank's circle of intervention to be all inclusive, especially in accommodating those left out since 1912, when the bank was established. If this can be supported by experienced Boer cooperatives, the development of emerging farmers can boost production whilst in the same breath addressing land redistribution concerns. This can, and will, ensure that commercial land remains productive and remains in the hands of those in the know.

What are the implications of these developments to agricultural development? On the surface they are three, viz.:

1. responsible land redistribution policies,
2. guidance and skilling of emerging and previously disadvantaged farmers, and
3. the ability to keep servicing the loans sustainably with a view to expand and strengthen agricultural development to boost production.

The encouragement of the investor partnerships with the Land Bank brings to the table responsible government policies on the land issue, and this is radical economic transformation or an evolutionary economic practice that encourages private ownership of farmland. The nationalization or capitalisation of the economy thus becomes the next consideration, to which the answer is that if land is nationalized, people are discouraged to develop it, but if capitalized, people are encouraged, as they seek to amass capital through the free enterprise economic system and practices. Russian history shows that when a socialist economic system was introduced, production decreased, but when a partly capitalist system was introduced, production increased, showing that investors seek private ownership, meaning that it is the only way of boosting investor confidence. The Land Bank's ability to serve farmers is thus informed by the people's spirit of nationalism—the next subject in answering the question, How patriotic are those clamouring for the socialisation of land and a radical economic transformation?

No doubt the Land Bank has transformed itself to be in step with current democratic revolutionary developments and sensitivity to the servicing of agricultural land to include the previously disadvantaged farming community. This should attract partnership with the bank by investors and loan applicants and recipients. It is a partnership that bodes well for democracy, which our democratic revolution should now develop further into an economic evolution to avoid the Tunisian revolution, which escalated into confusion when a young man burnt himself in a desperate effort to make himself heard. Our frustrations in South Africa will be fuelled by hot-headed rhetoric, but be encouraged by constructive debate to reach the right and informed conclusions to inform recommendations for implementation. It is no secret that it took one hundred years (1912–2012)for the Land Bank to develop the agricultural sector industry, and it has also taken the Vry Staat Koporasie Beperking (VKB) one hundred years to grow. This means that the VKB has benefited from the Land Bank's interventions and is now in partnership with global investors to invest in agricultural growth by skilling and servicing emerging farmers as the wheel of fortune keeps turning to reach another hundred-year milestone with land in the hands of those who not only love it but also have the scientific experience of growing produce. This is the strength of a patriotic spirit of nationalism that jealously promotes economic growth through a proper and scientific land usage.

THE NATURE OF NATIONALISM—ITS DEPTHS

Nationalism has always been a major part of historical political discourse over the years. It has played a major role in shaping the histories of nations. Whilst it could be as old as man himself, it started gaining prominence during the course of the nineteenth and twentieth centuries. It is derived from a reasonably widespread acceptance of what a people of any given territory see as constituting a nation and what they see as sufficient characteristics, strength, and sufficiency to make a people believe they have a common destiny tying them together in solidarity to make up a national identity. The symbol of that nationality must be worthy of their allegiance. Language is one such element required for nationalism to develop and for a nation to exist and acquire a national consciousness. This assessment is intentionally suggesting that the emergence of a national consciousness predetermines economic development as a dialectical process. Land is the sole legacy that ties a people into a common knot that instils a national patriotic consciousness.

No doubt the sound development of the South African economy after 1910 was driven by an Afrikaner ethnic nationalism whose roots are the Great Trek and the event traditional Afrikaner historians have called the Anglo-Boer War (1899–1902). The Great Trek made the Afrikaner a national entity that saw Britain as a common threat to their national identity and consciousness. The Battle of Blood River in 1838 gave the Afrikaners a national consciousness and strength that they have celebrated every year since then, and this was fused into a strong bond and spiritual belief in God, justifying their quest for their freedom. In chronicling this, the "Anglo-Boer" strengthened that identity, and leaders like J. B. M. Hertzog strengthened it by isolating the English in their midst and portraying them as a common enemy. A pragmatic reality, however, made them bedfellows with a promissory note when the time came, with a view to protect and promote Afrikaner political interests.

The causes of this war perpetuated a common national consciousness among Afrikaners whose origin is in the Great Trek of 1834 and who were reminded of where they come from as a nation. It made them one whilst the 1913 Land Act drew Africans together into a closely knit common allegiance, feeling a sense of loss that developed into "Ma yi buye – iAfrika!" (Come back, Africa). The exclusion of African interests and ultimate limited loss of franchise by blacks in the Cape in the Union of South Africa in 1910 precipitated the formation of the South African Native National Congress (renamed the African National Congress [ANC] in 1912). The South African 1913 Land Act became an issue, source, and driving force of African nationalism. This confirms the belief that for a national consciousness to emerge into a dialectical process for us to uncover the truth of ideas by discussion and logical argument, we need to look at ideas that are opposed to each other. In this particular case, Afrikaner nationalism and African nationalism locked horns and were pitted against each other for eighty-two years (1912–1994). It is these two isms that must now bring South African leaders from all corners of South Africa into round-table discussions to evolve a common African–Afrikaner nationalism. The leadership of the ANC, DA, EFF, and IFP, together with other political parties and important key figures in our revolution, can inform this ambitious view. Noteworthy is that we still have Chief Mangosuthu Buthelezi, former president F. W. De Klerk, and General Bantuboke Holomisa (my former prime minister in the Transkei) in our midst, as by virtue of their chronological and leadership mettle they can inform and facilitate this with a view to save South Africa from ourselves— and especially from our greed.

Nationalism as a living reality was highlighted by UK prime minister Harold Macmillan, who noted its tsunami-like strength as one of the major historical forces of the nineteenth and twentieth centuries in his address to the South African Parliament in 1960. This address was intended to strengthen the hope for African freedoms whilst strengthening Afrikaner nationalism, tightening its grip, and making apartheid more intransigent and even more diabolical and repugnant. In the same year the speech was delivered, Verwoerd withdrew South Africa from the British Commonwealth of Nations, and about five months later, hardly a year later after Macmillan's historic speech, on 3 February 1960, after a referendum on 5 October 1960, whose results showed 52 per cent in favour, South Africa was declared a republic. This occurred on 15 March 1961, exactly one year and twelve days after the famous—or infamous, depending on how you see it—Macmillan "Winds of Change" speech. The ANC and all liberation movements in SA were banned, and legislation was passed for the media not to quote or feature the pictures of the banned people. Literature associated with promoting the interests of African liberation was also banned.

Apartheid had moved fast to defuse any hope for a democratic revolution in South Africa. Whatever hope Macmillan had sowed soon dissipated into a sluggish but effective hopelessness for liberation movements. On 21 March 1960, the apartheid police shot at a defenceless group of 5,000 to 7,000 fleeing people who had gathered at a police station. This event, in which 69 people were killed and 180 were injured, became known as the Sharpeville Massacre. The "Winds of Change" speech clearly angered apartheid, and it made a resounding statement that equally angered the black leadership. About three years later, between 1 October 1963 and 12 June 1964, the Revonia Trial sentenced Nelson Mandela and his coaccused to life imprisonment in a trial that lasted eight months.

This history has to be retold, because for a nation to heal, the naked truth must be retold, as evidenced by the Truth and Reconciliation Commission. South Africa has politically developed into two major nationalisms with a dialectical component, as a Marxist view that all change results from opposing social forces which come into play and conflict because of practical, especially economic, needs. These found expression and fertile grounds in Africa and presently are pitted against each other, dangerously threatening economic practice and growth over land acquisition and redistribution. It is for us to give in to them or sensitively address both opposing forces' needs. We live on land, and if we destroy, we shall be the sufferers. What choice do we have but to love our land?

Our current rainbow nation is a development of these forces and nationalisms, but it was for the most part centred on one ism from two opposing perspectives, viz., Afrikaner and African nationalism, and a third, pan-African nationalism, which came into being when the pan-African wing broke away from the African National Congress in 1959. Its form of nationalism is a geopolitical national passion—people of one country feeling a common consciousness and allegiance to that country. Nationalism is also ethnic, such as in the case of the Basotho, who feel a oneness of spirit with other ethnic groups. It is these different nationalisms in our country that have generated the trauma we are analytically assessing.

At some point the Basotho resented the notion that an African liberator over twenty-seven years was of Amaxhosa ethnic origins, whilst this became a point of pride for the Amaxhosa. It thus falls on us together as South Africans to plant and then cultivate a new common allegiance to our country, whose roots should be forgiveness and reconciliation.

We dare not fail in this mission, because our failure will affect the coming generations—our children and their children. And leading in this exemplary nationalism is the VRYSTAAT KOöPERASIE BEPERK (Free State Cooperative Limited) whose headquarters are in Reits, a small town in the Nketoane Municipality. Its motto and grounding statement "for the LOVE of the LAND" expresses this national patriotic passionate love for South Africa.

The silos of this cooperative, storing the food for the nation, are in major parts of South Africa, and its one hundred years of growth are referred to in its advertisements: "100 years of growing and still going." This seems to augur well and in total agreement with the history of the Land Bank, which has been financing agriculture for one hundred years. This means it has taken VKB since 1919 to grow into the colossal giant it is today. This translates into the simple fact that agriculture is a patient scientific practice that requires skilful goal-directed scientific research over years of tertiary industrial commercial agricultural practice. The tragic Estina farm catastrophe, in which animals of quality breeds died because of neglect, is evidence of how sensitive agricultural practice is; that it requires experience and expertise is unquestionable. It is truthful reality that must guide land reform in South Africa. Any other approach will be more harmful than helpful.

The emergence of a national consciousness predetermines economic development, and the development of a national consciousness should be informed and be seen through a dialectical process. This draws the reader closer towards discussions herein explored. It becomes imperative to dig into our past and our political international relations to identify where we come from as today's nation—yes, nation, but a racialized, politically divided nation with no common positive identity. We have to identify a reason to develop a common allegiance for a common nationhood through business.

In my view, "for the LOVE of the LAND", in the picture above, seems to be the reason for that common allegiance, which can grow into a common love for one another and for our land so that it can keep producing a yield that will feed us and posterity. We should and must always keep in mind that what we have is not only for us but is also for our progeny. We should guard against our land dying in our own hands as Zimbabwe has, leaving the nation finding it difficult to rise from the rubble of its own self-destruction. We should always take a look back to see where others went wrong so that we do not repeat past mistakes but rather learn from them in loving our land for structural growth and further development.

Our past is subdivided into parts that may myopically be seen as the barbarous years and the productive years—barbarous in the sense that technology at first was in its barest, simplest forms, leading to those years being labelled according to their technology. Stone technology resulted in an era being labelled the Stone Age, and iron technology resulted in an era being labelled the Iron Age. The technology of both these eras was simple but sufficiently catered for the Abraham Maslow–related needs of the eras. We should take pride in those years because they define where we come from as a nation. We should know our past and take pride in it. This also assists us in understanding our present era and generation, and defining a future that will inspire our people. There is a need to dream—and dream realistically—along the lines of the great American dream spearheaded by Martin Luther King Jr to avoid dying together as fools, implying that we should identify what impedes and stunts our common growth as a nation, together analyse it as chronicled in this book, find common solutions, and together jump the hurdles.

Our life should be like our seeing our agricultural yields falling—not because of El Niño conditions but rather because of a rodent or rodents out in the fields eating our crops. We should together hunt the rodent or rodents and destroy them. This should be our way of life as South Africans.

No doubt, we will be blinded to racial differences as we together tackle what plagues our commercial agricultural yields. We must muster the courage to let those who know be our leaders and follow their wise counsel to enjoy another one hundred years of growing, and in 2119 the generation looking back at us should be proud, and its administration should seek to better our efforts and also boast of another "100 years of growth and still growing" for the love of the land!

This will make our nation and country proud. We may even start seeing our foolishness in removing inanimate objects simply because they remind us of a bitter past. As a traumatized nation, we understand why things turned out the way they did, and we can even be more understanding and appreciative when we take a stand to repair our own foolishness. Let us carve roads in the wilderness of a political ineptitude we created and make rivers in our own self-inflicted drought and desert of self-destruction made up of the sands of a loveless society. Let us together create an oasis of hope in this desert of hopelessness. Surely the pastures that we shall create and the fountains we shall build will help make our bitter past a sweet pill to swallow as we together put our shoulders on the wheel and rebuild our economy.

Our past is a result of a history we cannot change, but it is one we can together build on.

THE BIBLICAL VERSION OF A PATRIOTIC NATIONALISM

South African African nationalism was inspired by religious belief. Two of the African National Congress presidents were men influenced by a strong religious perception. Chief Albert Luthuli's statement indicating that the road to South African freedom is via the cross of Jesus was a result of his biblical influence as the son of a clergyman and his own experience as a lay preacher in Goutvlei, Natal. He was aevangelist at heart and sought peaceful means in South Africa and was opposed to any form of violence, like Chief Gatsha Buthelezi. This won him the Nobel Peace Prize, which, notably, the apartheid government allowed him to collect. He was also permitted to give an address in Oslo. This in itself is laudable and showed a lot of tolerance at a time when apartheid was intolerant of any opposition.

The young lions, as the youth movement became known, led by men such as Nelson Mandela, saw differently, and the result became Umkhonto We Sizwe (Spear of the nation), which turned the struggle for African liberation into a "soft battle" that hit soft targets like power stations, with no intention to harm people. However, this did not always happen, and people were hurt.

We are chronicling nationalism from a religious perspective. God himself loved the land he created, and the man he made was the apple of his heart. He created him with his own image and sought to govern over him in a type of government men of the cloth refer to as "theocratic" and not autocratic or democratic. God himself governed through his chosen leaders, the judges. The theocratic nationalism God bestowed on us makes our democratic version more tangible and more understandable and spiritual.

THE NATURE OF NATIONALISM—ITS RELIGIOUS ROOTS

John 3: 16 states that "For God so [much] loved the world ..." The rest of this statement is too painful to finish, and in it we find the true depths of a heavenly patriotism—a national consciousness and nationalism man cannot be sufficiently thankful for. In it there is evidence of the bitterness of the truth, which John teaches will set us free though it failed to set God's only son free. But Isaac was set free at the eleventh hour when Abraham looked and saw a ram caught in the thicket. This ram Isaiah prophesied to be the Son of God—a sacrificial lamb to free man from the dungeons of the sin of hatred, racist hatred, and to introduce him to and lead him towards the freedom the cross offers. Hence Chief Albert Luthuli identified the cross as the source of South African liberation to teach South Africa and the world interracial love. It is this that should inspire the burying of the hatchet and encourage focus on remaking the land and finding a new, inspiring love. If we do not, as a nation, look to the scriptures for true salvation, where shall we find it? We should be thankful and mindful of the perils Dr David Livingstone faced when traversing the dangerous living waters across oceans and the hostile African tribes to bring the Good Book to Africa. Jomo Kenyatta looks at it with disdain, blaming it for land grabs, conveniently forgetting that behind it was a man, Livingstone, who opposed everything colonial and was not a favourite of colonial imperial officers, who sought expansion at any cost. He was a disturbance to their consciences, and they denigrated and hated him.

Yet this truth, which St. John quotes as "Ye shall know the truth, and the truth shall make you free", is the very source of Africa's freedom from the bondage of the sin of racism. In one of Moses's five books of the Torah, Leviticus, God says to the children of Israel, "… if a stranger sojourn with thee in your land, ye shall not vex him. But the stranger that dweleth with you shall be unto you as one born among you, and thou shalt love him as thyself; for ye were strangers in the land of Egypt …" This means freedom is born out of a compassionate nationalism and is a give-and-receive kind of resource out of which emanates the working of an economy for human survival.

Nationalism is a biblical concept. It is not necessarily political, yet it is not apolitical. It emanates from God's covenant with Abraham, when God beckoned Abraham and said unto him, "Get thee out of thy country, and from thy kindred, and from thy father's house, unto a land I will show thee …" The *Good News Bible* has modernized this statement into "Leave your country, your relatives, and your father's home, and go to a land that I am going to show you." The two statements say exactly the same thing and relay the same message, each using language that belongs to the times in which the books were published. It is a divine injunction to Abraham, who was a God-respecting and -fearing person in the mould of Noah and Job in the Old Testament and Simeon in the New Testament.

The Old Testament is full of covenants, which are formal contracts and agreements between God and man. These agreements were constantly broken by man. The first can be said to have been between God and Adam when God placed Adam in the holy garden of Eden with injunctions. When Adam and Eve broke them, Adam blamed the transgression on Eve.

This was the first stage of a holy nationalism, for God so loved his creation that he placed it in a stupendously beautiful place. He had commanded the appearance of light to brighten and beautify the land he was preparing for a creation he was about to bring to life. The darkness that surrounded the outer cosmos was not a place conducive for his creation. It was meant to become beautiful and to be made in his image. When a master sculptor like Michelangelo plans his work, he does so with utmost care, diligence, and precession. He composes himself and prepares his mind before taking his tools to carve a special kind of stone. He goes into a state of meditation, and when his mind is clear of earthly troubles, he begins his craft. So deeply engrossed in his work he becomes that he carves every part of it into a state of eye-catching perfection to attract and impress an appreciating eye. When Michelangelo finished carving Moses from stone, he commanded him to speak to him, and when the statue's lips remained motionless, he struck it with his hammer, and where he struck it, a splinter fell off; this is visible on the statue. This explains God's creation with the soil that he took from the ground to create man out of it; he breathed a life-giving breath into its nostrils.

God must have sat back, as Michelangelo did, to behold his creation, and he must have been impressed. Because he is a loving God imbued with a nationalism filled with a spirit of heavenly nationalism, he now sought a perfect place for his creation, and none other than the garden of Eden was good enough. The garden was a symbol and expression of beauty.

The garden of Eden had all kinds of beautiful trees planted in it, and some of these produced juicy fruits. One in particular stood in the middle of the garden and gave life, and there also stood the tree that gives knowledge of what is good and what is bad.

The garden of Eden was beautiful. A stream flowed into the garden to water it, and beyond the garden it divided into four rivers. Their names were the Pishon, the Gihon, the Tigris, and the Euphrates. The Pishon flowed round the country of Havilah, where pure gold of the highest quality was found, together with rare perfume and precious stones. The Gihon flowed round the country of Cush, and the Tigris flowed east of Assyria. God associates the beauty of land with water. In the book of Exodus, God shows Moses a piece of wood to cleanse bitterness out of the water of Mara. God then gives the Israelites laws which he expects them to live by, and he leads them towards twelve springs and seventy palm trees where he lets them camp by the still waters. This shows that he is a loving, caring God who seeks nothing in return but obedience. His nationalism is of the highest quality, and he expects same from his creation. He trusts them to obey his laws in return for the natural riches that he gives them, these being nothing but land. Of all mankind's possessions, land is the most precious. It gives man a source of economic life and a place of abode. It gives man sanctuary, and it gives him a sense of security.

Because of the security land gives man, God entered into a covenant with Abraham that he should leave his original country, which he loved, and to go to a land that God would show him. Like the garden of Eden, it was a rich country that had everything. But imagine for a second that you are Abraham and you have been living in a country for over ninety years and have been instructed by the most high God to forfeit it and your people. How would you feel?

Obviously you would have your doubts. But not Abraham! His obedience to God was unquestionable. He was God's most honest, loving, and fearing creation. God entered into a covenant with him by commanding him to leave his country and his people. Abraham's spirit of nationalism in heavenly quests beats man's known desires. But because God knows that land is crucial for human existence, he promises his descendants a land full of all human desires for them to own. Abraham sees God as the provider and as his heavenly father, and he goes by his word and commandments. He is a religious nationalist and is imbued with a heavenly nationalism that prepares him for ownership of land away from bondage and want, working a land that does not belong to him.

The Israelites in Egypt were drawn together by a spirit of nationalism, and naturally they still fought among themselves, but Moses kept them together. As we know, he fled Egypt when he became exposed as a murderer by his own kith and kin. But because God saw some leadership characteristics in him, he called him for duty. He resisted God's calling, just as we sometimes do, but he finally relented and took the leadership rod to conduct God's mission without compromising it.

By and large, Moses was a die-hard nationalist. Joshua, Aaron, and Hur were equally enthusiastic nationalists who stood together by Moses during their most troubled times in the wilderness. They all four loved and cared for their people, the chosen nation of Israel. God chose them because he saw leadership qualities in them and he loved their patriotic spirit of nationalism, which we are going to give modern spectacles. Aaron may have been misled by the children of Israel into false worship and disappointed the leadership and God in person, but he was the spokesperson of Moses, whose speech was slurred. All four played a role at Rephidim in the great defeat in which God promised Moses, "Behold, I will stand before thee thereupon the rock in Horeb …" And stand he did when the children of Israel demanded water from him and then faced an enemy that required the role of all four to conquer.

Among the leaders of the African people there were such men, and the ultimate success of the struggle should be credited to them as well. The South African Defence Force was awesome. P. W. Botha had developed it into powerful war machinery, and no liberation force would match it. Its defeat required the intervention of a third force, and it was no more a paralysis than a defeat, because no power in Africa would defeat it. It was a paralysis that sought to make it moribund and inactive to avoid a hot war. Even the forces of African struggles were inspired by nationalism, which is the strongest of human feelings because it is inspired by love, a strong human emotion as evidenced between two people, resulting in an "In sickness and in health …" incantation or vow tying a couple together in holy matrimony.

As we shall see, nationalism comes in various kinds and shades. A person who loves his country falls in love with it for itself, whether it has gold or it does not have gold, whether it has diamonds or it does not have diamonds, whether it has water or is barren, and whether it has grass for cattle or does not. He loves his country because he has this invincible umbilical cord attached to it with his soul.

When a great famine struck an Israelite family during the era of the judges who ruled over Israel before God anointed the first king, such a love was demonstrated. Israel was under a temporal government led by God himself. He appointed judges, and those who are well known are Deborah, Samson, and Gideon. Enimelech, a man of Bethlehem-Judah, left his country and took sojourn in Moab territory. His wife, Naomi, bore him two sons, Mahlon and Chilon. Enimelech died, living Naomi with his sons, and they took Moabite women for wives. One was Orpah, and the other Ruth. Naomi's sons both soon died. The women had stayed in Moab for a period not exceeding ten years before the deaths of their husbands. After their deaths, together with her two daughters-in-law, Naomi returned to the land of Judah. When preparing to leave Moab for Judah, Naomi released her daughters-in-law and urged them to return to their kith and kin, whereupon Orpah took her belongings and set forth. Her other daughter-in-law, Ruth, refused to go back to her kith and kin and used strong words to stick by her mother-in-law, saying, "… wither thou goest, I will; and where thou lodgest, I will lodge: thy people shall be my people, and thy God my God …" She thus developed and evolved a new nationalism. On her arrival in Judah, her people recognized Naomi, calling her by that name. But she instead chose a name of bitterness, Mara, which depicted her bitterness for the loss of her loved ones. "Mara" means "as bitter as the water Israelites found after three days walking in the wilderness, thirsty beyond words".

What this suggests is that Naomi returned home not as a prodigal woman but as one that sought to be with her own people in her bitterness. She had requested the same of her daughters-in-law, but Ruth, her second, refused and vowed to be with her among her people, whom she adopted as her own. She developed a new national feeling because of her indebtedness to her mother-in-law.

Many centuries later, nationalism is seen as part of major historical forces worthy of a common allegiance in the course of the nineteenth and twentieth centuries. For this nationalism to exist, we must have a nation; and for this nation to exist, the population must acquire a national consciousness and be dialectically developed. This suggests the emergence of a national consciousness predetermining economic development. Without a nation, there can be no economic development to speak of.

In South Africa after 1910, there developed an Afrikaner nationalism whose strength developed the economy. These are a generation of Hollanders who came to South Africa seeking a halfway station to spice-rich India and to trade with her. Added to these were the 1820 British settlers who settled around Grahamstown in what is today the Eastern Cape. The Afrikaners developed an ethnic Afrikaner nationalism that evolved from the Great Trek, a vast exodus of Afrikaners dissatisfied by British "misrule" in the Eastern Cape. In the hinterland, it was strengthened by the Anglo-Boer War, which erupted owing to the British policy of encirclement. In its encirclement of the Boers, the English were ensuring that the Afrikaners would not get a port to their name, as the English feared a second power meddling in what they considered the British sphere of influence. Like the Israelites, who were fearful of Assyrians, the English did not want a strong neighbour in South Africa.

The English thus remained a thorn in the side of the Afrikaners. The causal factors of the Anglo-Boer War are based on an ethnic nationalism among the Afrikaners, as they felt they were victims of British interference, which they resented in their lives. The discovery of gemstones, diamonds, and gold strained relations between the two nationalities, proving, so to speak, what the source of all evil is. The Afrikaners sought republicanism, whereas the English pursued imperialism to protect British interests around the world. There was a saying going round in the 1980s: "The sun never sets in the British Empire." This statement demonstrates British imperialism in its most extreme forms.

The struggle between the two nationalities was essentially a struggle for political and economic power over one group. This dominated the South African scene during the nineteenth century. This clash of interests worsened relations and ignited the Anglo-Boer War in 1899. The results of the war escalated into a source of extreme anger for the Afrikaners and found a true pioneer of Afrikaner nationalism in J. B. M. Hertzog. He was a practising attorney in Pretoria from 1892 to 1895 and was appointed to the Orange Free State High Court. He became the driving force of Afrikaner nationalism—its prophet and its engine. Never in the history of nationalism in South Africa did the concept of nationalism find expression on the lips of one so passionate as this man. He was passionate and was comparable to none at the time. He was an alumnus of the University of Amsterdam, a Boer general in World War II, and prime minister of the Union of South Africa from 1924 to 1939; he served in this capacity during the reigns of George V, Edward VIII and George VI. He was the only head of state to serve during the reigns of three monarchs. He was an attorney who earned a doctorate in law in 1892 but always used the title of "General". His love and commitment to their cause made him see sense in committing his people to the Treaty of Vergeeniging in May 1902 as a means of stopping what he saw as unnecessary bloodshed.

It is for this reason that the Anglo-Boer War perpetuated and strengthened a common national consciousness among Afrikaners whose origins in the Great Trek of 1834 found a true source in it. The words "kreun van osse wa" (the creaking of ox wagons) expresses the difficulties the Boers were going through. These difficulties made them one, and they swore allegiance to a country they had adopted as their home: "Ons sal lewe, ons sal sterwe, onse vir jou Suid Africa" (We shall live, we shall die for you, dear land).

In their quest for that land, they unfortunately dispossessed its rightful owners just as the Israelites did to the original owners of the land God promised them; this created a tension that broke into a traumatic experience in 1994 that unsettled many people. The people of South Africa are still dealing with this trauma to this day.

After the Afrikaners had consolidated their power in the union of the four Boer republics, they stripped Africans of their rights and land through the 1913 Land Act, just three years after their union, with African resistance against it rising to a crescendo. Just as the Anglo–Boer conflict was the glue that kept the Afrikaners together, so was the 1913 Land Act to the developing African national consciousness Harold Macmillan saw raging throughout the African continent in the 1960s.

"Ma y'ibuye – iAfrika!" became the clarion call of African nationalism seeking to challenge Afrikaner nationalism. This inspired a desire for freedom. Chief Albert Luthuli became its true prophet. Being a son of a minister of religion, and himself a lay preacher, he realized that Africans were fighting a formidable enemy when he asserted that "the road to freedom is via the cross." It is this thread of religious belief that leads to the ultimate realization of freedom in South Africa. Of course, sacrifices in the mould of Moses, Aaron, Hur, and Joshua were made by African leaders. Various leaders in the struggle for freedom in South Africa were associated with these three biblical Israelite leaders. They gave up their kindred as Abraham did and became soldiers of liberation.

In the book of Isaiah, God promises to release the children of Israel from their second Babylonian bondage. Isaiah is the prophet of Israel during and after the Israelites' Babylonian exile. In Isaiah 3:19 the Lord says, "Behold, I will do a new thing. I will even make a road in the wilderness and rivers in the desert." This is a bold statement—one that gives hope to the hopeless, and one that inspires confidence in those who believe and who have found new strength and inspiration in such words because biblical interpretation is subjective. Man uses it to drive his agenda whilst worshiping and praying for God to deliver an enemy, just as Samson, one of the judges of Israel, did to free himself from Philistine bondage, preferring to die with them in the process than remain in captivity as a Philistine toy and blinded entertainer.

If Isaiah inspired a new hope among the Israelites, Chief Albert Luthuli's words also inspired unarmed African nationalists, whilst the youth felt that guerrilla warfare and change by violent means remained the only alternative in the face of government intransigence to changes in policy. At that stage, the leadership was divided. Older African nationalists were sceptical about the armed struggle, whilst younger nationalists believed it remained the only viable alternative.

When the Lilieslief Farm arrests happened, the older nationalists must have felt vindicated, and Chief Albert Luthuli's Nobel Peace Prize strengthened his resolve that even the world was acknowledging that apartheid was a sin against mankind but still required peaceful means to change it.

The United Democratic Front's leadership was spearheaded by men of the cloth whose activities weakened the beast of apartheid. Among them was a Dutch Reformed Church minister, Oom Bey, who felt that apartheid was bad policy.

The 1913 Land Act drew Africans together into a common allegiance of "Ma yi buye – iAfrika!" (Come back, Africa). The exclusion of Africans in the Union of South Africa in 1910 precipitated the formation of the South African Native National Congress, which was renamed the African National Congress (ANC) two years later. The South African 1913 Land Act became an issue, source, and driving force of African nationalism. This confirms Lehmann's closing line in his assertion that the emergence of a national consciousness is a dialectical process that allows us to uncover the truth of ideas by discussion and logical argument by considering ideas that are opposed to each other. In this case, the opposing ideas were Afrikaner nationalism and African nationalism.

As stated, our current rainbow nation is a development of various nationalisms. In one form, nationalism is a geopolitical passion—people of one country feeling a common consciousness and allegiance to that country. Ethnic and pan-Africanist nationalism also threatened the fabric of an overall common national consciousness. These nationalisms in turn generated the trauma we are analysing to find a common root and national consciousness. It falls upon South Africans to sow and then cultivate a new common allegiance whose roots have to be solidly constructed on forgiveness and reconciliation. These chronicles of South African history should offer reason for growth together.

A new national consciousness following the miraculous fall of apartheid from grace reveals the common nature of all colonial administrations from the Cape to Cairo, and a desire for liberty engineered by temporal interventions. The strength of colonial governments against their subjects made their subjects sitting ducks, and as with the Israelites in Egypt, theocratic love and nationalism had to intervene. What the Afrikaners prayed for came to pass and was acknowledged by them through a covenant with God. Religious practice at home, church, and school determined their lives, and it is this postapartheid government that must be copied.

Our schools must practise morning assembly as a devotional exercise to neutralize the lack of discipline currently prevailing. Sports and recreation must be part of the curriculum to fill the time of our youth productively, and this will also provide teams with development. Our national football team is deprived of this provision of material. Making the school curriculum broad for learners to express themselves and develop future careers should be a priority, because not all learners are academic.

We should appreciate that apartheid had its good aspects, which should form part of the new dispensation. One of these is its religious character, and there is no doubt South Africa was founded on a, perhaps ill defined, religious practice. Any situation without an acknowledgement of the Supreme Being cannot have a good ending. This is reflected in our current situation in an educational policy that does not put God at the centre. Crime has spiralled out of control, and all the bad elements are defeating our resolve to build our country and develop our people. Good and bad have become confused, and bad addictions are making our youth ungovernable and are a result of the trauma of political change, whose consequences are the bitter fruits we are reaping. Too much suddenly happened, and nothing prepared the people for it.

SOUTH AFRICA'S PAST IN HISTORICAL PERIODS

South Africa Prior to White contact
Stone Age
Iron Age
Modern Age
(Era of black and white people's contact)

The Jan Van Riebeeck Settlement (DEIC)—To the Great Trek

The Mfecane (a cultural revolution)

Missionary Contact and Influence

Reverend Tiyo Soga and Lady Janet Soga nee Burnside

Boer Republics and Their Merging: The South Africa Civil War

From Union to Republicanism: 1910–1948 and beyond

The Political Phases of South Africa

1910–1966: Union of South Africa

The Era of White Domination in South African Politics, 1910–1994

Era of Generals: Botha, Smuts, Hertzog, and Smuts, 1910–1948 (Thirty-Eight Years)

Era of Academics: Dr D. F. Malan 1948–1954 and Dr H. F. Verwoerd 1958–1966

1966–1994 Republic of South Africa

From Boer Republic to Democratic Revolution

Leader	Term	Duration	Alma Mater
• Dr D. F. Malan	1948–1954	6 years	Stellenbosch
• J. G. Strijdom	1954–1958	4 years	Stellenbosch
• Dr H. F. Verwoerd	1958–1966	8 years	Stellenbosch
• B. J. Vorster	1966–1978	12 years	Stellenbosch
• P. W. Botha	1978–1989	11 years	Voortrekker Hoer Skool
• F. W. De Klerk	1989–1994	5 years	Potchefstroom

Epoch of an All-Inclusive Democratic Government—1994
The Era of Nelson Rolihlahla Mandela

In forty-six years, blacks and whites developed South Africa, and we can together take South Africa forward as a united people with a new national consciousness by burying our past.

THE SOUTH AFRICAN CIVIL WAR

Until now we have called this war the Anglo-Boer War (1899–1902), and we shall need to deviate from this a little for reasons that shall follow and refer to it as the South African Civil War. This is one historical chronicle that was to shape the history of South Africa. If we are all in agreement that the Great Trek was the central event in South Africa's modern history, as traditionally referred to by Afrikaner historians, then the 1899–1902 war was a biological catalyst of that centrality that brought about changes in this event's effects on the conscience of men without itself undergoing any change. A biological catalyst brings about change without itself undergoing any change. When visiting the Soweto Freedom Park, finish your visit by visiting the Anglo-Boer War Memorial in Randburg and Johannesburg, also called the Rand Regiment Memorial, to know and fall in love with your history objectively. Other Anglo-Boer war memorials are in Graaf-Reinet and Uitenhage, and they also touch base at the Anglo-Boer War Museum in Bloemfontein. My appeal to schools and history teachers is to organize tours to these historical sites, remembering that a child in the commercials and natural sciences is also affected by history. Such tours should thus be for entire schools. This war, grounded on the Great Trek, going into the Union of South Africa eight years later, was to shape the history of South Africa in a manner none could ever envision.

This war was declared by the Boers on 11 October 1899 and tracing its chain of causes throughout historical developments in the country shows that it was triggered by gemstone discoveries. The British public expected it to be over soon, but it proved to be much longer than expected. It also became costly and bloody; about 22,000 British, 25,000 Boers, and 12,000 Africans lost their lives. It humiliated the British the most between the years 1815 and 1914. Agriculture suffered through scorched earth policy as a war tactic.

It was an imperial war, as were the wars in India where the English were engaged. History dubbed it the Anglo-Boer War, which triggered Afrikaner nationalism, whose engine and live wire was J. B. M. Hertzog. With the "South Africa First" speech (1912) in Nylstroom, Smithfield and De Wildt made Hertzog a hero in Afrikanerdom. He was a nationalist at heart—a fervent nationalist. General Smuts, to him, was a villain that could not be trusted with white minority interests and was ousted from power by Dr D. F. Malan in the 1948 with the "Swart gevaar" (black danger) sloganeering in the 1948 general elections, which were won by "apartheid sloganeering." This was to precipitate a war of another kind, also sparked off by nationalism as a dangerous new concept in a South African "war" that was not hot, as this chronicle was. It was an ideological war that was to consume the consciences of men and women between the years 1912 and 1994,—eighty-two long years of strife, which is a subject for another book.

The author calls it the South African Civil War, which should also raise eyebrows, making a reader wonder why. Some other authors on the subject call it the South African War and do not qualify it as a civil war; others still call it the Anglo-Boer War, as if Africans were an audience not affected and not part of it. Such traditional historians see it a white man's war, which an African would see as "fighting over the riches of our land" because it became a hot war just four years after the gold rush that followed the diamond rush. Between these events, especially in 1895, the tension that was building following two belittling conventions became thicker and thicker until the first shot was fired four years following the Jameson Raid. My quest to study economic history at the University of the Witwatersrand was turned down on application, which required me to teach myself this history, as I was feeling burnout from years of teaching political history over many years.

Jan Smuts saw the Jameson Raid as the actual declaration of war to the Boers in this conflict. The aggressors were the British, and they consolidated their alliance against the Boers. The Boers were grimly protecting themselves against this aggression for three and half years in a war the English could have perhaps avoided and would be have been best advised to avoid but nevertheless fought. At stake were the riches of the Transvaal before union.

In a philosophy of history class at the University of Fort Hare in 1979, Mr D. M. Moore then, and later Professor D. M. Moore, taught the class that South African history has two sides, or versions—the traditional Afrikaner version and the English. This history requires an African perspective basically because history is a subjective subject which E. H. Carr sees as a menu served by a writer according to the way the facts of history unfold in his view and how they speak to him. One such instance is the subject of the Mfecane in the Nguni languages, or the Difaqane in Sesotho.

English traditional historian writers see the Mfecane, or Difaqane, as a cultural revolution from which Africans trace their origins. The villains and heroes of the times, according to this prolific writer and historian, bear testimony to this version because present-day Africans pride themselves with the heroes of these wars. To the Amazulu, Shaka is seen as a hero that gave them a sense of nationhood (not "tribalhood", and there is a difference) through a tactical military superiority he changed from long-stabbing to short-stabbing assegais—or spears, if you like. Moshoeshoe is seen by the present-day Basotho people as an intellectual hero who saved their land from imperial annexation and domination by keeping it a British protectorate against the occupation of the land-hungry Boers, who, with what became obvious in the long term, he saw as a threat to his people's independence and nationhood.

This justifies that historical facts speak to a person in a very subjective way. The facts of history are sensitive, and this makes people studying it give them an interpretation that suits their subjective interests. The subject of objectivity and subjectivity in history has captured the interests of academics over the years, and writers see themselves as objective in what others see as subjective. Stone Age and Iron Age history to a traditional Afrikaner historian are ages of irrelevance, and acts of marauding barbarous tribes moving from one place to another inside South Africa do not relate these periods to modern and contemporary history.

Traditional Afrikaner historians in the 1970s and 1980s saw 500 Years of South African History. To such historians, South African history started in 1652 when Jan Van Riebeeck landed on South African shores to set up a halfway station between Holland, his mother country, and India to trade in Indian spices, which appealed to the West's culinary tastes.

This makes the naming of this 1899–1902 war a subject of interest to writers of history. Seen from any angle, it is a civil war in that it affected the lives of all people inside the country. It displaced many people and claimed the lives of South Africans in large numbers. It caused diseases and epidemics that affected the lives of many, and many died as a result. It attracted the sympathy of an English professional nurse who left her country to tend to the sick in concentration camps and made the English aware of the costs of the war with regard to human lives. Lloyd George tabled this in the British Parliament, resulting in the British government giving the English a blank cheque regarding African interests after the passing of the Land Act of 1913. The English felt justified to let the Afrikaners do as they pleased in South Africa to sugarcoat the bitter pill the war became to the Afrikaners, and in later years, they pitted the English against the Afrikaners.

This war was therefore a civil war whose wrath claimed the lives of many. The Afrikaners had a part to play to safeguard their interests and to say to the English enough was enough. The English saw it as a war they had to fight to safeguard their interests in South Africa by keeping it a sphere of British influence and no other power. Her policy of encirclement was a constant act of irritability to the Afrikaners who left the Cape in 1834 with the hope that the English would want nothing from them in the future. But they were wrong, because they would make ties with other superpowers, to the detriment of British imperial interests which came about in Francophone North and Western Africa, whilst the East—Kenya, Uganda, and Tanzania—had ties with the British. This triggered a Cape-to-Cairo imperial interest dream which did not come about, because of its ambitious drive and scant financial resources. This war—whatever you may call it, but it was an 1899–1902 war—was part of the struggles of attrition against the English that gave the Afrikaners no peace of mind. Present-day Afrikaners see some of its key players, especially President Paul Kruger of the Transvaal Republic and Emily Hobhouse (whose names are recognized in a national park in Limpopo Province and a town in the Free State, respectively) as their heroes and heroines.

The South African Civil War was a brutal war one English woman saw as the stupidest war the English ever fought. It developed from the crisis in the Transvaal at the close of the nineteenth century because South Africa then had four provinces—namely the Cape, Orange Free State, the Transvaal, and Natal. On the outside, the crisis was a result of the truculence of what became known as Afrikaners or Afrikanders, who evolved from the original Dutch settlers from Holland's Dutch East India Company (DEIC), who founded a shipping station at the Cape of Good Hope. These people were outnumbered by their coloured servants at the Cape, and their settlement resulted in a legacy of resentment against anything European. This resentment grew into an ideological philosophy and nationalism away from Europe that set up three antagonistic groups—English, Afrikaners, and Africans—against one another, each under leadership that shaped their growth and effectively carved South Africa accordingly into those three main groups. The Afrikaners are defined by their language, which became known as Afrikaans and is a derivation from the Dutch language. They became a strong, homogenous group that saw Africans as inferior beings they could not live with and soon saw the English as a threat to the type of master/servant relationship they sought to live by with the inferior beings. Of this group, the poorest were the trekboers, who wandered from place to place in search of grazing pastures for their cattle. This took them deep into African territory and inevitably resulted into clashes over land, of which the Battle of Blood River is the worst example.

In 1834 Britain abolished slavery in all its territories throughout its empire, precipitating the Great Trek, which is a historically recorded exodus of Afrikaners in the mould of that of the Israelites from Egypt after the seven fat and lean years to the Promised Land. This event took place over three years from 1835 to 1837, engaging 5,000 Boers and about 5,000 coloured servants across the Orange and Vaal Rivers. Among them, the voortrekker (pioneer) Afrikaners shared among them what Pakenham calls "one article of faith", this being to deny any political rights to the Africans and coloured people of mixed race.

When the Napoleonic Wars broke out in 1806, Britain occupied the Cape permanently for strategic reasons. The Cape was a naval base protecting English interests in the trade with the East. However, the Cape did not attract British immigrants, because it was dry and arid, and for this reason, the Afrikaners far outnumbered the English. Attempts were made to send the 1820 British settlers but did not solve the problem of numbers. In 1843 Britain occupied Natal, a voortrekkers area (note that it was no longer Zulu territory), creating a secondary colony.

In 1852 and 1854, England recognized the independence of the Free State and Transvaal Boer Republics. However, in 1877 she annexed the Transvaal with a view to create a federal state. In 1880 Paul Kruger and the Boers led by him revolted against the English and resultantly inflicted harm on the British, and this resulted in the Battle of Majuba in Natal. Gladstone returned as British prime minister and withdrew British forces from Natal, thus reversing British annexation. Gladstone's reversal policy gave the Boers an air of self-governance, but they still claimed overall paramount superiority in the area to avert any foreign-power interests in the area. Britain had full foreign affairs control of the Transvaal, but not as a colony or a member of her empire. Kruger consented on this in duress, and this was made formal by the Convention of Pretoria in 1881 and the Convention of London in 1884. Note that 1884 was the year in which Otto von Bismarck, the Austrian diplomat, scrambled for Africa and, summarily on a table in Berlin, divided Africa among the superpowers to divert French interests in Europe with a view to finalize his German unification efforts without Austria being part of that unification, though the two are in language and culture the same people. Kruger made it clear that he entered into that pact in duress and would, in future, remove British supremacy in the affairs of the Transvaal Republic.

Two multimillionaires, Cecil John Rhodes and Alfred Beit, entered into a conspiracy to take the Transvaal, which was rich with minerals, for themselves. The diamond rush to Kimberly facilitated the colony's way to self-government in 1870. Rhodes and Beit made a fortune out of diamonds, and the former became prime minister at the Cape. Together they founded a new African territory named Rhodesia (present-day Zimbabwe) on the north of the Transvaal Republic, thus adding to Boer encirclement in the region. The Boers found themselves encircled by the British at every turn. In 1886, the gold rush in the Witwatersrand, Transvaal, began in earnest. The Transvaal developed into the richest and militarily most powerful province in Southern Africa and increased the fortunes of both Rhodes and Beit. This inevitably triggered new tensions between the English and the Boers. Whilst the Uitlanders (foreigners) outnumbered the Afrikaners in the province, Kruger made the franchise difficult for the English. However, in 1895 the political hunger of the Uitlanders—backed by Rhodes and Beit's riches—offered the British a chance to win back the Transvaal, which had become a Canaan of Southern Africa in rich gold deposits. This pitted the Afrikaners against the British in a strife that was to spark a clash of alarming proportions—a monstrosity of a war that fanned hostilities and ill feelings among the English when news of war broke out in reports written Emily Hobhouse, an English woman who sympathized with the Afrikaners. This bitterness developed into racial hatred between the English and Afrikaners, fanned by J. B. M. Hertzog. In 1948 this developed into a policy that was to pit black versus white in a struggle that was to shape South African history in a manner untold. This became known as apartheid, which angered black South African nationalists and the world in the long term. Its atrocities against fellow humans shot itself in the foot.

Yes, unifications created new friends and new enemies, and so did revolutions in Europe. But the South African struggle was to become a centre for the evolution of political opinions and formulation of policies in Europe that were to result in a revolution that the world, including South Africans, is still trying to adapt to.

The South African Civil War, 1899–1902, is the beginning of that epic event that was to intensify into an internal racial and national hatred as well as international discord. The United Nations ran in circles until a South African diplomat dared the world to do its damnedest, and the result was sanctions that turned the wheels around to undo apartheid. What we, the current generation, are faced with are the consequences of that bold statement: "Do your damnedest!" The results were politically and economically severe for the apartheid state. Apartheid was brought to its knees and had reached its end.

POVERTY IN SOUTH AFRICA

Our poverty cannot at the moment be eradicated, but it can be alleviated by looking at how the apartheid state dealt with it. During the years of white governments, the poverty of ordinary Afrikaner citizens was a matter of primary concern. One area of interest in social and economic history against the backdrop of political influences has always been the subject of poor whites in South Africa. The apartheid state gave it full attention. At the time, poverty among blacks was considered not a problem but an acceptable natural phenomenon.

The phenomenon of history repeating itself (though it can only follow a cyclic pattern) is looming large in South Africa today. The years 1934 to 1948 saw the development of a fusion government in South Africa. Hertzog tried unsuccessfully to win Malan over into a fusion government pact. Malan sought republicanism, believing the British influence was jeopardizing Afrikaner nationalism. At the time, Malan was not as popular as Hertzog, who then turned to General Smuts. The National Party, Hertzog's creation, would collaborate with an imperialistic but Afrikaner South African party led by General Smuts to form the United South African National Party, with J. B. M. Hertzog as its leader and Smuts as its deputy, in 1934. This side-stepped policy regarding the roles of blacks, coloureds, and Asians, with the Cape having the franchise of blacks in the voters' roll. At the time, the ANC was ineffective because of divisive leadership opinionations—just as the case was a few weeks before the 8 May 2019 general elections. On the other hand, the Broederbond— inaugurated in 1918, its membership restricted to white males of Afrikaner origin and members of the Dutch Reformed Church—was promoting the Afrikaner language and culture. Malan joined the movement in 1933 and became its fervent apostle.

The fusion government's major concern was the poor white problem, which provides the reason why Hertzog's nationalistic passion made him compromise while still retaining his "South Africa First" views. His people were hungry! The Afrikaner economy had been plagued by industrialisation, the rinderpest, mining, a debilitating drought, and the Great Depression. In 1929 this poverty escalated. Some Afrikaners were landless and lived as *bywoners* (tenants) with no skills and poor training. Many Afrikaners had been affected by the "pull factor" industrialisation had on people and had been drawn to towns and required to adjust to urbanization, but because they were unskilled, they could not compete in the labour market. Despite their poor training, they regarded manual labour as being meant for blacks and too degrading for them—a legacy of the Great Trek regarding the maintenance of proper relations between master and servant. Today the tables have turned and local blacks regard some remuneration as too low for them and are accepted by foreign nationals.

Commissions after commissions were appointed to scientifically investigate the poor white problem. The Carnegie Commission (1929–1932) produced a report on the problem, resulting in the formation of a government department, the Department of Social Development, in 1937, two years after the Carnegie Commission had submitted its report. Unemployment among whites escalated into a political issue, and legislation promoting white interests was passed. The formation of the fusion government was intended to resolve the socioeconomic crises of the time, which are comparable to what South Africans are experiencing at the present moment. The cyclic philosophy of history is revealing this eighty-two years after it was first experienced. This time it is blacks who are mostly hard hit, but whites are also feeling the pinch; whereas begging in the streets was a black thing in the past, it has now crossed over to our white fellow citizens. Mentally sick people are strewn all over South Africa, and one in particular lives in an open veld between Frankfurt and Tweeling on the road to an intersection to Reitz, Bethlehem, and Petrusteyn in the Free State Province. Imagine a person living by the roadside with the sky as his blanket.

The poor white problem (1929–1932) is a chronicle featured in order to examine the ways previous governments dealt with the socioeconomic challenges which are main causes for crime. A problem nipped at the bud from its fundamental causes is a problem solved, and this is something the fusion government did admirably well. It is important to note that not all of our past is bad; the only bad apple in it has always been racism. From this past, we need to harvest good apples and make use of them. In truth, when I taught this history in my classes, I always felt resentment about the notion that poverty among my people was regarded an acceptable natural phenomenon. It was a very bitter aspect of our history to teach, but it had to be taught! It was in the curricula, and this showed how much the government cared for its people.

THE NATURE OF CONTENT

As its title indicates, this book is concerned with a chronicled analytic assessment of aspects of our history that have influenced our present as South Africans. It analytically chronicles the causal factors of a society plagued by leaders whose sole interests became their own interests and not so much national issues plaguing our country, its economy, and our communities. The devil's fork security fences that have become abundant in South Africa, the vicious dogs inside our yards and inside our houses, and the pythons guarding us are all indicative of the insecurity the postapartheid state has imposed on its citizens. In every township and suburb, security firms are raking in millions of rands because of the reigning state of insecurity. This book takes parts of our history and analyses their impact on our history, resulting in the current state of chaos and corrupt governance engulfing our new dispensation and eating away at our economy and our national pride.

Very few connected individuals are cashing in from the new policies designed to address the black condition of poverty, taking advantage of the Broad-Based Black Economic Empowerment government policy, and the looting of the national treasury is followed by costly commissions of inquiry. This has not only ruined the economy but has also dumped South Africa into a state of anarchy, as evidenced in the recent North West Province upheavals and South Africa's having been downgraded to junk status. These anarchical developments are scaring off job-creating investors. Imposing leaders preferred by powers that be in metros have had very negative results, as evidenced in Gauteng, Tshwane, and Port Elizabeth. In retrospect, what Trollip was doing as executive mayor in

Nelson Mandela Bay is what proper governance is all about, and if his example had been followed, we would be cruising towards economic recovery. But it was not to be. He was setting a "bad" example and had to be quickly removed through coalition between the ANC and EFF.

Apartheid has always been the cause of our problems since its inception. Yonder was the Union of South Africa, which deprived natives of every right, resulting in the formation of what was to be renamed the African National Congress just two years after the Union of South Africa in 1910. The 1913 Land Act became a lemon that soured relations between the two races. It culminated in the current policy of expropriation of land without compensation, clouding the much anticipated new dawn promised by Ramaphosa. His secretary general, Ace Magashule, is causing confusion in the Free State, and its municipalities are in a state of paralysis, and most are under administration. He is tarnishing and discarding whatever new dawn Ramaphosa has in mind, and this is confusing the voter as internal factions divide the movement.

Though apartheid is the causal factor of the pre-1994 malady, what happened after 1994 cannot be blamed on it but should be a shared responsibility, because removing racism from the constitution did not mean races would suddenly fall in love. The road to true freedom is still marred by the natural preference of doves being with doves, elephants with elephants, birds with birds, and zebras with zebras. In human nature, blacks are instinctively more drawn towards one another, and much the same with whites, without either necessarily being racist. South Africans should attune their minds to this and accept as fact and let state resources benefit all South Africans without regard to race or political affiliation. As South Africans, we belong to a common fatherland with national symbols which should blind us to diversity and encourage the remaking of our country as one with naturally preferred racial associations like those of our fellow four-legged and feather-winged creatures. In unison we can fly, but we may do so in preferred associations that are not necessarily intentionally racist.

The apartheid was built upon the segregation order which had developed along the industrialization of South Africa after the discovery of diamonds in 1869 and gold in 1886. Race and class relations in the industrial development era grew around the forms of domination and privilege which arose from the founding of the Dutch settlement in the

Cape in 1652. This should prepare the present generation to gather their thoughts and put their heads together to mend differences and map out a way to a common future as a nation.

As we do this, our country has become a new ground for local and international politics. We have in our midst a host of international settlers who play significant roles in reshaping South Africa's future. Foreign nationals of various nationalities have landed at Oliver Tambo International Airport to make a living far away from their lands of birth. They are a new reality that should be respected. For this reason, xenophobia and Afrophobia should be guarded against. Unfortunately, some of our foreign nationals have become a threat to our social fabric, introducing things that pose a danger to our societies. For this reason, where the guilty are proved to be such, the law should take its course.

South Africa, in its government leadership, has had a host of reluctant reformers, of whom former state president F. W. De Klerk is not one. His predecessors, like P. W. Botha, fall squarely within that group that existed during the time when apartheid was frowned upon. Some may argue that he was somewhat reluctant, but pressured by the circumstances of the times. Figuratively, he had a gun pointed to his head, forcing him to convincingly lead political change in South Africa.

P. W. Botha missed a golden opportunity to reform apartheid on 15 August 1985 under the glare of international expectation in a speech in Durban. Verwoerd also resisted Harold Macmillan's "Winds of Change" speech in the apartheid Parliament on 3 February 1960. It was a repetition of an address already made in Accra, Ghana, but it received media attention in South Africa. It reflected a shift in British policy regarding apartheid. If anything, the speech hardened Verwoerd's attitude, and his grip on power became defined by his protection of white minority interests.

Of interest are the opening lines of this historic speech, which need recitation:

> It is a ... special privilege for me to be here in 1960 when you are celebrating what I might call the golden wedding of your Union. At such a time it is natural and right that you should pause to take stock of your position, to look back at what you have achieved, to look forward to what

lies ahead. In the fifty years of their nationhood the people of South Africa have built a strong economy founded upon a healthy agriculture and thriving and resilient industries …

But it is the third paragraph of this historic speech that captures one's interest:

As I have travelled around the Union I have found everywhere, as I expected a deep preoccupation with what is happening in the rest of the African continent. I understand and sympathize with your interests in these events and your anxiety about them …

The next two paragraphs alarmingly and disturbingly take one's breath away:

Ever since the breakup of the Roman Empire one of the constant facts of political life in Europe has been the emergence of independent nations. They have come into existence over the centuries in different forms, different kinds of government, but all have been inspired by a deep, keen feeling of nationalism, which has grown as the nations have grown …

In the twentieth century, and especially since the end of the war, the processes which gave birth to the nation states of Europe have been repeated all over the world. We have seen the awakening of national consciousness in people who have for centuries lived in dependence upon some other power. Fifteen years ago this movement spread through Asia. Many countries there, of different races and civilizations, pressed their claim to an independent national life …

The next paragraph is a jaw-dropping inspiration and encouragement for the forces of revolution, as it was just after the breaking away of the

Robert Sobukwe group from Congress, when tension in the Union was very thick:

> The wind of change is blowing throughout this continent and whether we like it or not, this growth of national consciousness is a political fact. We must all accept it as a fact, and our national policies must take account of it …

South Africa's national policies did take account in a very recalcitrant, repressively abominable kind of way. Verwoerd very surprisingly proudly walked out of the Commonwealth soon after; it was not surprising but was not expected either. This was followed by the declaration of a republic in 1961, just like the Unilateral Declaration of Independence in Rhodesia when Britain dissociated herself from the Smith government.

Macmillan's following remark must have been the nail in the coffin of any hope for the success of liberation movements in South Africa at the time: "Well you understand this better than anyone; you are sprung from Europe, the home of nationalism …"

The South African government selected the right men to put in the right places to pursue racial segregation in the most repressive way. Yet the strength of African nationalism persisted nonetheless, and like a radicle pushing the soil for growth and exposure to sunlight, so moved African nationalism as defined by Macmillan, and Pik Botha took stock of it every step of the way.

South Africa's foreign minister, Roloef Frederick "Pik" Botha, well known for his forthrightness, was the only cabinet member and minister who had the guts to face reality. He realized that apartheid was a dream living on borrowed time.

He relented in agreeing that there was a possibility of a black president in South Africa, earning himself a backlash from South Africa's ultra-conservatives. He became the most interesting politician in South African Afrikaner politics—enterprising too. We loved to hate him, and we would laugh at some of his political antics despite the wicked, calculating nature of apartheid and his part in it. It was not surprising that he was also a member of the first democratic cabinet. Pik had the political clout to face the truth in an astounding manner and with a straight face, looking his colleagues directly in the eye.

Pik Botha was actually a kind of apartheid misfit, because South Africa was politically dominated by leaders who were hell-bent on making apartheid work against all odds, with P. W. Botha and Dr Connie Mulder leading the pack, but the latter was smudged by the Information Scandal. Pik felt the apartheid sting in his travels abroad upon seeing hostile international media. The state firmly pursued the policy and was prepared to spare the lives of its soldiers, whose anthem indoctrinated them with the doctrine of "We shall live we shall die for thee, South Africa!"

The discovery of gemstones promoted the forms of domination and privilege arising from the 1652 Dutch settlement in the Cape in 1652, resulting in the Great Trek in 1834. This draws a line between the master-and-servant relationships that developed. Piet Retief explained in detail why the Afrikaners were leaving the Cape. He wrote that they were dissatisfied by the freeing of their slaves as a result of the philanthropic movement that was developing. Yet it was not so much the freedom of their slaves that engineered grievances, he stated, but the manner in which they were freed.

He expressed the general feeling of the Afrikaners that they were leaving the Cape with the full assurance that the British government would not interfere in their affairs in future. This meant a separate administration of the races—as expressed in the views of Anna Steenkamp, a woman of Afrikaner descent—to keep black people enslaved to serve the white race. This the Afrikaners believed in, and it was to shape apartheid policy for many years.

The genesis of "apartheid" emanates from the above-mentioned situation. It was used as a slogan of the D. F. Malan–led National Party for the first time in the 1948 general elections, with General Smuts relaxed in believing that his popularity would win him the elections. He lost miserably.

Malan formalized proper relations between master and servant in what was beginning to shape into an ideology. He was the first conservative academic Afrikaner leader to become head of state after forty-six years of the Anglo Boer War's effects, which the Afrikaners still felt. This justified the view that the Anglo-Boer War was an unwise conflict that should have been avoided.

Emily Hobhouse, a woman of British descent, described the full horrors of this war to the British government in a report she wrote. We will explore this report so we can understand what strengthened Afrikaner nationalism and also why the Afrikaners made South Africa their jewel. The Afrikaners are a result of the making of a nation through the teaching of history and the development of a religion that made them confident and self-reliant. This development was facilitated by the Union of South Africa (1910–1961). Traditional Afrikaner historians refer to this as a shaping through an indoctrinating system of education, which was effective. I vividly call to mind these teachings in our history lectures at Fort Hare University. They were made by prolific visiting academics who espoused their own sources as Afrikaners at heart.

EMILY HOBHOUSE'S EXPOSITION OF THE 1899–1902 WAR

Hobhouse's exposition of the war is graphic. She compares it to a parish she knows very well in England and is apparently well known to the English people, too, where funerals were a one-off activity. What she was experiencing in South Africa, she wrote, was at least twenty-five people being buried on a daily basis. In her view, it was an unprecedented death rate since diseases had decimated English populations. Talking about death in the South African concentration camps became a normal daily occurrence, as she explained in her reports. People lay sick and dying and were buried with corpses, carried away at dawn. Her reports noted the smell of death and the burial of many in big trenches. A newspaper cartoonist depicted the Queen of England washing herself in innocence of these developments in South Africa. The reports had the desired effects.

Lloyd George, a British politician who later became prime minister, intervened and forced debates on the subject, alarmed by Emily Hobhouse's reports. As a politician, he was alarmed because it was the aim of the crown to subject the Afrikaners to British authority with a view to prevent a second power from taking over in Southern Africa. The aim was to make it a British sphere of influence, which thus necessitated wining the

Afrikaners over. What alarmed him most were child deaths, which he saw as discrediting British rule in Africa. His statements and assessment of the situation proved him right when the effects of the war fuelled Afrikaner nationalism. J. B. M. Hertzog was its most fervent, passionate, and most vociferous prophet. He took the war and all its painful consequences personally and resented everything English—even the language!

Lloyd George's view shaped and influenced the British reception of the African nationalists' delegations to London in protest against the Native Land Act (no. 27 of 1913), which Sol Plaatje saw as making South African blacks more than slaves but pariahs and polecats in the land of their forebears. This, as shall be seen, became a source for major concerns regarding land issues, escalating into the expropriation without any compensation in our time that will surely make investors take a step back to consider their options. Who in their right minds will risk such an ill-advised and unworthy of consideration enterprise? Implementation must tread carefully and very lightly, like one walking a tightrope. It is a disastrous recipe in a land plagued by unemployment in a stagnant economy that is failing to create jobs. Economic activity in all countries is promoted by a stable political situation. Governments do not create employment but create conducive conditions to attract investors who are job creators to make profits. Healthy policies and a stable labour market become attractive to investors, and job-related strikes are an impediment to job creation, as was the case in South Africa when unions were empowered to be representatives of workers' interests. It soon became clear that in the Council for Conciliation and Mediation Arbitration, workers were more empowered than employers and that work stoppages discouraged investors.

This was a digression showing that as much as the Afrikaner was aggrieved by the 1899–1902 war, so was the African by the brutality of the 1913 land dispossession. Such aggravation can find expression in work stoppages that become harmful to the very jobs governments seek to create. This means people should realize that some policies can actually be albatrosses around the necks of their very socioeconomics. Historical events that affect economic current developments emanate from the hostilities between the English and Afrikaners, in which Africans became sacrificial lambs to broker reconciliation between South Africa's "master races". Be this as it may, vengeance should not cloud reality and pragmatism, as this will surely make the situation worse than it currently is.

Emily Hobhouse's description of the effects of the war situation is harrowing and heart-rending. Lloyd George's reaction gives us the full picture of the effects the Anglo Boer War had on the British conscience. It also makes one understand why and how the war shaped Afrikaner nationalism. Hertzog became the man of the moment, and his heart went out to the Afrikaner cause, and it deepened his spirit of nationalism to pursue Afrikaner self-determination. The pictures of concentration camps in the media tell a tale of their own. Emaciated Afrikaner children in refugee camps and in coffins, as well as the executions of Afrikaner men, all tell a distressing story, making people understand where the Afrikaner comes from as a nation imbued with a spirit of nationalism—a national togetherness and consciousness that was to generate and inspire an Africanist national reaction when their cause deprived Africans of their ancestral land via the 1913 Land Act.

Yes, in a country that was not theirs, they systematically took land from its rightful owners. But still the reader understands present-day Afrikaner reactions to democratic change. They were never prepared for what was happening, and this is what reconciliation should take cognizance of, despite Macmillan's advisory speech, which in retrospect became counterrevolutionary in that it made apartheid policies even more repressive.

On the other hand, the Afrikaner should also feel what Africans feel from an episode history recorded as the "national suicide of the Amaxhosa" as a result of Nongqauze's false prophecy, which was suspected as a British ploy to domesticate the Amaxhosa. This was the first step of what was to become the dispossession of Africans in their native land. They were rich stock farmers and landowners who saw whites as land predators; the Amaxhosa were duped into believing their ancestors would drive whites into the sea if they destroyed their crops and slaughtered their cattle. The poverty that followed ensured their complete domestication through employment and even slavery. To the African, the national suicide of the Amaxhosa became analysed as a tragic incident, further straining relations among races. Dingane's treachery and betrayal of Retief's trek party added to the Afrikaner's psychological bleeding as the African's wound over the loss of their precious land festered.

On arrival in Natal, Piet Retief and his followers sought land. They met Dingane, whose cattle had been taken by his enemies, and promised the Retief party land only if they could reclaim their cattle from a powerful neighbour. After successfully swiftly recovering them, they were invited to a celebration feast and asked to leave their armaments outside the king's kraal. This was a sly disarmament the trek party did not suspect. In the midst of the celebrations, Dingane commanded his warriors to kill the Afrikaners with a war cry of "bulal 'abathakathi!" (Kill the wizards!). The long and short of the story is that it resulted in the Battle of Blood River in 1938, so called because the Ncome River turned red with Amazulu blood. The Afrikaners had vowed to God that they would build a church in his honour if the enemy were delivered into their hands. Many Amazulu (10,000 to 15,000) were killed in a vengeful war of attrition that followed with the Ncome River becoming red with Amazulu blood, resulting in the naming of the conflict as the Battle of Blood River.

This sealed a hateful rivalry and mistrust between Africans and Afrikaners. This victory became annually celebrated on 16 December first as Dingane's Day, which was changed to Day of the Vow and later the Day of the Covenant. Each celebration added salt to the psychological wounds festering on both sides of the racial divide, hardening racial attitudes and making people tense, with racial hatred brewing and solidifying over the years. Every drop of the races' blood over the years intensified racial strife and silently bred racial hatred, which was intensified by riots against racial oppression. These incidents planted and nurtured racial stereotypes and attitudes in the races' hearts, where human emotions are bred, nurtured, and stored.

Today, to promote and breed generational and genealogical reconciliation, this holiday, 16 December, has been renamed the Day of Reconciliation; but its true history must be retold to make this truly conciliatory in the making of a new South African nation. Referring to South Africans as united in diversity is actually divisive. Unity must be blind to diversity and must highlight similarities for the races to be genuinely reconciled.

THE EVOLUTION OF APARTHEID

Malan, Strijdom, and Smuts had the same sentiments, though the latter was progressive and more aligned towards international matters than the Afrikaner nationalism that was gaining momentum and strength. There was a determination by the trio to preserve white civilization, and this was threatened by a liberal race-based policy that would destroy it. On the international plane, Smuts had to be in complete accord with Malan and Strijdom. Smuts thus addressed the international family in accordance with maintaining a desire to harmonize whites towards a common purpose of preserving white interests in a South Africa that was shaping a policy which was being expressed in South African institutions with very far-reaching effects in the future civilisation of the African people. In South Africa, there developed a practice of giving natives their own separate parallel institutions. On these drawn parallel lines, we may yet be able to solve a problem which otherwise may be not solvable. We, the current generation, must be resolved to try to make black and white stay in the same system and live together in harmony. Our political institutions have to promote this desire and be designed to be accommodative of all cultures and all people from all walks of life. What is admirable is that our public institutions, shopping malls, and some buses and other forms of vehicles have room for physically challenged or alternatively abled people, because in our societies, we do not have disabled people.

This is affirmed by South Africans who are trying to find and reach one another through sports, as we often see white South Africans in their favourite teams' attires in stadiums across the country. These are incidents South Africa should promote in song and in all other forms of social interactions. African reactions to the practice of giving the natives their own separate institutions on parallel lines with whites started first as consultative and begging reactions. African leaders like Chief Albert Luthuli (1952–1958), Nobel Peace Prize laureate, began seeing the struggle and its desires through a glass ceiling they could see through but that refused to be broken. This practice should not be practised by postapartheid governments as reverse racism, because we are all not so different after all. Our human needs for belonging are the same and interactive sports should draw South Africans together, now that what used to be a 'glass ceiling' has now been broken by the 1994 revolution. It is every South Africans wish to actualise. This can only be achieved by state interventions of levelling the ground for all racial groups to actualise their potential. Reverse racism is a sin against mankind just as apartheid was a sin against mankind. Two wrongs can never make a right! None other than Nelson Mandela himself said during the Rivonia Trial that his struggle of achieving equality in a land of unequal opportunities was a struggle he hoped to live for and achieve, and if needs be, it was a struggle for which he was prepared to sacrifice his life for. The South Africa that was a land of contrasts now has to be a land of equal opportunities without regard to race, colour nor creed. This is our only hope for a stress free life and existence on earth.

Our past in General Smuts's policy on the native issues had been one of inconsistencies, but during J. G. Strijdom's administration it became firm. Between the years 1939 and 1948 under Smuts, it had been more inclined towards liberalization on native policy, but his actions defeated its realization. His inconsistencies on native policy made him unreliable to white minority interests and led to a loss in faith that was expressed in the 1948 elections when Dr Malan toppled him from power. Malan and Strijdom after him became firmly rigid, and Verwoerd took it to the next level. Luthuli's frustrations were real and could be empathized with only by the Nobel Peace Committee when he was nominated and won. Referring to this is an attempt to say it does not go unnoticed that it did happen but should not stand in the way of reconciliation. It is our duty, the current generation, to redeem ourselves from this sad inconsistent past to build a future that is based on consistencies to remake our land.

Smuts's inconsistencies during the First World War found expression in the futility of subjecting black and white administration to the same machinery of governance, yet seeking liberal policies. Against his convictions, he stated that black and white were different in colour and mind, as well as in political status, and therefore should have separate political institutions. It is this that later developed into apartheid's obnoxious signs in public amenities: "Swartes" "Bantu" / "Blanke" "Whites" / "Nie Blanke" "Non-Whites", etc. These amenities were separate and unequal in maintenance, as those for blacks were cheaper and dirty while those for whites were spotlessly clean and kept clean by the very Verwoerd-created inferior education policy that produced cheap black labour as farmhands and not labourers. Black markers of matriculation examination papers in Pretoria were given government first-class train tickets from their places of abode whilst there were no first-class train coaches for blacks, and this infuriated a lot of markers. This separateness today, however, must be used to foster racial integration and keep the past in the past.

Smuts ended up defending separate institutions for blacks and whites, and their inequality as well. He was liberal and progressive in mind but was forced into a policy that compromised his deep-seated political convictions. His inconsistencies put him and Afrikaner nationalism at a crossroads that would result in his defeat by the apartheid sloganeering in the 1948 elections, which he lost by banking on his popularity. That there was a time when racial integration was actually considered by some white partisan groups should spur South Africans on towards acceptance and moving forward to make South Africa a racially integrated society.

The apartheid vision evolved into government policy after 1948, and separateness was met with a bitterness that grew over the years into growls of anger and public outcries of "Away with Afrikaans" and "Away with Bantu Education!" Schoolchildren reacted against Afrikaans as medium of instruction in a Bantu education policy Congress denounced in 1954 as being designed to create docile cheap labour for mines, farms, and related industries. Resistance is also a positive thing that should assist the interracialization of the people of South Africa, leading from negativity to positivity.

For the sake of clarity, South African leadership can be divided into two periods, viz. the "Era of Generals", with Generals Smuts, Hertzog (the supreme Afrikaner nationalist), and Botha as its leaders; followed by the "Era of Academics", of whom Drs Malan and Verwoerd were the mainstream and most supreme, with Dr Malan's conception of "apartheid" being a warning against "die swart gevaar" (the black danger). Dr Verwoerd shaped this into what was to become an ideology infused in government policy as institutionalized racism, becoming part of every aspect of South African life. Sandwiched between them, J. G. Strijdom (1954–1958), a University of Pretoria alumnus, was an equally uncompromising Afrikaner nationalist nicknamed the Lion of the North. These perceptions should show us where we come from as a nation and scientifically help us to live together harmoniously.

In B. J. Vorster's administration, apartheid grew into a catatonic, schizophrenic monstrosity that was to occupy white minds for years as institutionalized racism that had always been there but had not been defined by government policy when conceived by Dr Malan as apartheid. Verwoerd, after Strijdom, systematically and ruthlessly shaped it into policy as an ideology into native administration and education—one superior and the other inferior. B. J. Vorster sadistically enjoyed it, later to fall with a thud in a scandal, at which time he passed the baton to P. W. Botha, the finger-wagging prime minister.

Under Botha, focus was firmly on the independence of homelands, and white superiority deepened to keep blacks inferior. Enmity between the two races also grew by leaps and bounds. P. W. Botha was a university dropout—in effect a matriculant produced by Voortrekker Hoer Skool (high school) in Bethlehem Free State, seventy-five kilometres from Qwaqwa. His hometown is Paul Roux, and the house he grew up in is known to the locals and is shown to tourists; it is a humble house just like Nelson Mandela's homestead in Qunu.

In 1968 to 1969, to highlight South Africa's policy of white superiority, the government spent a paltry fourteen rands for every black child in education, and a huge chunk for every white child's education, with buses carting children from their home gates to school and from school back home in the safety of their parents. This disparity in educational provision was attacked by Abram Tiro as Student Representative Council president at Turfloop University, leading to his harassment by the system, which prompted him to flee the country to Botswana, where a parcel bomb killed him. Education for whites was compulsory, whilst for blacks it was not. What made it compulsory was that the parents did not pay for it. Also compulsory was military training at the age of eighteen.

If this does not highlight the assurance of white superiority and black inferiority, nothing will. Over the years, the quality of education of the white child steadily grew, whilst that of the black child deteriorated. Afrikaner governments became insanely wicked, and their repressive policies grew just as reactions against it abounded and grew to an eardrum-piercing crescendo from black reactions. It is this that has partly caused stagnation of economic development, because all South Africans were caught in a situation in which the majority were uneducated and could not be absorbed into the economic mainstream. However, the Carnegie Commission had shown that scientific inquiries solve such social maladies. It should have been copied for a scientific intervention rather than the twenty-five-year-old trial and error of 1994 to date that has dumped the country into junk status.

From 1910, the time of the formation of the Union of South Africa, apartheid was an undefined sociopolitical way of life. The year 1912 marks a formally politicized black reaction. In that year, it became clear that blacks were alienated from social, educational, political, and economic life and were not part of their fatherland. This dissatisfaction led to the formation of the South African Native National Congress, later renamed the African National Congress (ANC). Professor Z. K. Matthews played a prominent role in black reactions against inferior education in South Africa, resigning his Fort Hare post and becoming Botswana's representative in the United Nations, where he became bigger than that country.

The ANC grew in strength until 1959, when the Pan-Africanist Congress broke away, feeling that the struggle for liberation was compromised. Its emblem and coat of arms reflect the pan-Africanism that was developing in Ghana's solo black star, along with a hammer and a sickle on its national flag, showing its socialist inclinations. However, apartheid developed unabated and gained strength. This was despite Macmillan's warning and advice in 1960 in the South African Parliament in his sweeping tour of Africa.

In 1974, in the course of a speech given by B. J. Vorster, who was to fall from grace because of the infamous Information Scandal, a foreign female journalist made a remark which raised his ire and showed his sadism. The remark was based on the realization that there was no indication that Mr Vorster, or any of his cabinet ministers or their white constituency, were prepared to denounce apartheid and to allow black majority rule in South Africa. To this Vorster slowly but surely, with a rising tone of anger from deep inside, replied that apartheid was now equated with refusal to facilitate black majority rule and that members of the apartheid government were now being accused of not being prepared to allow black majority rule in South Africa. Vorster put the record straight, stating that there would be a black majority in the Transkei, which was on the verge of becoming independent, and that there would be black majority rule for all the Zulus in Kwazulu, Bophuthatswana, Lebowa, Venda, the Ciskei, Qwaqwa, and Gazankulu, but in white South Africa, only whites would rule South Africa, and there would be no black majority rule. One has to wonder how he would have reacted had he lived to see black majority rule in our time.

Apparently the Stellenbosch University–trained Afrikaner leaders D. F. Malan, H. F. Verwoerd, and B. J. Vorster had a common political and ideological DNA streak, and apartheid blood passionately flowed through their veins. J. G. Strijdom, with the University of Pretoria as his alma mater, shows that the Afrikaner bond was not an academic matter only but stemmed from the Anglo-Boer War and was shaped into policy by Afrikaner academics.

Yet there is something in these developments that the current crop of leaders should perhaps learn in Afrikaner politics, this being that the Muldergate Scandal claimed B. J. Vorster's political scalp and career, as he had to resign in shame when implicated, to become state president—a ceremonial office he was later forced to relinquish. He died a broken, miserable, shamed man about four years later. The evident silent lesson is that apartheid administration did not condone corruption, no matter the good intentions of the perpetrator. I wonder if we can unashamedly say the same about the present-day black administration. Corruption deploys the high and mighty to parliamentary membership in order that they may keep enjoying the good life—a practice that must come to a screeching halt!

Balthazar Johannes Vorster's term includes the ruthless suppression of the Soweto riots and Mapetla Mohapi and Steve Biko's deaths in detention, leaving Jimmy Kruger, minister of police, cold ("dit laat my koud"). This caused the blood of blacks to boil, and their reactions reverberated countrywide as apartheid evolved, growing into a resolute, intransigent monster. This followed Mapetla Mohapi's death in detention on 5 August 1976, allegedly by suicide. The alleged written suicide note was addressed to security police officer Captain P. A. Schoeman, whom I knew from Alice, a town next to Fort Hare Universiy in the Eastern Cape, and read, "Death Cell, Kei Road, 5 August 1976, bidding goodbye Captain Schoeman, challenging him to carry go on interrogating his dead body and sarcastically hoping he would what he wanted from it, asking him to pass his warmest regards to his family and his people." However, as we followed this case during an inquest, a handwriting expert testified in court and showed the differences between the writing on the note and Mapetla's handwriting, declaring it a clumsy imitation.

Mapetla was a Steve Biko associate, together with Dr Mamphela Ramphela, the now failed South African academic politician, and all three were banished to the Eastern Cape. I attended both Mohapi's funeral at Jozana's Nek, in Herschel Eastern Cape, and, in 1977, Biko's funeral at Ginsburg, near King William's Town, as I was at the time a student at Fort Hare University. The Eastern Cape print media wrote that never were Fort Hare students as united in purpose as they were by Steve Biko's death in detention. One newspaper editor earned the wrath of B. J. Vorster, and he lived like a prisoner in his own home until, in disguise as a priest, he escaped into Lesotho over Tele Bridge in Herschel, met his family, and flew with them to safety in London. It was a very narrow escape indeed!

P. W. Botha inherited this politically volatile situation on 27 September 1978. We were traumatized but strengthened. Riots broke out in Soweto in 1976 when we were en route to university after the holiday, and these were followed by unprecedented police reprisals, causing a new deep wave of international disgust. Black protest literature predicted in a black renaissance convention in Hamanskraal in December 1974 that one day Soweto was going to burst. Indeed, one and half years later, on 16 June 1976, Soweto burst.

These riots and police reprisals added to the psychological trauma of the time. Reading papers on our way to the reopening of Fort Hare University after the winter holiday, we were shocked and traumatized. We knew immediately on arrival at the university that we would be heading back home pretty soon. As it was, we did not have to pack our luggage, and some of us had a wasted academic session, but we registered for the following session.

The suddenness of incidents such as these make change in South Africa psychologically traumatic, as they lie dormant in our minds and our memories. The system of apartheid and the hate and distrust it engineered among races is so deeply rooted and seated that it will take generations to undo. Sanctions were not expected to have the strength to uproot the system, and when they did, the revolution became an exciting, anxiety-filled psychological trauma, which also entrenched it in human memory.

Too much blood had flowed in South Africa and in neighbouring states, as recorded in songs by a Lesotho-based musical outfit, Uhuru, whose change of name to Sankomota records a horrific cross-border incident in which the South African Defence Force attacked places in Lesotho suspected of harbouring freedom fighters the system called terrorists.

All this was harrowing, horrific, deathly, and repressive—traumatic—not only to the victims of the attacks and their families, but inside South Africa as well, and for those in the diaspora abroad. It rippled to the periphery of the world, sending shockwaves every kilometre of the way. That is why apartheid's fall resulted in black jubilation and white anxiety as the system met its end and responded to its death knell. White anxiety was obviously fuelled by fear for vengeance, which was allayed to very little effect. Musicians celebrated freedom in joyful recordings, and the excitement spread like wildfire.

Truthfully, every incident resulting from a desire to end apartheid and its retaliation was reflected in the Hector Pieterson incident, showing that the apartheid system had shot itself in the foot. The sanctions that followed repressed the oppressor, strangled the economy, and eventually squeezed life out of it and had to be dismantled, and this traumatized all and sundry, including its leaders.

That generation of academics' glimpses into the future saw the political mood of the time, when collaboration with the apartheid state was seen as a nauseating factor by the educated elite's defiance of apartheid. Chief Gatsha Buthelezi was an outspoken opponent of apartheid policies but experienced the hostility of black radicals. All homeland leaders became strait-jacketed as puppets of the apartheid state, and all these developments did not bode well for South Africa's future. Glimpses into the future showed an unalluring situation under a radical black regime.

These glimpses into the future after Vorster's administration envisaged the mayhem of postapartheid South African society, which could not ever have fully predicted what would follow through the anxiety that sparked off a trauma resulting in a catastrophic loss of human lives. The loss of human life that was unprecedented in our time, though this was a common event in the fall of colonialism in formerly colonized Africa, shattered and traumatised the nation. Also, Johannesburg had many traumatized domestic animals left by their owners who fled black majority when bans over liberation movements were lifted.

It is this that is psychologically traumatizing, and it is this that needs to be addressed to free South Africa from the remnants of apartheid still clouding our minds, allowing us to carve out a future for our progeny without regard to race, colour, or creed. Reconciliation can be practical only if we can identify what the causal factors of postapartheid discord became and address them. We must remember that denials will not dress the wounds but affirmation will help seek redress going forward and heal the nation. Denialism will not help.

Our common destiny, however, is to heal the economy, and the need for bread and butter is what has to inspire reconciliation.

Perhaps 6 April 1969 became a turning point in the viciousness of the apartheid state when police in Sharpeville opened live fire on peacefully protesting people, shooting them whilst they were fleeing, nine years after Harold Macmillan's speech.

The casualty list was disturbing, and a sad reminder of this spectacle was the 1976 Soweto riots, which escalated racial tension. The banning of liberation movements triggered Resolution 134 by the United Nations Security Council, effectively making South Africa the polecat of the world.

Reacting to this with conceited pride, South Africa walked out of the Commonwealth of Nations in 1961, and on the 31 May of the same year, it became a republic. On the whole, this was a painful but eventful period in the history of South Africa. An uncompromising intransigence hung like the dark cloud that once hovered over Hiroshima and Nagasaki in 1942. Apartheid, like Shaka when his mother Nandi died, had gone mad!

Verwoerd was authoritarian and socially conservative and sought to at all costs preserve white minority rule over various black ethnic groups, including Khoisans, coloureds, and Indians who were the majority. He expanded apartheid policy and relayed it to equally resolved Afrikaner leaders to implement what was characterized as good neighbourliness. Yet it was a domination that made blacks a subject people until 1994, when a new constitution drafted by Cyril Ramaphosa and Roelf Meyer was adopted with a new Bill of Rights.

If on 6 September 1966, Dimitri Tsanfendas sought to kill and destroy apartheid when he killed H. F. Verwoerd, its architect, he only added to its intransigence and recalcitrant stance, as B. J. Voster succeeded him. J. G. Strijdom, who had preceded Verwoerd, had been equally bent on making the policy work. Verwoerd brewed apartheid into a concoction that became a discredited polecat of the world, exploding into the 1976 Soweto riots. He was the last prime minister of the Union of South Africa, which he led into a four-province republican administration in 1961, after the Macmillan Winds of Change Speech in the South African Parliament.

When we became a republic in 1961, I was eight years of age doing substandard B (grade 2 in today's education system). I vaguely remember holding a small flag I did not understand and having a gold-coloured medal pinned to my blazer, which I also did not understand. The small flag and the gold-coloured object I did not understand were symbols of a system bent on denying me, at that tender age, my citizenship rights in apartheid South Africa, the land of my forebears. They meant I had no political future in my native land. Where would I have a future, with rights that go with citizenship? In a homeland, Bantustan, for Botswana, Bophuthatswana, whose map no genius could draw. It was a banana republic strewn all over South Africa from Thaba Nchu to Rustenburg and Mahikeng, Mmabatho. Dr Lucas Mangope was its father. Eddie, his son, whose tragic death I read in the media about, was my colleague at Fort Hare University.

Whilst the Nongqauze tragedy in the Cape can be said to have been self-inflicted, the Sharpeville Massacre was an unprecedented racial killing of unarmed and defenceless people, including children, and it was to become a turning point in the history of apartheid. It demonstrated the lengths apartheid was prepared to go to, to defend the indefensible. It was a message to black nationalists that white South Africa was staying put and was not prepared to move an inch or a fraction thereof to share South Africa with them. The Soweto riots of 1976 and how the apartheid state dealt with them were a shot to its foot. The incident was to activate the mineral-stifled voice of international conscience when it became audible after the Hector Pieterson photo that dominated international media to become Pik Botha's living nightmare and caused sanctions to be put firmly in place.

South Africa's inflexion point was in 1910, when she became a union. This was engineered by Britain with a determination to bring about peace between the Boer and Britain, the colonial superpower, which turned a deaf ear to black aspirations and literally left blacks in a lurch, where they were to stay for almost another century. This was the British policy of pacification to redress Afrikaner hostility and its cries of sorrow after the Anglo-Boer War. Black suffering became a pacifier like the dummy a mother sticks in a crying child's mouth to keep it quiet. Hence the failure of the Sol Plaatje Dube–led delegation to London.

This was to change when Macmillan gave a polite but firm denunciation of apartheid in his "Winds of Change" speech to a shocked press audience in the South African Parliament, to which Verwoerd reacted with tragic intransigence. Apartheid tightened its grip on power. Unrest and mayhem followed, and the South African Bureau of State Security was strengthened. Verwoerd was shot by a deranged farmer, but he recovered and became even more repressive than ever, but South Africa's international isolation deepened. It put the apartheid state on its back foot, leading to her ultimate self-ejection from the Commonwealth. The United Nations became its bane where she became battered.

Having blacks totally at their mercy, the Boers carved South Africa into national states and shared a big chunk among whites just as Bismarck encouraged the scramble for Africa on a table in Berlin in 1884. Barely three years old, the Union government passed the Native Land Act of 1913, which was to become the bedrock of apartheid that denied blacks political and land rights outside homelands, which constituted only 13 per cent of South Africa.

The formation of the South African National Native Congress, later ANC, became a natural reaction to this repression, but delegations sent to London in protest yielded no fruits. Britain sacrificed blacks like pawns to the Union government, with no intervention whatsoever. Steve Biko was to sloganize in Black Consciousness sixty-three years later, "Black man, you are alone!", to awaken a consciousness that was to make him the enemy of the apartheid state, with dire consequences. Steve awoke a sleeping giant, and he was to pay the ultimate price for it in a horrific death. When this sloganeering took root, we were tertiary students, and we heard it loud and clear as we were conscientized to be proud of being black. It fuelled a unity of purpose that also attracted liberal white student support. All these developments also attracted the sympathy of Afrikaner men of the cloth, such as Reverends Beyer Naude (whom Govan Mbeki referred to as Oom Bey) and Theo Kotze in the early 1970s. It is such conscience-heeding emotions that will help heal our trauma and allow us to be men and women enough to say that the very African National Congress that fought the evils of apartheid has now betrayed the people of South Africa.

The greed for land by Afrikaners, which clouded any sense of sanity, shifted gears in the ANC from peaceful negotiations to aggressive reactions, leading to the formation of the ANC Youth League in 1944, and its adoption of the Programme of Action in 1949 has now become the greed of the powerful in postapartheid South Africa.

A sense of anger and urgency engulfed the ANC, especially when the apartheid-minded National Party came to power in 1948, dramatically changing the peaceful tone of negotiations with Afrikaner officials into a violent struggle. This became the beginning of a protracted struggle for power, and African liberation movements gained momentum, proving Macmillan more than right after 1960.

All these things today lie forgotten in the minds of greedy leaders. They have forgotten the defiance campaigns that ensued and the adoption of the Freedom Charter in 1955 in Kliptown, which planted the seeds of the total liberation of African people. The means of achieving liberation resulted in a split of ideological opinion within the ANC and split the movement into two, ending up with the formation of a pan-Africanist liberation organization, the Pan-Africanist Congress (PAC), which preempted planned ANC demonstrations against the pass laws, triggering the Sharpeville Massacre of 21 March 1960.

The once banned African liberation formations are now losing the respect of South Africans. The South African black subjects who were automatically politicized against apartheid when freedom movements went underground are now politicized against the forces of revolution. The Marikana incident, in which black miners were mowed down in a hail of live fire, called to mind incidents of black political suppression in apartheid South Africa because the revolution is failing the people dismally. The psychologically scarred and traumatized people of South Africa are disillusioned and losing hope in the revolution, the policies of which defeat their development, demanding a rethink on how to bring the people together to learn from one another to take South Africa forward.

The scars of psychological trauma are silently deepening and becoming evident in explosions of anger that flare up from time to time in destructive *toyi-toyi* (dances of excitement) that destroy the infrastructure. People are destroying and burning the little they have in their expressions of anger, and some schools are scenes of horrific violence that flares up from time to time. These things must be addressed through healthy policies that must identify where we went wrong. The fact is that in the Department of Education, only academics can scientifically put the rot right by putting into place policies that define human production. Politicians can only further their interests and those of their political parties to score points; they are unable to come up with practical and effective solutions to better the provision of education informed by a policy governing all nine provinces. Provincial administration must also be revisited, because as it is, the state is employing ten cabinets, nine of which are provincial legislatures. How effective is this system of administration, and does it not require further analysis? Secondly, do policies from the central government effectively channel into provincial administration to effectively control local and district municipalities? And finally, how effective are district municipalities in effecting government policies? These questions have to find right answers in an attempt to make governance effective, because in the past, municipal mayorship was a ceremonial position without political power.

Chapter 2

THE P. W. BOTHA YEARS—
INTRANSIGENCE

The P. W. Botha years were politically turbulent. P. W. Botha was under extreme pressure. He was grappling with very serious economic problems of an ailing economy under the violent siege of international sanctions and cultural boycotts. As a result, Botha lost interest in what he saw as petty issues. His anger was easily excited, and he sometimes overreacted. Those who were around him knew his wrath and nicknamed him the Pangaman for his ruthless removal of anyone who displeased him. His temper was volatile—explosive! Some people he physically manhandled experienced the psychological discomfort of being at close quarters with Prime Minister P. W. Botha's angry face. He grabbed them by the lapels of their jackets and shook them furiously, admonishing them about bothering him about petty issues when he was dealing with very serious pertinent matters and having to worry and be concerned.

He unceremoniously threw them out of his office door into the corridor, seething with anger. Such a fuming character in the corridors of eroding power reflects not only the character and anger of the man but also the extent of the trauma exerted by the feeling of an imminent, unavoidable revolution. The Rubicon had to be crossed to ease sanctions, but there was still hope in P. W. Botha that something could be done. But nothing could be done. The Rubicon had to be crossed, and he lost that opportunity on 15 August 1985.

Pieter Willem Botha's character and personality were those of a man who believed in the invincibility of the apartheid machinery, as portrayed in his "Rubicon" speech in Durban on 15 August 1985. Instead of loosening the apartheid grip, he tightened its screws with a firm institutionalized racism to appease his constituency and the whites of South Africa in general, giving them trust in the state and conscientizing their nationalism.

The system of apartheid was in place. Its army was strong and well resourced, with P. W. Bothat having been its builder. He held portfolios as both prime minister and minister of defence for two years. The army was the strongest in Africa and second to none. When Magnus Malan took over, he would boast that he could attack Africa at eight in the morning and have lunch in Cairo! That is how strong the South African army had become. Every white male above eighteen years of age was a trained soldier as policy, with a strong standing army, infantry, navy, and air force together making up the South African Armed Forces.

But its full might was never tested, because it was fighting an at times invincible enemy when guerrilla tactics became the only means of weakening the system. The finger-wagging head of state governed with threats which seemingly were empty, because as commander-in-chief of the South African Armed Forces, he could not command a full-scale war against unarmed and defenceless people he knew very well were opposed to the insanity of apartheid. It would have been an act of insanity and total mental derangement. His hands were tightly tied behind his back, leaving him frustrated.

P. W. Botha became his own enemy when Die Groot Krokodil nee The Pangaman (The Big Crocodile) opposed and firmly stood on the road to the political reconstruction of South Africa. At the back of his mind, P. W. Botha, like all his predecessors, had his constituency, which sought and could only support an aggressive, tough-jawed policy of retaliating against black resistance. He therefore found himself between the devil and the deep blue sea—between a rock and a hard place. He was seeking to please his *verkrampt* (conservative) support base, yet faced with hardening sanctions that were destroying the white economy and its hegemony, which his supporters could also not take and endure.

P. W. Botha went into a state of trauma that resulted in a destructive, life-threatening stroke as he resisted a Rubicon he had to cross, preferring to find refuge in the laager of his alma mater's name, Voortrekker Hoer Skool in Bethlehem—a conservative Eastern Free State Afrikaner town. His cabinet lost faith in him left him in the laager, and they prepared South Africa for the F. W. De Klerk years—albeit reluctantly, but under extreme economic sanctions' dictates. Sanctions were constricting the system, and something drastic and traumatic had to be done. It is not surprising that F. W. De Klerk started his administration with a "national" referendum for a mandate.

Yes, the nation moved from P. W. to F. W, who proved to be the man of the moment and led his people and South Africa out of the laager and towards a new political dispensation, albeit reluctantly. The question is, What was in his mind? Was it to genuinely bring about a transformation that would lose the Afrikaner its grip on political power? Answering this question in the next chapter will be tricky.

The P. W. Botha presidential years were tough for the apartheid state. They were years of reckoning because the system of apartheid had become a nauseating polecat. Its nauseating smell made apartheid unacceptable, and sanctions were squeezing the life out of it. Archbishop Desmond Mpilo Tutu became its nemesis. He became a sour and bitter taste in P. W. Botha's mouth, challenging Botha to a television debate. Botha's reply was that Tutu should focus on religion and he would focus on politics, and the debate was foiled.

Because of Tutu's weaponry of salvation through faith, Botha could not use force in silencing him; the Nobel Peace Prize raised his profile as a cleric and man of the cloth. Tutu's image grew and inspired his attempts to dismantle the apartheid state machinery. He realized and even commented that the Afrikaners are a God-fearing people. The United Democratic Front, active as an organization, and the African National Congress, in exile and underground, engaged in activities of rendering South Africa ungovernable, shaking the apartheid state to its very roots.

Succeeding B. J. Vorster, Pieter Willem Botha (P. W.) became the last prime minister of South Africa (1978–1984) and the first executive state president (1984–1989). He saw things differently to F. W. De Klerk and disfavoured the former's referendum, against which he campaigned for a no vote for a change to South Africa's constitution. He had suffered a debilitating stroke in 1989 and was coerced to vacate the presidency. He, like Chief Gatsha Buthelezi, preferred a federal system of government to an egalitarian democracy, based on the principles of separate development along equal lines, which nationalist radical black leaders were vehemently opposed to. In retrospect, this would have de-traumatized South Africa and saved the economy from ruin, as this system of governance is fully functional in the United States and in Germany.

What have been the P. W. Botha years' effects on conflicting transformation and adding to the trauma of change? Immense!

The stroke Botha suffered is a significant result of this psychological trauma. Imagining black majority rule was itself life-threatening for him, and the stroke was a result of his resistance to change apartheid. It traumatized him and his followers. Research of psychological trauma during his presidency should reveal this. New patients emerged, and their symptoms escalated, and today we see mentally deranged people in our streets living with us, but their behaviour is abnormal as a result of psychological trauma. Knowing and accepting that racial equality will never happen traumatizes when it happens or seems evident. But even leading a racially divided electorate is itself psychologically traumatic. A one-term presidency leading into a first term of democratization (1994–1999) would be enough, and focus on a pragmatic policy of reconciliation would be the only realistic route and option. However, its strain must have been difficult to cope and deal with.

The time from P. W. Botha's tenure to the first years of postapartheid governance was unsettling. The time from F. W. De Klerk's tenure to the first years of postapartheid governance was settling because the people were now semiprepared for the inevitable through a referendum that had been inconceivable under P. W. Botha's administration. P. W. Botha became a victim of his own obstinacy. One wonders how many of his followers were crushed and crippled in spirit and equally traumatized by his attitude. I may not have the credentials to evaluate this, but human behaviour intra- and cross-culturally tells a story of its own that Frantz Fanon and his ilk can best explain in works such as *The Wretched of the Earth*.

Human nature is complex—predictable and yet unpredictable. Only psychiatrists can correctly explain it. We ordinary professionals can only speculate on it. Yet attorneys at law can manipulate it and are good at doing so such that they can use it to sway a case in their favour to win it.

The P. W. Botha Years—Reforming Apartheid

Trying to reform apartheid proved to be a self-defeating cosmetic enterprise because it hit back. The Riekert Commission Report (RCR), commissioned to investigate reform, recommended the legalisation of black labour unions. This resulted from the apartheid state's crisis when its capitalist system was facing its deepest recession since 1945.

The government was trying to find ways and means of increasing productivity. Realizing that the labour movement was powerful and could not be crushed, industry and government were pushed into a corner and had to allow unionism in the black labour force, and thus government set up a commission on labour legislation in 1977 that was called the Wiehahn Commission. This commission called for the legislation of African trade unions, affecting the influx control laws' elasticity to accommodate the rapidly changing economic and political challenges. It required manpower.

In addition to the Wiehahn Commission, the Botha administration had to appoint the Riekert Commission to look at ways of adapting influx control laws to the new economic challenges and their political overtones.

The Riekert Commission was named after its chairman, Dr P. Riekert, who was advisor to B. J. Vorster. Stricter control of blacks without urban residential rights was recommended, but the seventy-two-hour rule (referring to the period to look for work in urban areas) was implemented for "qualified" black workers, whilst "disqualified" black workers would have to have to first register at assembly centres to be established along the borders of their homelands. Its report was published on 8 May 1979, indicating that the "qualified" black workers would receive preference in seeking employment.

As can be seen, the economic condition of the apartheid state was giving Afrikaner leadership sleepless nights. However, implementation of its recommendations proved to be prohibitively costly, and it was thus only partially implemented. This was seen as a clever piece of work which would maintain and promote the status quo of a relatively small privileged African group to avoid unrest. Qualified urban Africans were meant to supply labour for industries requiring a skilled African labour force and create a layer of comparatively privileged urban Africans that would emerge to pacify black masses. This resulted in the creation of a black middle class that would divide black people and thus minimize their political aspirations.

This also enhanced the hope that privileged urban blacks whose quality of life would improve would lessen their demand for political power and serve to stifle the forces of revolution for some years to come. They were buying time, and by and large the Africans became divided, as some accepted municipal council leaderships that were laced with burning tyres and died horrific deaths, being burned alive as political "sellouts".

Nat Nakasa, a gifted black journalist who committed suicide in the United States in 1965, summed this dream up as just that when he saw Africans in this country had not shown a fervent interest in their political advancement. His view was that the oppression blacks had suffered for so long and the lack of individual initiative produced by a black tribal system had prevented blacks from developing a militant spirit. He was convinced that the distractions of urban life—the bright lights and football matches and American clothes—had a lot to do with this state of affairs. Ironically, he saw these very aspects of the good life as whetting black people's appetites. Blacks had tasted enough to make them realize what they were being deprived of by the apartheid state, and it was this which in the long run would make them transcend their present preoccupation and awaken their political aspirations.

The dream indeed lived on borrowed time, as what blacks tasted was sweeter than honey and resulted in demands for political rights that would at several intervals pit servant against master. But the reluctant reformers persisted, and intransigence strengthened and resulted in a country being ripped from a people's hearts in 1994. P. W. Botha's hand on repression was stronger than his hand on reform, which in his administration stalled and became stifled to the point of being strangled into a lifeless form. P. W. Botha had to go! He left as a shaken and forlorn man and disappeared into the political wilderness until his passing.

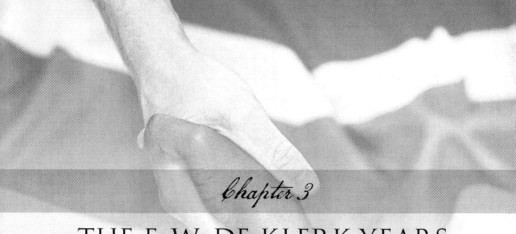

Chapter 3

THE F. W. DE KLERK YEARS:
THE ERA OF REALISM

His strength was his inspired courage to do what his predecessor, the reluctant reformer, could not do—cross the Rubicon—and this precipitated positive change from the P. W. Botha leadership crisis. Yet he did not really have the drive to inspire black majority rule; hence, immediately after releasing prisoners, he toured the world to give a sermon on the lifting of sanctions, but he was thwarted by the fact that apartheid was still in place and the voters' roll was still exclusively white. This was his undoing.

At the time, feeling on top of the world, the apostles of change followed and made certain that sanctions remained in place until the apartheid system was dismantled. De Klerk took the back seat in the violence that broke out in black townships, letting Mandela take the driver's seat as if he were president. Not suspecting that he was being used, Mandela addressed the violence, urging the people to "throw [their] weapons into the sea." Letters to the media—especially to what was then the *New Nation* newspaper, made Mandela take notice. Promptly, in a press conference he called, he declared, "I put the problem on De Klerk's door."

Yet president F. W. De Klerk, truth be told, was a realist and an original in the world of photocopies; 'n man wat sy man kon staan' (a man who could stand his manhood); a man of obstinate character in what he believed in, and a true leader of the Afrikaner volk (nation). Yes, he compromised African lives and was more drawn towards Chief Gatsha Buthelezi than any voice of a once imprisoned black conscience.

Chief Buthelezi was a man of conscience and steel and had advised the apartheid state to free the imprisoned and incarcerated prisoner of conscience. Yet he spent not one day in a prison cell, for he played by the book and was too obstinate to accept homeland independence. He sought peaceful change for a greater South Africa. He believed in a federal system of governance, which can still be experimented with.

F. W. De Klerk was a realist but was more of an idealistic realist (if you know what I mean) in that his unbanning of liberation movements, followed by the release of political prisoners, was inspired by a desire to dislocate economic sanctions—no more, no less! The white economy was struggling, and resuscitating it required drastic and genuine political change allowing a free democratic nonracial political activity.

This made him an idealistic realist. In many of his dealings with African nationalist leaders against Afrikaner nationalist leaders, he played a mediating role, though his Afrikanerdom naturally took the better of him. He was first Afrikaner, and only then South African, whilst the voice of conscience sought to close the gap between the two and became too reconciling, to a point of compromising African nationalist ideals and political values of total freedom, giving them political but not economic freedom, which, as we have realized, is worthless.

It is not fair to write about someone totally truthfully during his lifetime—especially someone one respects for daring to make the decisions that he did make, which placed his very life in danger. The fact is that the Afrikaner Weerstandsbeweging (AWB) founded by Eugene Terre'Blanche in 1973, led by Steyn von Ronge, was a cultural, not so much a political, movement inspired by apartheid politics and policies. It is described as a neo-Nazi separatist paramilitary white supremacist group with a swastika flag as its logo.

This organization must have been close to President De Klerk's heart, and yet he could not openly embrace it and entertain its lunacy. He is a product of Potchefstroom University, a Christian tertiary education institution, and educated at law. This thus placed him in a position to subjectively, albeit objectively, interpret jurisprudence to the advantage of a new beginning—the dawn of a new country. He had to admire the

AWB's tenacity and its cultural and political integrity, but he also had to question its sense of reality. In the period during and just after the Great Trek, it could have been opportune. In the early to late 1900s, it was a reactive rather than a realistic organization and was bound to collapse as it did. It also reflects a psychological trauma induced by a revolutionary transformation.

F. W. De Klerk became the leader of the moment in Afrikanerdom and in the politics of understanding the volatility of what he was dealing with, he moved with caution, measuring his every step like a man walking a tightrope.

Remember his son's courting of a coloured South African woman? This really placed him between a rock and a hard place and tested his politics of change. He was walking a tightrope in the true sense of the statement, and the prospect of a black makoti (daughter-in-law) in his household was present. What would the volk think? Most importantly, what would the volk say? This must have played at the back of his mind precariously, and he had to be as diplomatic as he could. This closes my exploration of that as a sensitive domestic and personal matter, and not a political matter.

He was a realist and indeed a man of the moment, and the current generation of South Africans owes much to this man and his legacy to South Africans by daring to cross a line which at the time was politically dangerous territory. This places him at the centre of this book, following his unbanning of repressed black nationalists political formations in preparation for the release of political prisoners. Was this an admission that apartheid was wrong? Tacitly, yes it was.

Chapter 4

THE UNBANNING OF BLACK LIBERATION MOVEMENTS

If you remember well, in the early 1990s our television screens flashed the alphabet letters ANC in a news bulletin and then disappeared. This was followed by the announcement of the unbanning of black resistance movements. South Africa was being prepared for what had happened in formerly colonized Africa when leaders recognized by the people were released from prison. This happened in Ghana and in Kenya, and in Namibia next door. It was about to happen in South Africa, and it did.

F. W. De Klerk's realism came into the picture, with P. W. Botha being against any form of concessionary actions and deeds to compromise Afrikaner liberty, which was still influenced by traces of a war the English should not have fought but that carried on for more than three years, resulting in Hertzog making General Smut's administration difficult in the extreme owing to that war. This war delivered what was engineered by the Great Trek—a movement defining the Afrikaner's sense of identity, just as the Mfecane defines African identity colourfully, as described by traditional English historians, and as a cultural revolution, and not as a singular crisis that smashed tribes, scattered others, and dashed the tribal fragments into new formations, meaning and implying that it was a crushing or destructive incident of no historical significance or relevance.

To relevantly digress a little, just as the Great Trek was a central event in South African history, the Mfecane was equally central in African history from the Great Lakes, because the tribes that fought over land in the Mfecane emanated from the Great Lakes shores, which they left when they stricken by a debilitating drought. The Mfecane, on the contrary, produced heroes Africans still identify with, and villains as well, and these were to shape the survivalism and endurance of South African tribes— including, of course, the Afrikaners.

This digression reflects the polarization of South African society, and F. W. De Klerk was beginning a process of bringing the two racial poles together. But he was first Afrikaner and only then South African! It would prove a very tight rope indeed to walk, because the racially polarized nation wanted a share of the cake and appeasement, and redress was to become the new challenge. The Afrikaner had worked the economy, and blacks were mere cheaply paid labourers in the cog well of a white-dominated economic machinery and activity. This incapacitation was not of their making. By offering blacks an educational raw deal, the apartheid state had shot itself on the foot, and this crippled the postapartheid economy with a white-only boon, which the media attacked. This was during the Thabo Mbeki administration and this was to result in his recall.

President De Klerk's administration was crossing the Rubicon across a great racial divide. There was black excitement and expectation, and there was white anxiety, distress, and despondence, yet whites were anxious whilst also negatively excited, with blacks positively excited by the dying, revolting, much-hated apartheid system.

South Africa's change was an exciting experience, both negatively and positively. It was a tale of two races—one white, the other black—which became good and bad, bitter and sweet, in that order to both races. But then again, it was the best of times but also the very worst, defining the effects change had on the black and white races of South Africa in extremely opposed degrees of comparison.

The era of change was one of wisdom but also extreme stupidity. There were those who believed in positive change and those who saw change as foolish. As events unfolded, they became incredulous. There was light at the end of the tunnel, but there was a darkness that was brought about by conservatism. Hope was also there, but it was also dampened by despair. As South Africans, we had everything, but we also had our stupid pride. The Arms Deal proffered a time of ill gains to suddenly equal white riches overnight, allowing some to lead lives of luxury. Ordinary South Africans had nothing before them, not even an RDP house. Some were built in computer files but were not there in reality. I know one such case in our area and wonder how many similar cases there are elsewhere in the country. This soon shifted into a gear of hopelessness, which currently prevails going into the 8 May 2019 general elections. Gone is the electric energy that inspired the revolutionary elections of 1994, and not even the use of the Mandela's name inspires hope.

Whilst many fought the vile system of apartheid, with cracks over it clearly visible, none ever believed it would start to be dismantled; hence it is described as the epoch of incredulity. Yet it was an era of transformation that would result in the disappearance of four provinces and the emergence of nine new provinces in a new transformation resulting from a constitutionally negotiated dispensation won by sanctions and external and internal resistance of mixed races, even from the Afrikaner community. Reverends Naude and Boesak also led the proceedings of change as men of the cloth, together with Bishop Desmond Mpilo Tutu and Theo.

Who will forget Dr Van Zyl Slabbert (2 March 1940–14 May 2010) as Progressive Federal Party leader (1979–1986), with Stellenbosch being his alma mater, acting as the salient voice of change coming from deep inside an Afrikaner's conscience? It was very noticeable indeed, in Lusaka, Zambia, and inside South Africa and in Parliament. He must have died the most disappointed politician by the turn of events that played quite an important role in ushering political change in this country. He needs to be immortalized with a statue and an avenue named after him, which a genuinely reconciling nation should positively consider. It is such considerations that will help a healing nation dress the wounds of the past and heal the psychological trauma threatening to tear apart its very national fabric. From known recorded material, Dr Van Zyl Slabbert facilitated change at a time when talking to banned organizations would be considered un-Afrikaner.

True to detail, education became apartheid's destruction, because by educating, colonialism sowed the seeds of its own destruction. Teaching revolutions precipitates revolutions (which should be followed by evolutions) from colonial apartheid to a new democratic dispensation undefined by race. Indeed, education proved once more to be a subversive activity. Yet, by oppressing, apartheid planted a desire for freedom as blacks sought to break the glass ceiling and get their hands on what lay beyond but was denied them by apartheid. They could see the greener pastures but were unable to reach them. By subjugating and offering the oppressed so little, it planted a desire for more and better pastures.

The unbanning of black liberation movements began that process. Yet it would prove difficult and painfully psychologically traumatic.

Many people would die horrific deaths before that happened. The dying system claimed lives. Civil war seemed inevitable, forcing leaders across oppositional fronts to work together. One death on 10 April 1993 in particular threatened the very talks that were ensuing, yet it galvanized the date for the first democratic elections that were set for 27 April 1994. The pistol fired by Janusz Walus no doubt ushered in the very liberation it sought to confuse and destroy, and that an Afrikaner housewife alerted the police was in itself a reconciling factor which was to quell unrest and restiveness to heal the prevailing psychological trauma.

Through this assassination, a veil of uncertainty which hung heavily over South Africa threatened the talks and political transformation. Expressions of anger became decibels of cacophony through the length and breadth of South Africa. How could one survive and defy death in the bush during the struggle and be struck by a foreigner's bullet at a time when his safety was almost guaranteed? Yet it happened!

Psychological trauma had dealt South Africa a severe blow. Races were thrown around and felt the first most extreme painful birth of a new nation. The baby's head was too big and required birth by Caesarean section. Political doctors converged as midwives in the maternity ward of talks to assist in the baby's psychologically traumatic and traumatizing birth. A sacrificial lamb for elections was offered, and they were successfully held.

THE RELEASE OF
POLITICAL PRISONERS

The release of political prisoners marked a new era in South Africa and was just as psychologically traumatic as the repressive apartheid regime in dealing with its subject people in 1976. When the first prisoners were released from the penal political "university" island, irrespective of political affiliation, they ushered in an era of hope that the apartheid monster was collapsing and breathing its last. Yet it proved to be a coiled python monstrosity that was to claim several lives before it lay prostrate, coiled, and lifeless in international history books.

These prisoners were tried and tested martyrs, each one of them. Others were in a self-imposed exile in the diaspora, having been driven from their homes by a vile system that did not recognize their talents. This was a kind of a prison that kept them in foreign lands, exposing the vile system of apartheid. I remember seeing Miriam Makeba and Hugh Masekela on the cover of *Drum Magazine* on horseback just across the Mohokare (Caledon) River, gazing into a motherland they could not perform in. South Africa, a land that gave them birth, had ejected them into a world of the arts that was to be their home.

When detainees were released, they too were released. Jan Smuts International Airport (now O. R. Tambo International Airport) received them. One wonders what the feeling was like when their jets raced down the tarmac, resting birdlike with staircases materializing to take them down to the fatherland, which some of them kissed and then strolled into Arrivals to hugs and kisses from family members that had given up hope of ever seeing them again. When Miriam Makeba collapsed on stage in Italy, it was as if she was destined to be buried a foreigner with her mortal remains as ashes, becoming part of the ocean. That she did not lead the Ministry of the Arts in the first cabinet still strikes me as odd.

The release of political detainees preceded the birth of a new nation. After all, prisoners could enter into contracts but could not take part in negotiations. This was the surest signal that apartheid was dying, but it was still breathing; its prisoner of conscience was in Victor Verster Prison.

Chapter 6

THE RELEASE OF THE VOICE OF CONSCIENCE— THE REAL TRAUMA

The release happened in three stages. The first was from Robben Island to Pollsmoor Prison, the second from Pollsmoor to Victor Verster Prison, and lastly, step by step to freedom on 11 February 1990. Apartheid was still alive, but it was very frail and sick, lying on its deathbed. P. W. Botha was also frail and sickly, but he remained defiant to the bitter end.

When you prepare someone whom you have held for years, you have to make sure that when he ultimately gets what he wants, he will turn around to make new friends with you. Otherwise you could be digging your own grave.

The voice of conscience can be a voice of a cornered person who has come to realize that death is imminent in a case of high treason. Such a person is also like a coiled poisonous snake, ready to spit venom in the form of the truth. The Sesotho-speaking people say, "nnete ke thebe" (the truth is a shield) When the truth is spoken, it is unlikely that the speaker will be condemned to death, but the truth has to be carefully, very carefully, spoken. So the truth is not so much a voice of conscience as a voice of defiant defence. In it, it carries a people's hopes and aspirations, and when listened to, it invokes passionate support against the fate of the speaker. Such a voice is passionately convincing.

When this one particular release during the epoch of human incredulity happened, I was in Bloemfontein. It was on 11 February in the year of our Lord, 1990. I had driven there from Qwaqwa to visit some friends.

On arrival in Bloemfontein, there was a frenzied excitement and cacophony all around town. I did not quite understand what was going on. On enquiry, I was informed that I was the only one worldwide who did not know what all that excitement was about. Indeed, I had stopped watching the news on television and reading papers because all this did not make sense to me. The suspense had been too much to deal with. That's how psychologically traumatized I was.

Being a prisoner of conscience makes one the most famous prisoner in the world, because what one is protesting against is on everybody's mind and conscience as a world-acknowledged truth with the power to set all free, unconditionally! The fact is that for as long as apartheid was in force, every South African was a prisoner of conscience, because everyone, including the oppressor, knew the system was vile and wrong and unjustifiable.

It was comparable to the fascist system that made Adolf Hitler the most hated man on the planet—a pariah whose ghost still haunts those who hobnobbed with him, committing a holocaust of horrific atrocities that horrified a shocked and traumatized world.

The atrocities of the holocaust were something right out of a horror film; its emblem, the swastika, was adopted by an equally demented group whose blue Mercedes-Benz in Bophuthatswana when Mangope fell is still a picture in my mind, and what followed is best forgotten! Traumatic indeed!

When the voice of conscience finally strolled into freedom that year, South Africa's conscience was also released, and the first steps out of prison towards a negotiated settlement were taken by all South Africans as its prisoner of conscience, silenced for years, departed Victor Verster Prison. He was released from Roben Island to Pollsmoor Prison, then to Victor Verster, and then step by step into true, unconditional freedom.

Yet it proved to be another Rubicon to cross, as the sitting president of South Africa was negotiating himself out of a plum job. His voice of conscience would be stifled by the psychological trauma of being unemployed, tantamount to selling the "volk, die mense" (the Afrikaner nation, the people) out. This traumatized F. W. De Klerk out of the second vice presidency, out of power, and out of the first democratic cabinet.

This intensified the reigning psychological trauma as people also went through it with anxiety and disbelief. After all was said and done, and the franchise extended to everyone eighteen years of age and above, the voters' roll was redrafted, and the new nation was about to be born in 1994.

Political parties extoled the virtues of their offices, and people went to the polls that snaked through every part of South African townships and white suburbs. Some whites had been traumatized into leaving South Africa, and Hillbrow soon became infested with stray cats and dogs left by owners avoiding quarantine regulations in their new destinations.

Uncertainty over a black government sowed traumatic seeds of doubt and challenging of the unknown. As the new South Africa was unmasked, so did it unmask Africa beyond the Limpopo border to educated South Africans who did not go into the diaspora. What we saw was poverty and famine, and this became unsettling and anxiety-triggering. The mild psychological trauma felt introduced a new approach-avoidance defence mechanism (i.e. approaching freedom anxiously whilst discomforted by the scary psychological scars of the apartheid state and its system).

To add to this subject of psychological trauma, South African standards deteriorated into just another African state, and in later years people trickled into voting stations as they came to realize that their votes were not giving them any new lease on life, and they began to be politically disgruntled and despondent, further traumatizing them psychologically. Every promise made proved to be empty. The reconstruction and development programme and its process proved to be an expensive sham. It was strikingly beautiful on paper but very impractical.

The result of the deterioration of standards is economic collapse and escalating unemployment. These depressing conditions resulted in stressful situations, adding to psychological trauma when people realized that political freedom does not equal economic freedom. The South African parliamentary system became a haven of drama when new members of Parliament in red overalls strolled into Parliament. A scary scenario was to develop and escalate into scuffles of parliamentary discord and disharmony. At the moment, new political bedmates are emerging, and the future still stands as uncertain as it stood at the beginning of freedom; it is still psychologically traumatizing, but enterprising, one could say.

The release of the voice of conscience died away as politicians scrambled for earthly possessions. The literal death of some leaders became the literal new lease on life for emerging new leaders. Today the difference between the rich and poor defies human imagination, with the rich too rich and the poor too poor. Some of the postapartheid rich elite own up to twenty top-of-the-range vehicles and live in homes fit for kings and queens, princes and princesses; they are far from the bridges that have become home to the homeless in snake-infested habitats that have become human habitats as well.

In his statements, Donald Trump made new enemies and won new admirers when AfriForum visited America as part of the protests against expropriation of land without compensation. Trumpian comments following this visit apparently attracted sympathetic ears on land matters in South Africa. Does this define a new psychological trauma? I will leave that to readers' minds and intellects to consider and interpret. Economists warn that the expropriation of land without compensation will have devastating consequences. Indeed, President Cyril Ramaphosa will have to be a magician to pull a mouse out of a hat to effect this without strangling or damaging economic growth.

The fact is that statistics never lie. Economists show that merely talking about this policy has already affected economic growth. The markets reacted upon every utterance of this policy. We have seen that in the negative gross domestic product's growth; in capital formation, which is 7 per cent lower than it was about eleven years ago; and, obviously, in the unemployment rate. Lessons in economic history prove this, and economics takes it to the next level of clarification. It needs no genius, just a simple analytic assessment.

Even the economy has become traumatized, the difference being that it does not have a psyche as people do, making them able to address psychological trauma to save the economy, for progeny to be saved when their progenitors leave the wretched earth to a place yonder. In this there is a silent but audible voice of conscience warning us to carefully consider policy in the face of empty supermarket shelves in Harare. Learning from history could be our making; disregarding its lessons, our unmaking.

We are blessed with a living example of reckless unrealistically idealistic economic policies that threaten what we already have and put us at the mercy of huge, lofty Chinese loans we can ill afford. Maybe we need to send students to Singapore to study how the Singaporeans do it. It sounds a fantastic idea. The criticism by the Singaporean leader that Dr Nkrumah's administration gave the vice chancellorship to a brilliant linguist at its premier university when Ghanaian independence required economic development may help us see things anew.

The voice of conscience has power and strength and is convincing to those listening to it and brilliant to those who heed it. It can educate, as a Sesotho proverb suggests, so as to empower people not to bank on the riches of pregnant heifers, as heard in popular leadership statements. "Don't count your chickens before they are hatch" is the English caution, and before they are hatched, the eggs should not be put in one basket as the traditional English phrase cautions. This sounds philosophical and if philosophy is a life view, why not use it to answer today's questions?

The voice of conscience can be sharpened on both ends and yet remain utterly safe between. It can silently make those listening to it to go to hell, such that they look forward to the trip. And we proceed to call men and women statesmen as their subjects live their lives in what they call the Blue Train, in parks which its passengers do not want to leave; neither do they enjoy the comforts of home.

The voice of conscience can be as conscienceless as those who perpetrate evil upon a defenceless people, making politics full of "politricks" as journalist wordsmiths say. The tongue of a politician is as forked as a snake's and just as double-edged. Learn to listen carefully—very carefully and analytically—before casting a vote, should you decide to.

The release was to precipitate violent reactions that swept over townships. Even white suburbs were disturbed as was demonstrated with domestic workers telling their masters that when violence broke out, they would be the first ones they would shoot.

Such tasteless conversations took place in 1988, when the apartheid system was set to crumble. It was a sad prediction of what lay ahead and a sad reminder that when whites are turned to loving, blacks shall be turned to hating. It is a monstrosity of a conversation which today is in people's hearts, yet with smiling faces, they are hiding daggers in their hearts. This spells doom to the land of our forebears, as it is destroyed by giant elephants fighting, leaving one wondering what the winner will get—burnt crops, making it necessary to start all over again. As history teaches, violence only begets violence, with winners winning nothing. The release of the prisoner of conscience, perhaps the last human opportunity to find one another, was the release of a new lease on life, and it can still save us and what's left of South Africa. One wonders how a man housed in a prison house can model his house as the same prison house that held him captive. Was he sending a message, and if so, what message was that? Perhaps we shall never know; only he knows, and he has been swallowed by the cruel, insatiable earth with that knowledge. We can only speculate and ask, "Was he perhaps saying he would remain imprisoned all his life?"

Did he, in retrospect, understand—*really* understand—the new world he walked into after so many years in captivity? We shall never know; we can only speculate.

What goes through the mind of a wife who used to be mother, father, grandmother, and grandfather all rolled into one when suddenly she has to be told what to do, how to do it, and when to do it, as is the custom in African tradition?

Perhaps that is why with this release there came a new release expressed in a league of women that feminine freedom from the rudiments of African life was also to be agitated for. Patriarchy had to be challenged, and patriarchal–matriarchal equality had to be phased in. What kind of a psychological trauma does such a woman go through? They were several, not just one woman. But one in particular endured long, lonely years as her husband remained in the hands of his captors. She suffered perhaps the worst atrocities to weaken the voice that kept her husband prisoner, trying to get her to let go and accept conditions that would compromise his freedom and that of the people he was leading. She had to endure all this. Various media outlets have quoted her as saying that she is "… a product of the masses of [her] people and also a product of [her] enemies," and maybe the wounds those enemies inflicted on her soul damaged her irreparably inside. Perhaps those who have engaged with her have lived the most painful chapters of their lives by seeing a once loving mother and wife turned into a hatred-filled woman whose soul was tortured beyond repair.

Upon release, having been hardened by the system of apartheid when she was torn from her beloved children at odd ungodly hours by the police, how would she be the spouse she was before her husband went into prison? Would that be possible? It proved difficult—and indeed impossible.

She had become a man and at the same time a mother to her children during those long, turbulent, painful years. Her heart was solidified and hardened by a system that took away her womanhood. It had unsexed her as a woman; it made her a man dressed in feminine clothing, and she was unsexed by the immortal evil spirits of her experiences.

"The 18th of July, marking the birth of a great leader in Qunu village, South Africa, should thus be considered a day of international and national reckoning. The white Zulu anthropologist, Johnny Clegg (may his soul RIP), dedicates a song "A si mbonanga" (We didn't see him) which calls to mind Nelson's 27 years absence from the South African political scene. Nelson Mandela was not only humanitarian, forgiving and conciliatory in spirit, but he had a genuinely cross-racial loving and compassionate big heart. It is this that makes him iconic. His divorce to Winnie, undoubtedly the love of his life, was actually a divorce from hardened residuals of apartheid arrests and persecution and let go - to heal. So deep seated were her wounds that she could not find it in her heart to yield to forgiving, let alone reconciling, because the first step to reconciling is forgiving – to heal. For the sake of statesmanship and diplomacy, he parted ways with her 'without any recriminations' in his own words; no hard feelings at all, and he got married to the politics of forgiveness and reconciliation. In this, he got support from an understanding new spouse, Graca Machel, and he led with pragmatism, clad in his Afro-shirts, his fashion statement."

Yet Winnie was God fearing and her hymn *'Nzulu ye mfihlakalo'* (an isiXhosa language John Wesley Methodist hymn glorifying Jesus Christ) suggests this.

That the Mother of the Nation died just after being part of an Easter church service she left before Christ's seventh word on the cross is indicative of the Christianity deeply implanted in her sore, deeply hurt heart. She was clad in her red-and-white Methodist church Young Women's Christian Association uniform—and yes, that when they are turned to loving, we shall be turned to hating is creative literature's seemingly valid opinion. She was turned to hating when they were turned to loving. She even questioned her husband's sharing of the Nobel Peace Prize with his jailer. She had indeed been turned to hating when they were turned to loving.

Our characters can be shaped by forces of thunder around us and make monsters of us, or these forces can have the very opposite effect of shaping our characters to transform others—especially those that perpetrate unforgivable trespasses against us. This is affirmed by the clash of characters that the voice of conscience and the Mother of the Nation had—one forgiving, the other vengeful, aggressively vindictive, and unrepentantly, mercilessly unforgiving.

I leave it to the reader's mind to ponder over the questions posed above, as well as the one that follows: Would she be the spouse her beloved husband left her very many years ago, swallowed by a system that targeted her to soften her heavily politicized husband to renounce violence as a means of change?

The reader's assessment of facts may either vilify her or vindicate her.

In her own words, in undated rich statements akin to archaeological artefacts lying on the surface and not related to a particular civilization, she expressed her love for a man she had little time to know and love. She confessed that that love survived over all those years of politically forced separation. She states that perhaps if she had had time to know him better, she might have found a lot of fault in him, but she only had time to love him and long for him as the system suffocated him and his political ideals.

What does your conscience say? Mine says she was the most wronged woman in the world and that I cannot judge her. Let history be that judge. We should take cognisance of natural human folly and master the ability to forgive. She died without forgiving because the pain she felt was too deep. The apartheid wound festered inside of her throughout her life. She could not understand her husband's pragmatism of letting go to avoid being caught up in a past he could not change. Apartheid shackled him in chains for 27 years and there was no way he could change that and forgiving to him was a remedy and medicine to his wounded soul. Winnie could not make sense of that and we should understand and empathize with her.

Chapter 7

AFRICAN EXCITEMENT

The release of political prisoners brought about an excitement that rose to a crescendo and twenty-four years later died down when freedom did not deliver on its promises. "A better life for all" became a better life for a chosen few and the very best for those who strolled into plum jobs.

First came the excitement of the release of the voice of conscience. It was unbelievably, absolutely electrifying! There was excitement everywhere! This excitement, which had been expectantly awaited on 15 August 1985, came as a breath of fresh air with jubilant outcries throughout South Africa and the world. But human nature can be surprising. Not everybody was positively excited. There were others who wondered what was to become of what they had worked for all those years—especially political leaders.

Many expected homeland leaders to throw in their lot behind unbanned liberation movements. But alas, that was not to be. Only one did, and he was soon disillusioned into a new political formation opposing the very freedom leaders he had helped usher in, which had alienated him from his masters in Pretoria.

South Africa and neighbouring states were boiling with excitement. During these times, I was in a hotel in Lesotho, relaxing on my way to my home in Sterkspruit in Herschel, Eastern Cape, through Van Rooy Border Gate near Wepener.

As I sat at the bar of Hotel Victoria, just across from Maseru Hat, I struck up conversation with some white guys, talking politics. I remember saying to them that the AWB (an Afrikaner cultural organization) was not a political formation but a deeply cultural movement or organization. To a huge receptive acknowledgement, and as we got to frankly and candidly talking about quite sensitive political topical issues across the South African border, I curiously enquired who I was talking to as we delved into more sensitive political territory.

The main white man I was airing my views and opinions to said he was a lecturer at the National University of Lesotho and originally from Australia. But his accent was heavily Afrikaner.

After a while, not showing any signs of discomfort, I left the bar like someone going to the loo, with my glass half full left on the bar's counter, and went into the hotel's car park and pulled out. That was how exciting the political situation in South Africa was. It was both positively and negatively exciting because we were not out of the woods yet. The positive part was the anticipation of what lay ahead.

The apartheid state was still very much in power, with the AWB very much opposed to the new developments. Sounding off in hotel bars was not such a good idea then, especially to white strangers. I drove away from Hotel Victoria.

Political excitement escalated. People died miserably. Civil war seemed inevitable. For the first time, the scars of the apartheid state became sharply clear as Zulu fought Xhosa and Xhosa fought Zulu. The Transvaal became politically tense. Hostels became hellish. Men fought and killed one another in the most gruesome ways. Indoctrination played itself out lethally, brutally, and horrifically.

In the midst of all this confusion, a Polish immigrant who once did business in Qwaqwa shaping bottles into glasses in the old industrial area did the unthinkable in Dawn Park—he shot and fatally wounded Chris Hani!

All hell broke loose!

The talks were jeopardized, and frantic efforts were made to quell the havoc and mayhem to save the situation. It is still a miracle that this state of emergency died down and was quelled so that talks could resume to conclude the traumatic revolution. That this unfortunate traumatic event facilitated the revolution cannot be denied. However, it must be recorded by history that it defined and reflected the level of trauma inside South

Africa. During the years of struggle and strife, Chris Hani was the most wanted man by the internationally discredited white minority government. He was the most sought after revolutionary but proved elusive. When his freedom was almost guaranteed, an assassin's bullet cut short his life, and his assassin is still languishing in prison, his freedom denied despite his having served more than twenty years of his sentence. The nation was in awe and in a state of traumatic shock and stress; its very soul was touched and broken when the assassin's bullet hit home and put him down.

Chris was an icon. He was the heartthrob of the revolution and in public rallies stated that the ANC was going to keep the promises it was making. His sad passing was to mark his words in every revolutionary rally when the movement he fought for and the South African Communist Party (SACP), in the hands of Dr Blade Nzimande, sold out. A social leader became part of the many leaders who lived luxurious lives in bling cars that rode on the very lives of the marginalized and disadvantaged masses as a revolutionary government started stealing from the poor. What he had fought for became a distant dream, a mirage on the tarred road as the vehicle of corruption sped on, defying resistance and defying journalists' criticism in newspapers, editorials, and analytical political insights. Letters to the editor by the reading public cried foul, but the gravy train sped on relentlessly, defying all and sundry. Solomon Mahlangu's blood dis-watered the tree of liberty it had once watered. Chris, no doubt, was a nationalist par excellence whose vision of freedom was blurred by the greed that followed his untimely death.

Not even the voice of conscience could outdo him. He was the peoples' very heart—their very soul!

Of all excitements, this one remains central. Of all psychological traumas people went through, Chris's remains central. Of all leaders in exile, Chris stood firm and remained central. Even Oliver Tambo could not quite absorb his passing. Shortly thereafter, Oliver, the father of South African nationalism in exile, sadly passed on after his wife agreed to the disengagement of his life support machinery in hospital. The nation was in mourning, and this defined the trauma the nation was going through, because whilst expected to change by force, the fall of apartheid became a traumatic incident that tore men and women apart psychologically.

Realities of life faced the newly emergent postrevolution South Africa.

Excitement made men crazy. Ever heard of "talks about talks"? Sounds crazy, does it not? Oh yes, before talks began in earnest, we first of all had talks about talks, which to this day sounds insane.

This is indicative of the psychological trauma the nation was going through. It is not in the interest of this book to delve into these talks, but just to overview and highlight their effects upon the prevailing situation in the country—the way they impacted the building tension. They added to the excitement. They added to the drama. They added to the psychological trauma. The media went into a frenzied excitement. I remember having to buy three weekend newspapers to read various editorial opinions the papers were sharing with a view of making sense of developments at that time.

Excitement made change hectic. Each new dawn had its own story to tell. Hippos and nyala in the townships were running around with soldiers also deployed in the township.

When excitement went into overdrive in Thokoza, Natalspruit, a hippo full of South African defence soldiers stopped us. A young Afrikaner-sympathetic soldier asked me where I was going, asking me why I had not watched the news before driving into Natalspruit. He proceeded to advise me where to go and stay until morning, as it was at night. I remain eternally grateful to that young soldier and hope he is still in the defence of our common fatherland. He advised me to switch my car lights off and drive to a place of safety he directed me to, which to this day I cannot identify. I stayed there until the morning. It was scary!

Excitement can be ruinous, yet it is part of human nature.

During all this drama, the voice of conscience led on, directing the twists and turns towards our new destiny. Excitement had very nearly resulted in a ruinous civil war because there was too much at stake—even the loss of the very lives that were leading the revolutionary transformation.

F. W. De Klerk had made it clear in a carefully worded statement that the state was no longer responsible for the safety of the voice of conscience after releasing him. His safety was henceforth his own baby.

South Africa is an African state that tasted colonialism longer than any other on the African continent. It is further made complex by its composite ethnographic nature. It is an ethnically composite culturally diversified state that was divided and ruled over for many years in balkanised homelands that reflected its nature. Perhaps this alone justified federal constitutional governance, which the forces of revolution refused.

Its tertiary institutions were organized along ethnic tribal lines, and its homelands were likewise tribal. Everything was organized along tribal groupings; even hostels in locations where workers from homelands stayed were tribal. Townships were organized along tribal groupings. The best example of this is perhaps Soshanguve Township, whose name is an acronym for Sotho, Shangaan, Nguni, and Venda. This made the excitement modelled along these tribal persuasions. Song renditions made the excitement very traditional. When African people get excited, there is a tendency to destroy what they already have to clamour for what they do not have. They will burn and destroy bakeries and the next day queue to buy bread!

By the time the excitement died down, a lot had been destroyed, and what we are doing now is rebuilding, reconstructing, and developing—even the ruined economy. Perhaps it is this that will remake South Africa as we together build the Tower of Hope as a new nation, laughing at our own stupidity.

Chapter 8

THE VIBRATIONS OF POLITICAL CHANGE

Political vibrations are felt but not seen and heard. You feel them each time you meet someone of a different hue. When among your own, you do not feel them, but you do when you meet someone of another hue. This will go on for as long as the old generation is mixed with the new generation. The old Israelites who left Egypt for Canaan were swallowed by sand dunes in the wilderness. Of those who left Egypt, only two entered the Promised Land; these were Joshua and Caleb.

Moses did not enter the Promised Land either, but he saw it from the plains of Moab, atop Mount Nebo at the peak of Pisgah. Joshua was to take the mission over. This gave the people of the Promised Land no comparisons, and they should have been the most united of people and believers to beat all. Yet they were not, and they went into a second misery of seventy-two years in exile in Babylon, having forfeited their freedom. Is this another reflection of the psychological trauma human nature experiences?

The Afrikaners after 1902 were a united front, maybe because of the psychological trauma of the Anglo-Boer War or South African War; perhaps they remembered and called to mind the concentration camps. Like the Mfecane, this war is the nucleus of Afrikanerdom, the very source and soul of its nationalism, emanating from the Great Trek and solidified by the "kreun van ossewa" (the creaking of ox wagons) and, of course, a common "volk taal" (national language)—Afrikaans.

In a way, the psychological trauma of the South African War affected every South African. After years of oppression—which in retrospect affected both races—we have gone into a new oppressive system of poverty and want, comparable to a situation of war, as a result of being at each other's throats rather than rehabilitating the economy to sustain the new nation.

We are behaving like enemies in a war situation, applying a scotched earth policy on our own land, destroying what should sustain us. A new racism prevails in municipal tenders defined to suit the new situation— formerly marginalized people. But the system still favours family members employed by the municipalities and government departments, and the unconnected remain unemployed, not getting tenders and therefore going hungry.

We must find a way of directing our energies and sinking our teeth into something worthwhile, this being an economic renaissance wherein we use our gifts and talents to prepare the ground for growing an economic base that will make our country the workshop of the world. We are blessed with natural resources which we let leave our shores raw and which resurface as finished products. This is the slumber we need to wake up from if we are to create jobs for South Africans. Producing gold, diamonds, iron ore, etc. and shipping them out to coming back as finished products is counterrevolutionary.

Looking at Singapore and her economic rebirth; we could be looking at a nation that defeated negative political vibrations to grow a new country—a new people.

As we go into a neocolonialism of huge Chinese loans, we should find ways of enticing rich countries to open up workshops in our country and producing finished products locally and selling them abroad. This must be a new focus that will attract foreign currency for a healthy economy. The Industrial Revolution made Britain the world's workshop, and colonies became markets with profits channelled to the island country that ruled the world economically and linguistically. The language used is colonial, in a state of freedom.

This can happen only if we use our new political vibrations positively and stop seeing one another through racial spectacles but begin seeing one another as one composite nation united in diversity—a nation of South Africans. That would really heal and dress our psychological trauma, and only by salvation through faith can we receive the grace of our renaissance—a rebirth that will sustain us and our generations to come.

Should we fail, we can only have ourselves to blame as a people who have made our freedom benefit and work for foreign nationals, with us becoming looters of their stores rather than competing with them commercially.

Chapter 9

THE REAL TRAUMA OF POLITICAL CHANGE

The real trauma of political change is the question of land acquisition.

Losing what you believe to be yours, no matter how you acquired, it is traumatic. Namibia and South Africa very much have the same problem. Land is still a dilemma and a very sensitive issue that seems to threaten and slow the attraction of new investors. The heavily politicized land redistribution issue has become the 2019 general elections' leading issue; the governing African National Congress Party is holding it central in its manifesto, to resist the Economic Freedom Front's nonsensical political rhetoric as international governments look on with bated breath. What the polls reveal will define whether the twenty-five-year trauma will subside for the nation to begin a healing process that will revitalize economic development recovery.

The Land Bank has expressed its concerns over the redistribution of farms and the ability of emerging previously marginalized farmers to service those farms. In *The History of the Land Bank: Financing Agriculture for 100 Years* (2013), edited by Dr Makhura, there is a warning suggestive of treading carefully and very lightly on land-related policy issues.

In this book's foreword, the CEO of Land Bank in 2013, Phakamani Hadebe, stoically, and in an authoritative, philosophical manner notes that "the purpose of history is to inform the present [and], in so doing, shape the future."

Hadebe unveils and reminds us of the fateful 1913 Land Act and Sol Plaatje's shocked reaction to it. He goes on to explain how the Land Bank, in a discriminatory way, empowered tertiary industry, favouring white farmers only. The bank financed the buying of land by white farmers on Crown land when South Africa was still a union. For 100 years (1912–2012) the bank financed white farmers, and today, through tampering with Section 25 of the Constitution, the revolution has reversed that with the flip of a coin.

This is where the traumatic revolution may become a suicidal national risk we may live to regret and be unable to remedy, owing to a political excitement, thus becoming food for vultures because of populist rhetoric rather than informed, realistic, pragmatic politics.

THE HISTORY OF THE LAND BANK

Financing agriculture for one hundred years (page 103) has it on good authority that to establish the target of emerging black farmers requires government assistance over a long period, meaning that after expropriation, time will pass before government interventions become effective. Secondly, the high price of land is another complication, which expropriation without compensation apparently seeks to remove to facilitate land reform. Lastly, and importantly, is the escalating cost of farming equipment being worsened by the limited national resources in the National Treasury and further weakened by the corruption and poor planning of the traumatized revolutionary state. A new political party leading up to the 2019 general elections, the Afrikan Alliance of Social Democrats, led by Itumeleng "Pappie" Mokoena, warns in a stoic fashion that "corruption steals from the poor" as it seeks its provincial legislature and national recognition with a peoples' mandate. This warning should not be taken lightly, because it emanates from the nine years of a Gupta-captured state that the African National Congress is licking its wounds from after two trial-and-error leaderships that were recalled. As a result of these frantic trial-and-error leaderships and their unscientific quick fixes to postrevolution challenges that have proved ineffective, the nation has been swallowed into a quicksand of a sinking economy that requires a sustainable long-term transformation. It is this that should justify a government-facilitated Land Bank to change by evolution. If the one-hundred-year tertiary industry-growing intervention strategy worked, so will it work as the VKB pursues its vision with government support. It should be seen as a relay in what educational psychology refers to as accompanying the child to adulthood as the VKB assists emerging farmers towards commercial farming, appreciating that this is a one-hundred-year process and not an event. Patience thus becomes important because insensitive political rhetoric fired by racial hatred is an ill wind that will blow the nation no good. It will only hurt the marginalized on either side of the racial fence that have already turned to begging in the streets, with their dignity impaired and insulted. This is what should shake the nation from the its twenty-five-year trauma and wake it up to the breeding of an all-inclusive interracial national harmony to build a National Tower of Babel to keep our silos full of grain to feed the nation and neighbouring states—especially Zimbabwe, whose leaders have destroyed a once vibrant economy. The Land Bank's cautions should be heeded, and its vision facilitated to grow commercial farming.

The bank warns that costs incurred on entering agriculture make it difficult for beginners to financially survive the entrance phase, which one black farmer recently demonstrated by his inability to pay a hospital fee for one of his injured farmworkers. It is doubtful that this farmer did not have R40 ($2.10) in his wallet to pay the hospital fee, but he simply may not have wanted to take on a responsibility that would set a precedent among his workers. Be that as it may, this reflects the futility of land expropriation without compensation as a solution to black postapartheid economic freedom aspirations. We need to realize that it takes years to gain economic liberation, and multimillionaires created since 1994 can only have come about by becoming national lottery winners or, of course, through corrupt means—not through arduous hard work. It requires emancipation from a state of dependence and a quest for self-reliance to be rich.

The apartheid state, whose political theme then president Julius Nyerere of Tanzania captured in his Ujamaa philosophy (which relates to education for self-reliance) went into overdrive to prepare whites to rely on themselves through an effective, well-planned education system that inculcates and nourishes scientific knowledge.

Armed with this, the apartheid state empowered whites only and, through the obnoxious Verwoerdian 1954 Bantu Education Act that Z. K. Matthews loathed so much that he resigned his Fort Hare University post, prepared the blacks to be drawers of water to irrigate white farms for slave wages, ensuring that they would report for work the next day for a sack of mielie meal for pap (porridge) and wheat for bread, together with milk for pap. To change and eradicate this mental slavery requires a new nonracial mindset and can be implemented only over years, at a snail's pace, heeding the Land Bank's advice to newly emerging formerly marginalized farmers.

If you want to build a solid economy, it becomes a generational process and can never occur overnight. It can only be done in five-year plans over several years, as Stalin did when building the post-revolution economy in Russia. To change this overnight or in a year is delusional and counterrevolutionary. It will only spiral the nation into a state of economic disrepair.

National economic recovery in agriculture will come in stages as in scientific project management, wherein one can never put in window and door frames without first constructing walls. Given time, the Land Bank can and will erect such walls and painstakingly put the window and door frames in place as it develops emerging farmers for the national good. It is a one-hundred-year process as economic history in tertiary industry has shown. Figures in commerce ledger books cannot lie. Man can lie, but statistics never lie, as research after data analysis shows.

Chapter 10

THE REVOLUTION AND RESISTING RECONCILIATION WHILST PREACHING IT

The 1994 revolution ushered in a new era.

The hope that it would shift gears to evolution soon dissipated when racial divisions went into the new nonracial state, carving people into apartheid creation under democratic rule. A new apartheid evolved. The divide and rule of the past left the dream of a rainbow nation just that—a dream!

What really shattered this dream into smithereens is playing to our differences and not identifying and strengthening similarities that bring us together to promote Maslow's primary and secondary needs as a new nation. Instead of wedging into one another, we grow apart and as a result fail to effectively work the economy.

Former workers seek to be new owners and thus strangle the economy. The socialist Mozambique Frelimo government economy was strangled by bank clerks becoming bank managers and executives overnight.

In our case, academic philosophy behind or inside academic disciplines does not define our schools' disciplines, and neither does scientific overview inform emergent leaders for a practical, workable policy definition and implementation. In a tour with Robert Mugabe at Fort Hare University, his alma mater, he stated that "the policy is still the same, but now in black hands." This statement has stayed with me to this day, as it spiralled into confusion and a mess requiring redress. The utterer is a known despot whose beard style is suspiciously Hitlerian, which could make Hitler part of his DNA.

In truth, the emergent leaders used what the apartheid government had left in reserves and failed to grow those reserves because of lack of fiscal discipline. The national treasury was plundered with reckless and wasteful expenditure, with billions going into waste that no auditing can account for, "corruption" seemingly becoming the new watchword. Dignified government diplomatic black sedans almost overnight changed into expensive vehicles the print media dubbed "bling cars." This is the naked truth, and populist rhetoric became South Africa's number-one national enemy as politicians had a field day in toyi-toyi-style celebrations and the singing of struggle and freedom songs blaming everything on apartheid.

Liberation movements gave youth leadership an unsupervised leeway, and this tremendously destroyed the economy as young ministers lost direction, with some being coerced by their seniors into approving corrupt deals. Social media became a haven of destruction for our young ministers. Had they bitten off more than they could chew, leaving the playpen before it was time to delve into territory well beyond their age? Young leaders found new toys in their pants, and they abused them. They literally fell on their sword in a manner reminiscent of a tragic Shakespearean scene, playing it out in reality.

Becoming party leaders whilst still in diapers should begin to make us wonder whether the restriction of the appointment of ministers to age is not required and ascertain that under no circumstances can such be amended. Added to that, perhaps there should be a minimum education level requirement.

It sounds tough but realistic. Ideals do not put food on the table, but pragmatic realism does. A cabinet minister should be a mature person of at least fifty-five years of age, and party leader eligibility should likewise be restricted by age.

Revolutions are aimed at bringing about positive change, and they have done so in many countries. The Industrial Revolution grew an economy and opened up new markets for the English. However, it also had its social evil sides, consistent with suddenly growing places in industrialized cities.

Our revolution has had very negative side effects on our economy because the energies of leaderships focused on "mine" and not "ours"; the nation came second, and personal needs came first as the notion of "what is in it for me" persisted, rather than "what is in it for my country?"

Our revolution became only political and not even slightly economical. It inherited an uneducated majority and was not structured to address the malady of Verwoerdian education policies; instead it compromised standards to allow through a generation of people with little expertise to grow the economy. Mathematical literacy paved the way for this dropping of standards. Surf the internet for school exam questions and review school exam questions, and note just how infested with objective questions they are. Questions requiring analytic assessments to test insight have disappeared, and this has fed the revolution with poorly informed, uncritical professionals.

Ours was a bloody revolution, and violent outbreaks claimed people's lives mercilessly and heartlessly. It had to be so after years of institutionalized racism. Painful is the fact that even amongst Africans there are fellow Africans who focus more on African disabilities than abilities, and when such disabilities are identified, they are not addressed through enabling training workshops.

We preach reconciliation, and yet we resist it at every turn.

The revolution has been a mission compromised as those entering Canaan firmly shut the door to those still crossing the river Jordan. Seeing things through the glass ceiling still very much persists, as it looks like equality with some is not for others, just as Verwoerd explained his policy. Some are still very much more equal than others.

At the dawn of democratic change, the new elite preached reconciliation with a forked tongue, and it soon proved to be a farce and a complete failure. This practice changed when the real enemies of postapartheid society emerged with a president that seemingly was only de facto rather than de jure. He was a man of no moral muscle of power, as he gave it to a family that seemed to have no, or very little, respect for him. He made a sham of his leadership when a military airport served its interests and the economy served its insatiable greed for sudden riches, mercilessly and unashamedly looting the national treasury.

Postapartheid politicians were to confuse and confound as they preached "forgive and forget", but with the same breath and tongue they blamed everything on apartheid. How is that conciliatory?

Perhaps the most reconciled, in retrospect, was the voice of conscience—the nemesis of the apartheid state and system. The most wronged man on earth who put apartheid on trial in a court case that shook the international conscience; and held it to ransom for many years became the most forgiving. His children had been left destitute and fatherless, his wife husbandless, but he became the most forgiving and reconciling and enterprising.

Five years after a new postapartheid constitutional political term, people still blamed everything on apartheid to cover up their failures, their greed, and their corrupt activities as the rand took a knock. Reconciliation proved an unreachable mirage. The more it was approached, the farther away it went, shining in the distance—unreachable! It still is unreachable, and this reconciliation is the only means to release tension and heal the nation's psyche and psychological trauma. A forgiving, reconciling heart is baggage free; it travels lightly.

Man's soul can be healed only through faith by a second invincible power whose power ensures salvation from hatred and revenge, and encourages people to seek one another in a genuine effort to find one another through grace.

Resisting reconciliation only adds to children going wayward in their expressions of their psychological trauma, tearing South Africans apart and leaving drug lords smiling all the way to the bank. Parents lose control of their children; the community also loses control, and so do schools. The law loses control because of the Child Justice Act (75 of 2008) and inadvertently puts children at the risk of being abused by adults and coerced into committing crimes. This Act absolves children below seventeen of crimes they commit, and criminal adults use them to commit crimes—a phenomenon the Department of Social Development has dubbed "Adults Using Children to Commit Crime". It is actually the reason we started a nonprofit organization, Qwaqwa Youth Against Crime, and drew our attention to the need to protect children from a life of crime. However, its funding could not sustain it, and running it is a struggle. International organizations, however, are playing admirable roles that at least do something to those children they can reach, lightening the plight of some children to help them lead better lives.

A laissez-faire kind of life ensues, and psychological trauma gains momentum. Crime escalates. The nation needs a remedy to end its psychological trauma because of the traumatic nature and effects the revolution has had, and what came after was still traumatic because the deaths experienced—even worse, witnessed, and to a lesser degree heard— were traumatic. This experience calls for a redress that only sanity and objective, pragmatic minds can provide. What we are going through and experiencing is a situation of hardship prevailing among our people all over the country. It is tough!

Despondence reigns supreme, as it becomes folly to be wise in trying to deal with a youth that seems to know it all but is oh, so ignorant! Becoming wise in such a situation should entail consultation, discussion, and reconsideration for redress. We need one another more than ever for a constructive reconstruction and development—a reconstructive surgery of a psychopolitical, rather than medical, nature.

Our souls are scarred and scared, our psyches ill at ease and psychologically traumatized.

Like a troop of monkeys in their commune, grooming one another in the sunshine, we need to come together as a people to groom one another and get rid of pests and parasites so we can start counting our gains.

One way to address trauma is to identify our similarities, stop the blame game, and breathe a new lease on life into our economy to create jobs for those leaving our schools. One thing for certain is that we need one another, just as our hands need one another to wash each other, as no one hand can wash itself.

The initial years and their setbacks are a result of a change that has no depth. It is just on the surface. It is as though a different agenda was tabled by the governing party compared to the one tabled in its election manifesto. Chris Hani insisted at every rally that all those promises would be met. They apparently died with him, as the nation is struggling to find its footing.

Twenty-four years after a revolution that probably was the last on Earth, the nation is still empty-handed and still barren, with nothing to show except new, very beautiful shopping malls enjoyed by a few whilst the unconnected are in township slums eating '*kotas, diskopo, maotwana* and *mala mohodu*' (tripe). People who can afford pizzas are few, but franchises are growing nonetheless, and their customers are the envy of the latter as the glass ceiling is opened or broken through by a select few.

Twenty-four years after the revolution, we find many youth qualified academically but roaming the streets with no jobs, hustling for a living. This is where we need to find one another. It is here that we need to put our heads together to grow a job-creating economy by giving a chance to every South African, not only the politically connected.

Many economists are very sceptical about current developments to turn the economy around, and their concerns should be taken in a very serious light and regarded as cautionary. Populist rhetoric has lamentably killed African economies. Some youths with practical certification from top universities are seeking jobs. How do you go job hunting when you hold an agricultural qualification? Does it make sense?

Yes, one can do so, but if he does not find a job, he should practise what he is qualified to do to put bread on the table. There are many examples that can be cited to support the one given affirmation. Skills have been acquired, which should make the people who have them apply their minds to self-employment, which will of course need capital, thus requiring government interventions.

Rich BBBEE tycoons should also be advised to reduce their tax assessments by reaching out to the have-nots and giving them a lease on life. What, indeed, is the point in owning a fleet of top-of-the-range vehicles? Most likely have dead batteries because of infrequent usage. But if the money used to buy those fleets were instead used to support community development for community service, it would be money invested and not spent. Owning a fleet is a sad, senseless, and insensitive display of ill-gained wealth. Adopt a school and renovate it, build its laboratory and library and stock them with a computer laboratory, adopt well-performing learners and pay for their tertiary education, identify a road in the villages and pave it—do anything communal rather than buy a fleet!

That done, declare your community outreach programme to SARS and earn its sympathies and receive a "due to you" tax assessment. Consulting an auditing firm on how to go about that would be most wise!

Chapter 11

CONCLUSIONS ON REVOLUTIONARY CHANGE

It is wise to conclude and only then make recommendations aimed at correcting what has been scientifically determined as causal.

The gaining of our freedom—that of both blacks and whites, was a psychologically traumatic experience because both blacks and whites in this country were in a psychopolitical bondage that kept one group separated from another, whilst in reality blacks were in both psychological and political bondage, with whites being more bound psychologically.

I once met an extremely beautiful white woman in a car rental company at the height of apartheid. Struck by her natural beauty, I said, "Oh my, but you are so beautiful!"

After her terse acknowledgement of "Thank you" to the compliment, we went through the processes of the car hire like automatons. The rest, after that, is a private matter, but the resultant reactions were a traumatic experience in white South Africa. My interactions were less traumatic in Qwaqwa a week later at the Qwaqwa Mountain Resort, where apartheid was unheard of.

The South African wealth gap must be a cause for national and international concern. It affirms that those who sacrificed their lives for liberation indeed did not go into the struggle to be poor, as Smuts Ngonyama once arrogantly stated.

The wealth gap in South Africa and indeed fellow African states is well documented. We see this in postcolonial Namibia, where youth leaders challenge the wealth gap as a colonial legacy. Having said this, in my community we see it on a daily basis. We live with it. It is a sad reality where poor people walk long distances because they cannot afford a taxi fare.

In South Africa, white wealth was steadily built over the years from 1913 to the 1994 revolution through intensive government intervention programmes and a facilitating education system. The white education system was a well-oiled development machine designed for a healthy wealth-creating economy. School, college and tertiary programmes skilled whites scientifically. Native education was designed to create a cheap labour pool for whites to do odd jobs. Black workers on white-owned farms were seen as farmhands doing unskilled labour, just as Verwoerd had planned. Present-day post-1994 administrations have not addressed this as it was addressed by white hegemony to develop its people to develop and strengthen the economy which only education can empower. The 1994 revolution lost sight of this and should be corrected in a racially all inclusive manner.

The now defunct Verwoerdian education system, influenced by Lord Lugard's divide-and-rule system in Nigeria, became Verwoerd's way of facilitating white supremacy and wealth in South Africa. White academics built on this system over the years, with the government setting up state structures like the Land Bank to nurture, build, and sustain white monopoly capital with the slogan 'Ons bou ons nasie' (we are building our nation). It worked like a charm, and blacks were systematically dispossessed but lay in wait to generate anxiety for change versus excitement, meaning white anxiety versus black excitement.

Development corporations were set up in autonomous homelands aimed at encouraging banana republics like the Transkei and Ciskei for Amaxhosa and Bophuthatswana for Botswana in the long term. This was based on the divide-and-rule principle promoting racial policies along cultural divides, ostensibly to protect diverse cultures.

The Basotho in their homeland had the Qwaqwa Development Corporation; the Amaxhosa, the Transkie Development Corporation; and so on. These corporations loaned money to facilitated black business interests to create wealth for blacks in their politically designated areas constituting 13 per cent of South Africa after the adoption of the 1913 Land Act, which virtually expropriated black land without compensation.

After 1994, these were transformed into provincial development corporations, which have since become white elephants under poor and questionable provincial administrations. The Free State Development Corporation is in a state of collapse and total disrepair.

We need to resuscitate these corporations to develop wealth among South Africans scientifically—to breathe life into them in such a manner that they use skills gained through schooling to build wealth and grow the economy. This should not be done through reverse racism by excluding white youth having viable business plans and a capacity to grow job-creating enterprises. The racial makeup of the employment force should include all races. White youths are also South Africans who pay taxes, which should also benefit them.

At the centre of the creation of a postcolonial wealthy black middle class is land reacquisition. However, the truth is that we have very few blacks interested in farming. A senseless land expropriation without compensation will negatively impact investment in the country, just as a 51 per cent ownership by Zimbabweans failed to attract foreign investments to resuscitate the Zimbabwean economy.

It is one thing to seek to narrow the wealth gap between whites and blacks in South Africa and fellow African states, but quite another to implement policies that will sustain this without acknowledging and rewarding other races' hard work towards a better future. A senseless implementation of policies aimed at changing the status quo will hurt the very people such policies seek to help. This is a catch-22 situation in which present-day South Africa should be very careful with implementation.

Emphasis should be placed on skilling the youth, our future, before they can be trusted with huge budgets that whet appetites for top-of-the-range vehicles, eating at their own budgets to grow their wealth-creating enterprises. The buying of these vehicles only promotes the trend rather than arresting it.

When a black middle class is thus created, it should offer bursaries to poor schoolgoing youths to build black wealth, and this must become a genealogically relayed practice. In this way, poverty eradication over time will be based on a sound scientific foundation that will produce and grow a balance between white and black wealth. Education remains the root for harvesting the fruits of development, and the creation of wealth and must be carefully nurtured.

By including rather than alienating postcolonial powers, all Africans, not only South Africans, will have the potential for reducing and, over years, eradicating imbalances between white and black wealth by evolution. A revolutionary implementation will not yield fruits; it will only generate anxieties, as it presently does.

We need sound educational programmes as a sine qua non of transforming South Africa from black dependence on state grants to the creation of wealth. Focus should be on youth development programmes along Agenda 2063 lines, meaning over periods of fifty years, with the VKB having set the example with its Vision 2020 programme.

Agenda 2063 is another solution for South Africa that is administered very carefully and sensitively as a means to attract, not alienate, foreign investors to get South Africa out of the economic quagmire it has been plunged into.

On the other hand, Africa needs a reconstructive political surgery as well. The base and very rock of such a reconstruction is nationalism. The source of this opinion is the emergence of Afrikaner academics' objective scientific study of nationalism. Traditional Afrikaner historians were transformed into historical objectivity. Stellenbosch University, which at the time was a heartland of conservative Afrikaner educational production, underwent an academic revolutionary transformation. Her academics began seeing sense in Kwame Nkrumah's pan-African view that "the African struggle for independence and unity must begin with a political union." These emergent academics express a sense of regret that these words appear on the huge statue of Dr Nkrumah that stood outside the Houses of Parliament in Accra, Ghana, but was destroyed during the coup of 1966. This was a regrettable, senseless act like the removal of colonial statues in postapartheid South Africa, which removed important landmarks of our history and, I believe, tourist attractions, similar to the slave castles in West African countries. One can regret a past and be nauseated and repulsed by aspects of it, but that it is undeletable is a naked truth!

Well-known international jazz musicians expressed their feelings about African slave castles in concerts in Senegal's Door of No Return overlooking the Atlantic Ocean, through which captured African slaves would never return after they went into captivity in America. Such songs induce a bitter sadness that should challenge attitudes.

Of interest are traditional Afrikaner academics that are historically objective. They inspire the hope that academics with a deeply rooted ideology that shaped their upbringing as Afrikaners in a country whose policy stood firmly against Macmillan's views after the Second World War are changing their tune. This struck me as interesting and resulted in this plea for the reconstruction of Africa nuanced in such academic views where an objective scientific definition of nationalism finds expression. There are many such books.

Nationalism is an offspring of love for one's country, its people, and its very flora and fauna! If we love Africa—indeed, if we love South Africa—we need to reconstruct her. And when you reconstruct something, you must start from the start.

We need to identify our origins from the Stone Age through modern and contemporary times. Things that shaped us as a people and the geopolitics of our continent, and as a continental nation in contemporary Africa, influenced by the music of the likes of white South Africans identifying with the struggle, are encouraging. African musicians who ply their trade abroad also reflect a deep-seated African nationalism. Some Afrikaner musicians even make this nationalism the sweetest and are musically captivating and inspiring. If song cannot bring people together, nothing else can.

Such a reconstruction of Africa needs the scientific objectivity exemplified in traditional Afrikaner writings. Their political tones lack racial attitude, having a scientific purity of mind whilst belonging to an era that saw Afrikaner nationalism as the bastion of "Afrikanerdom". Some of these books were written by Stellenboch University, which bred apartheid's mastermind.

They look at nationalism as being detached from the sociopolitics of their immediate nationhood shaped by the Great Trek (1834), from which "Die Stem Van Suid Africa" (The Voice of South Africa), the Afrikaner national anthem, emanates. This detachment can trigger in the reader positivity about a reconstruction of Africa that will delete Afrophobia, which African journalists write about. Indeed, Africans cannot be xenophobic about their own; they can only be Afrophobic.

These Afrikaner academics have mastered the courage to see differently and can thus be the catalysts that change the political outlooks of those who cannot. But for this to happen, their books must be known and be read in schools.

A traditional academic seeing Africanism positively can even be recruited into a government department to help redefine African nationalism for a positive reconstruction of Africa into a common nationhood. I believe we can be able to do this. All we need is to cultivate the ability to make such Afrikaners part of change. Their objective purity can change even the minds of extreme fundamentalists to realize that the world has become a globe lit with various cultural colours that make it a glittering rainbow requiring intercultural exchanges through scientific book knowledge.

Finally, it is from the scars of apartheid that we should discern a common spirit of oneness. The preamble to the newly adopted constitution of South Africa, partly taken from the Freedom Charter, states, "We, the people of South Africa … Believe that South Africa belongs to all who live in it, united in our diversity." The selfsame people of South Africa must wake up to this to achieve such oneness. This is the covenant, or contract, that binds us as people of South Africa and Africans in general—Afrikaner or Africans, so to speak. For this to be realized, we must begin a process of healing our psychological trauma as a nation and revisiting the traumatic events herein referred to that befell us to find closure. Without closure, we cannot nation-actualise. Does that make sense?

Closure will draw us together to make the best of our situation and stimulate economic growth from its stagnant 0.07 per cent, and create crime-avoiding employment, since unemployment aberts crime. Abraham Maslow gives a hierarchy people need to self-actualise as individuals. This can be adapted to nationhood to provide a sense of belonging to satisfy our primary physiological, safety, love, and belonging needs. We can then together make the economy work after acknowledging that we all belong to this lovely, rich country and work to realize our higher needs and its rich culture.

Of what use is social science if we do not use it to realize organizational behaviour for economic growth? Why spend so much on education but fail to apply the scientifically acquired knowledge to build an economy the Afrikaner built, albeit with cheap farmhand labour and cheap mining labour, to reconstruct our primary and tertiary industries? Cheap labour can be compensated with worthy wages by understanding our archaeological genesis as South Africans and understanding our people as ethnoanthropological realities, allowing us to realize the unwritten human contract of 'ubuntu' (humanity) that binds us as South Africans.

We need to shape our raw materials into job-creating finished products for exportation as bedrock for a growing economy because imports repel income and exports attract income and strengthen the rand. We should objectively view conservatism from both sides of the racial political spectrum. This will show that black radicals have become conservative while white conservatives have become liberal in mental orientation. This means the once radical blacks have become conservatives regarding land matters and want land totally for themselves, thus introducing a new racism. Marxist views today must be modernized into constructivism and revisited to give answers to today's challenges. The haves must not resist a desire for the have-nots to be haves, whilst the have-nots should not seek to swallow more than they can chew. Class struggles must wear new spectacles to avoid starving the nation in the midst of the plenty our natural resources provide. We need to draw strength from one another over the next one hundred years of an economic renaissance.

Chapter 12

OPEN LETTERS

Open letters are a means of reaching our leaders by putting our concerns in the public domain and putting our leaders on the spot. Following are some such letters addressing issues of public interest directly affecting us. The first letter is to the president of South Africa, and the next is to the premier. The third should have been to the mayor; however, this was deemed unnecessary because we interact with him in our municipality.

The reason for my including these letters here is because we only have their contact details given on their websites, which they apparently do not take seriously and never reply to. We have emails from the business cards of members of the Economic Council, and our letters are still never replied to, and our concerns never addressed. Politicians do not seem to see the need to reply to letters from a public that mandated their ascent into power. They have become too powerful and seem no longer to be servants of the people that gave them power.

The reason for this could be that they do not receive our correspondence. We hope, in platforms such as this one, they will read our letters and hopefully address concerns therein expressed, even though they may not reply. Adding to this, writing to people holding high office does not mean we want to tell them how to run their offices—far from it! It is just one of the many ways of making them aware that their decisions or, at times, failures to take action affect us immensely. A case in point is to encourage the minister of police, Bheki Cele, to react to violence when invited by communities to do so. The question is, does the government, and such sensitive departments, not see the need to react to needs of the public without being invited by taking the initiative? After all, that is exactly why they are appointed!

Democratic governance and practice are participatory in nature. Crime is one phenomenon that is eroding our economy and needs communities' social cohesion and participatory democracy to fight it. Crime forums currently have no effect on crime prevention. This concern was referred to the president of South Africa, Cyril Ramaphosa. It was followed by an open letter to him after no feedback was received from him. Putting it in the public domain is aimed at conscientizing the nation that crime watch is a communal responsibility and can help reduce crime. Let us together consider the proposal below:

BROTHERHOOD-SISTERHOOD BAND OF HOPE AGAINST CRIME (B-SBOHAC)

Neighbourhood Crime Watch—Together against Crime!

Crime has become so widespread that it no longer is the government's concern only. It emanates from our communities. It plagues us and is eating into our economy. The surge of crime affects investment opportunities, and we the community need to play a leading role in nipping it at the bud to attract job-creating investors.

You know your neighbour, and your neighbour knows you. You know areas in your community that are prone to crime, and you know houses that sell drugs to our youth. *That makes you the first police officer. If you do not know them, then you are the first detective.* If not concerned, remember that your child knows these places and his or her friends, through peer pressure groups, will lure him or her into them to create a circle of abusers so that dependence on them can be fed. You are therefore one of the Brotherhood and Sisterhood Band of Hope against Crime members. Join hands with us and be part of the band of hope to squeeze criminals out of our communities and hand them over to law enforcement officers. Abandoned buildings in our communities are homes to criminals, and they must be either sold or demolished.

Crime knows no denomination; it affects all denominations. B-SBOHAC is an interdenominational association of brothers and sisters involved in fighting crime. Much talk and many sermons have been made inside our denominations and their conventions. Many strategies have been suggested to take crime by the scruff of its neck. In the Methodist Church, our former president of the Young Men's Guild (YMG), of which I am a member, Reverend Bosman, suggested school visits and adoption to bring about awareness and means of fighting crime. In the Methodist Crusade (20–21 October 2018) in Sterkspruit, Herschel, Evangelist Mdwaba made a passionate and fervent sermon and prayer plea against crime. He read from St. Luke 10:31–32: "And there by chance came down a certain priest that way, and when he saw him (a man who fell among thieves), he passed on the other side. And like-wise a Levite, when he was at the place, came and looked on him, and passed by on the other side." The evangelist made a passionate plea sermon explaining how *people look the other way* like the priest and Levite when crime is committed. He related his sermon by applying it to our situation, where people do very little, if anything at all, to engage in crime fighting and prevention. This is communal betrayal of the highest degree and is sans holiness—a priest looking the other way, less concerned!

It is this sermon and plea in this Methodist Crusade whose theme was "Time with God" out of which this organization, B–SBOHAC, was conceived. Having been previously involved in crime prevention and training by the Free State Department of Social Development, I decided to take up my cudgel and take up where I left off in our organization, the Qwaqwa Youth Against Crime NPO.

Our strategy to engage in crime fighting is as follows:

1. Visit schools and engage learners and educators in crime fighting and prevention.
2. Engage out-of-school youth in income-generating projects, to check unemployment and encourage entrepreneurs to give those leaving school a chance to build their experience.
3. Bring awareness to substance abuse as a causal factor of home burglaries, robberies, and shoplifting.
4. Bring awareness to schoolgoing children that committing crimes gives them records which will impede employment when job opportunities emerge.
5. Promote sports and recreation in various codes in schools on Wednesdays (or Saturdays if the school programme is full) to

engage the youth productively and meaningfully by filling up their free time. It is during these free times that their minds turn into the devil's workshops! School sports also give learners an opportunity to explore their talents.

The living legend Jomo Sono is a local best example. The current freeze in sports in schools is not helping development, and this explains why Baxter (the national Bafana-Bafana coach) is on the spot. Producing the class of 1996 (the Phil Masingas, Doctor Khumalos, Lucas Radebes, etc.) is neutered by a school curriculum that has excluded sports and recreation with focus on 100 per cent matric results. However, Saturdays can be set aside for sports and recreation to make schools part and parcel of sports development. This will help boost development and assist South Africa to stop struggling against sides with low national statistics, such as Seychelles, appreciating that development is a process, not an event.

6. Bring awareness to and prevent peer pressure that engages the youth in crime.

7. Importantly, unveil St. Luke 15 (The parable of the *prodigal son*— the lost son) and relate it to youth lost to drugs, alcohol, and crime perpetration, to encourage their turning around (like the prodigal son) to a crime-free life and gaining the ambition to build a future by exploring their talents in singing, traditional dance, arts and crafts, sports and recreation, chess, etc., as occupations that will unleash youth talent and exploit it to the fullest extent. School psychology and career choice and counselling sessions shall be held to build their ambitions as a strategy to keep them in libraries as internet research in groups of five.

8. Create a band of hope with schools, churches and the wider community to build a crime prevention and fighting band (ring) of fellowship by strengthening this fellowship with our "Together against Crime!" motto.

PAROLEE RELEASE HALFWAY HOUSE

The aim of this project is to prepare the parolee for release and let there be contact between the parolee and his or her victim to work on their

119

reconciliation to be accepted and reintegrated into society. Cases of rape are the most common and severe. A rape victim feels most insecure, and the violence against such a victim is irreversible and unforgettable. The release for reintegration into society of a rapist parolee is in itself a traumatic act, and reconciling the perpetrator with the victim requires psychological skill and should thus be placed in the hands of social workers and psychologists with a view to reconcile them for the perpetrator's societal reintegration.

Our theory is that when the community sees the two together in a peaceful union, the parolee will hopefully be accepted by community members, and this will thus facilitate parolee reintegration.

PAROLEE REHABILITATION PROGRAMMES

Parolee second-chance programmes will identify a parolee's strong points and passions to occupy them on full-time income-generating projects or work. Such programs will do the following:

1. Work hand-in-hand with the church elders to take interest in giving a parolee a second chance.
2. Make parolees part of church activities, such as the choir and church classes, and identify his or her skills to be shared with the church.
3. Let the parolee mix freely with congregants and share skills acquired in correctional services with the youth.
4. Encourage church members to work on their prejudices and give the parolee time to rehabilitate and become a responsible member of the community.
5. Allow parolees to visit schools to bring awareness to students about the futility of committing crimes.

The stigma of committing crimes is a perpetrator's albatross, and each time a crime is reported in his neighbourhood after his release, he becomes the first suspect. This should be guarded against, and whilst it probably could be, sufficient evidence must be produced to prove such an allegation.

Be involved. Join us in fighting and preventing crime for the economic growth of our country, and the safety and security of our people and our progeny!

AN OPEN LETTER TO THE PRESIDENT OF SOUTH AFRICA

Brotherhood–Sisterhood Band of Hope against Crime (B–SBOHAC)

Dear Honourable Mr President Cyril Ramaphosa,

Ndaa (good day), Mr President!

It has been a while since I have written to you soliciting government support in the endeavour to fight crime, and I have received no reply. I understand that the demands of your high office make it difficult for you to address personal letters. There are huge national and global matters demanding your undivided stoic attention to address the concerns we are raising in such letters. This is understandable.

However, crime is one of the issues that should give your presidency sleepless nights, the major challenge being to restore the integrity and credibility of the African National Congress, which in itself is a tall order. This is no easy matter, and I fully appreciate that you have inherited a corrupt state requiring reconstruction and redress. Your predecessor has left unenviable tasks, and for this you have my sympathies.

Be that as it may, Mr President, the issues at hand require your attention for facilitation from the ground because you need our help. If you want to develop people, make them part of their own development in participatory democracy. To do this, you need ground soldiers to oil your administration's machinery. This will make you go into our history books as the man that restored integrity, credibility, and respectability to the African National Congress—as the man that restored unity in a divided organization the media is feasting on, revealing disturbing matters between even you and your secretary general.

I believe, as all sane and patriotic nationals should, that Solomon Mahlangu and all past cadres of our movement who sacrificed their very lives so we could be liberated from the repressive yoke of apartheid want to see from yonder a changing organization. We, the people of South Africa, also want to see that, Mr President. We want to see the new dawn you preached so that the people can believe in your vision.

The trauma of liberation distorted your movement's focal point to improve the lot of our people and restore their dignity. This requires foot soldiers to hit the ground running and be facilitators of the presidential machinery on this matter.

But how do we do that if letters raising issues that can help facilitate this go unanswered?

For how long are we to knock unheeded on locked and barred doors, as President Chief Albert Luthuli did on the apartheid government's door? Are we, as ordinary nationals, to receive the same treatment from the very door of your government and administration?

During our years as students, we stood defiant to the system of governance our forefathers stood opposed to. We are still to enjoy the fruits of our liberty as role players, not be mere spectators as the case is now, and only you can facilitate that.

I beseech you to reply to letters from your compatriots as president of the country, because the automatic reply, as you may well know and be aware of, is not enough and serves no purpose.

In all sincerity, this simply and only acknowledges receipt and nothing more, Mr President.

I thus, with much respect, request you to come to our assistance as a brotherhood–sisterhood against crime so that we can proudly say we had a hand in facilitating the hope your administration instils in the nation and the world, finding expression and inspiration in the visit to you by former US president Bill Clinton and his wife, Hillary. This statesman and his wife have a proud executive administration history in the United States, and their visit was a diplomatic message of their belief and support for your administration. This visit gave us hope.

This is one of the many windows through which we see this hope shining in the distance, and it is our wish to give this hope strength and mobility for realization, making it more than the mirage it seems to be at the moment.

Your silence, Mr President, is like a kick in the teeth. Hereto attached please find my African National Congress membership in good standing.

Your reply will keep the hope going strong and make us proud and prove that our investment in education, and sacrifice in our lifetime, does not go into the sandy, dusty wastelands of despair.

I remain yours truly

[NB: The writer has since lost confidence in the African National Congress and is now a member of the Afrikan Alliance of Social Democrats under Itumeleng "Pappie" Mokoena, the founding president going into the 2019 general elections.]

An Open Letter to the Free State Premier

Why Our Local (Rural) Municipal Economy Is Failing

Dear Madam Premier,

Local municipalities are cesspits of a few connected individuals who give kickbacks for lucrative tenders resulting in very poor municipal services. Their tarred roads are a case in point, with insufficient tar that gets eroded by the first soft rains. Other examples are hidden and more intricate. Those getting tenders are self-serving, and some do not pay the very staff they employ decent salaries, whilst others do not pay them at all.

I should know; I am one of the victims. Pleas for intervention fell on deaf ears.

Events held do not benefit our communities. Dipontsho Tsa Maluti and MACUFE, which word has it is an international event, justifying featuring American artists at a price you can yourself imagine, as one such artist in Ghana cost $1,000,000, (a cool R14,510,000) at the time of writing

The acronym MACUFE, structured from Mangaung Cultural Festival, indicates the cultural nature of the event, and Dipontsho Tsa Maluti is also supposed to be cultural, but these are both misnomers. "Dipontsho" means "show" and should ideally showcase Basotho culture, viz., traditional music, arts, and dress. The event should also ideally showcase animal husbandry and the growing of produce, with a view to show rural people how to raise animals scientifically and till land productively in their back yards and communal plots.

But alas, this never happens! What we see are musical events and stall owners coming from afar, but they do not earn enough to sustain their craft, because the public, though supposed to be buying, does not have the money. Most are unemployed, and some of those who are employed earn a pittance and cannot afford the luxury of an art collection—a luxury afforded only by the well-heeled, connected tender entrepreneurs, whose eye for art is stunted.

Our local artists' skills do not find a suitable market to promote their craft. Visit our local public library and see their quality portraits and related works of art. They are breathtaking!

Local artists need to be promoted by the local municipality's Sports, Arts & Culture Department and the Local Economic Development Department. The youth producing these works are clearly gifted; they need the exposure afforded by the municipal departments. Basotho Cultural Village is becoming a white elephant, apparently unbudgeted or insufficiently budgeted for by the provincial government, and this adversely impacts and negatively affects tourism.

Those getting government tenders create jobs for their families, effectively leaving locals out. Tender entrepreneurs do not contribute to community projects like crime prevention, welfare, and religious organizations. Businesses that fund institutions of faith are our spiritual bedrock to promote spirituality, helping in detraumatizing their congregations.

Tender entrepreneurs own top-of-the-range fleets of vehicles, and one in particular hovers in the air in a helicopter purchased with ill-gotten wealth to reduce his tax liabilities. When it is pointed out that he should be funding communal projects and NPOs, he promptly changes the subject.

As long as our municipal budget is enjoyed by a few, we can forget about municipal economic growth and the reduction of unemployment. One of our two provincial teams in the National First Division League, the Free State Stars, changed its home to Bethlehem because of alleged maltreatment from our local municipality.

The economy in this way will fail to generate growth and create employment within the municipality. Some industrial firms lie desolate because the Free State Development Corporation (FDC) does not assist with loans, whilst people have business plans requiring financial assistance intervention to create jobs. The FDC, Small Enterprise Development Agency (SEDA), and our Municipal Local Economic Development Department are all not coordinated to generate economic growth. SEDA is fighting a lone battle, with some support from Thabo Mofutsanyana District Municipality.

This letter serves to bring our plight to your attention and that of the national government. Enforcing by-laws would also help keep Harrismith and all its neighbouring locations, Kestel and Phuthaditjhaba—especially the Setsing CBD—clean! Presently, the putrid smell of urine is present in every part of our CBD. Our environment is a mess of litter—a sore eye to tourists. Your intervention can help save the situation.

An Open Letter to the Media—Print and Electronic

The African Has a Very Long Way to Go!

When Donald Trump unleashes his disgusting verbal venom, we become, as I do, disgusted! I definitely do not affirm or condone his disgusting racist paranoia and racially divisive utterances, but let us face it—Africa is a cog well of corruption and is the only continent in the world where corruption has become a state of normalcy.

Africa is a citadel of corruption through and through and does not have colonialism to blame, as insinuated in African literature and by her political leaders. Some in South Africa to this day still condemn apartheid, as they have been doing since 1994, whilst three fingers point back at them. When the Afrikaners finally came together in a union, the atrocities of the Anglo-Boer War became their source of strength and bitterness, and they focused on a 1912–2012 nation building that grew the economy, albeit through unjustifiable racial policies. This is something the revolution is not considering but that it effectively eroded. The wealth the state has lost is today reflected in our multimillionaires and billionaires after twenty-five short years, as if to indicate that these suddenly wealthy politicians and well-connected individuals stole from the state.

Africa is riddled with self-inflicted corruption holes that can be remedied and dressed to heal by her only through fiscal discipline. Africa is an example of assisted suicide to beat all I have heard of. However, Rwanda never ceases to amaze as a striking exception. Her heart-rending history has unfolded into a heart-warming story that must be duplicated throughout Africa. The African leadership's problem is a lack of fiscal discipline that Thomas Sankara sought to put right, only to be assassinated by insatiable greed that removed the man. However, his ideas are filtering through to this day.

South Africa has seen many billions of rands going unaccounted for in corrupt, underhanded Reconstruction Development Programme deals between government officials and tender entrepreneurs since black Africans took over from white Africans. In these deals, huge sums of money exchange hands in paybacks delivering very shoddy services, such as roads coated with tar that is washed away by very soft rains, leaving the roads worse off than they previously were. And yet truth be told, this corruption runs amuck among black Africans, who still cannot look at how apartheid built a strong, solid economy, even though this time they are looking through racially inclusive practices. A scientific analysis of the poor white problem answered the question, and the state put in place solutions enabling economic development in order to build a solid, self-sustaining economy. These solutions unfortunately enabled a section of the population with a view to justify a black poverty–fuelling white economic development that Verwoerd enabled through a wicked education system wherein mathematics was irrelevant to the mental endowment of the black child. It was a system designed to produce "free" slaves through evil, subhuman, repressive policies that ascertained the Afrikaner nation where Verwoerd stood to keep the National Party in power! The statement he uttered in a rally is tongue-blistering!

In the new South Africa since 1994, and worse still during the past ten years, the Verwoerdian condition went on unabated. The corruption worm dug deep into the strongly built economic development inheritance, with some government projects well beyond projected management–scheduled time charts, resulting in most projects costing ten times their actual projected costs. Road construction projects between Qwaqwa and Bethlehem swallowed millions of rands and took a long time to complete, with a telling negative effect on economic development because means of communication are inextricably tied to economic development. Truckloads of time were wasted in road construction stops where one side of a road was under construction.

Auditor generals uncovered huge deficits in municipal audits which were swept under the carpet like nothing had happened, with rabble-rousers pushed under the bus. One such case in point is the Estina farm disaster in the Free State, where millions went to one godforsaken Gupta family whilst its beneficiaries were left destitute! The farm's purebred dairy cattle were left unkempt, starving, and dying as a result because money meant for them fed one family. Disgusting!

Politicians can lie in smear campaigns, but a picture of ill-kept dairy farm cattle in the media at Estina farm in Vrede, where R220 million was allegedly paid to the Guptas by the Free State Department of Agriculture, can never lie. The people of the Free State and affected emerging farmers are still demanding answers to bring the matter to rest and find closure.

A raid of the Free State premier's office raised hopes that the plight of these emerging farmers for whom the money was intended would finally be addressed. However, this soon dissipated, or so it seems. It looks like the National Prosecuting Authority (NPA) is powerless to prosecute the high and mighty, thus making some more equal than the others in a democracy designed to serve people equally. The newly appointed director of the NPA, Shamila Batohi, could be our last hope and may have been most effective during Thuli Madonsela's tenure. Does Thuli require an introduction? I guess not!

Today's African should be ashamed to look in the mirror and say, "I'm black and I'm proud!" as we did during the Steve Biko Black Consciousness years! But we cannot afford to lose hope. It is a comfort zone we can ill afford. Bringing all South Africans together seems to be the only face-saving ideal to address the rot and seek remedies.

But there is an immediate remedy, and that is to take action against all corrupt leaders without wasting taxpayers' money (most of which is presently out of circulation) in commissions of inquiry. If an audit can be taken to determine how much money has been printed and how much of it is in circulation, a huge deficit can be uncovered, because money gained through corrupt deals is not in circulation but is rather in offshore accounts and ground vaults to avoid discrepant incomes of corrupt officials in their bank accounts. This hurts an already afflicted economy immensely! When such corrupt officials die, as they do, what becomes of that money?

Government officials earn incredible salaries! The recent cabinet ministers' salary adjustments raised eyebrows. Word has it that these salary adjustments have not been implemented yet, but that fact is that they were tabled when they should not even have been considered!

Africa is a sick joke, a presently occurring disaster, and it has a marathon to run before normalizing the line between the poverty stricken and the well heeled! As it stands, it is abnormal, because to add insult to injury, tender entrepreneurs employ family members, meaning that taxpayers' money is circulating among very few "lucky" postapartheid black families, and a trickle goes to the poverty-stricken nationals! These new lucky families do not even know what to do with their sudden ill-gotten wealth. This means that our rescuers and liberators from the Verwoerdian apartheid mindset have become our new colonizers, perpetuating colonialism in another form—a post neocolonialism stage of imperialism that can be defined as liberated colonialism. We need a national dialectic engagement to reverse the ongoing status quo for total liberation. We must and have to develop a liberating national consciousness; only then shall we have lasting peace.

Very few political parties have the peoples' interests at heart. In retrospect, only one African political party had its peoples' interests at heart, and this is the National Party, but it was discredited by its racist policies! The new government must adopt this by seeing all South Africans as its people and dropping the racist definition of "die mense" apartheid. Colonel Muammar Gaddafi may have been what the media claim he was, but he cared for Libyans and African peoples deeply! This is something our provincial and national government leaders lack in leaps and bounds!

Today, few political parties care for the people and one of those with an element of credibility, the Democratic Alliance, is viewed as interested only in safeguarding white monopoly interests. Predominantly black political parties under government policies justify Broad-Based Black Economic Empowerment (BBBEE) policies, thus introducing a new racism that favours even very few of black people! Only those who are politically connected gain from BBBEE. Look at it any other way, but such policies will remain just that—racist to the core! That it favours the few connected individuals is obvious, and this has stagnated economic growth because those gaining from it only employ family members and a few outside family members. Service delivery is also politically motivated. Areas that do not vote ANC are hit by water and electricity cuts simply because they vote Democratic Alliance and this as can be seen is undemocratic and unconstitutional.

The ANC has completely and utterly sold out, and there seems to be nothing that will ever change it—nothing! It has become a party for selected families and persons, and not a caring national party safeguarding national interests. Its leaders are self-serving, with no regard for the people of South Africa, the home for Africans and all those who live in it and call her home. The people are disgruntled.

Even journalism has a hand in this. Letters raising such concerns receive scant publishing because their piercing truth is too much! It is a truth from another angle, another perspective. We need such truth to uncover evil practices and to work towards working for the people of South Africa and the peoples of Africa. Only then will the economy respond towards growth. The Chinese bettering what the West can do has generated an economic growth that has grown its wealth by leaps and bounds whilst we still adore colonialism and live out of its bowl. The Western lifestyle we live is proof of this assertion, yet we have natural resources aplenty; our problem is an inability to learn that it is small things like time management that are actually big things. Yet there is nothing wrong with Western lifestyles. The only problem is that the living and feeding of them has made some insatiably greedy.

Brothers and sisters, beyond racial divides we need one another to turn our freedom from narrow racial divides into true liberty. Nelson Mandela's view ("As I stand before the door of my freedom, I realise that if I don't leave my pain, anger and bitterness behind me, I will still be in prison") makes self-imposed imprisonment worse than that imposed by an inability to forgive. He is one of the many our history will recount, just as the Americans trace their liberty from men such as Abraham Lincoln, Dr Martin Luther King Jr., and one woman in particular, Rosa Parks, who refused to vacate her seat in a bus for a citizen whom racism defined as more refined than her. It is people like these who will be milestones along the route to a liberty we have yet to attain, shining like a mirage ahead of us. We still need more men and women of this calibre to create a new state, a new people, a new country. You could be one of those to free Vickie Momberg from a literally physical self-imposed imprisonment.

We as Africans indeed have a long way to go, remembering that if our passports and identity cards say we are South African citizens, we are Africans. We still have a long way to trudge together to remake Africa. We have a long way to go to achieve that freedom. As Nelson Mandela once said, it is a long walk, and at every vista we shall pause and take stock; we shall realize just how long the walk to freedom is. It will take us well over twenty-seven years, but to achieve it we must work and walk towards it every step of the way on a daily basis. If activists can walk long distances to make themselves heard, so can we, as a nation, to realize true economic freedom and be released from the prison of mental slavery. To achieve this, we have to strive for racial equality.

Chapter 13

RECOMMENDATIONS AND THE WAY FORWARD

Putting recommendations after a conclusion is a method of scientific writing that applies its findings to a problem under consideration with the purpose of providing scholarly analysis for scholars and readers. I hope readers will realize that as much as we strive to strike a balance between the haves and have-nots, we must sincerely note past and present disparities. However, attempts should be made to make opposing parties note where we come from as a nation. We must realize that the centre of our political discord in this country is land, which one side, like a rag, is pulling from the other in a dialectical struggle that threatens to tear the land apart. You cannot let something you love be destroyed or be torn apart—no one can afford to!

Two bull elephants are at each other's throats, and as the saying goes, the grass is the sufferer! In the rag analogy, as the struggle ensues, the rag (land) becomes torn, implying that what suffers is the land. The source of discord gets destroyed, with both sides ending up being losers. In a situation such as this, it becomes difficult to make recommendations; it is easier to draw scenarios that will make people sit back, evaluate the situation, and come to their senses for the general good.

So to speak, a simple recommendation is for us to start from the start, based on a sound educational system developed and facilitated by a reconciling people. We can suddenly love one another cross-culturally as though we are actors in a soap after the director shouts "Action!" All we need is to *try* and *act*, and then, after the director shouts "Cut!", we can call one another names under our breath, having worked out the economy through acting as if we had suddenly found love for one another. Without this mindset, our economy will fail to take off and sustain us.

Yes, tempers will flare at times, but forgetting a mishap will be better than nursing a tortured heart and a bruised ego. The personality we study in psychology is imbedded in us, and only we can develop ego-protecting mechanisms that will help us find one another.

University education should start preparing the product to fit easily in society and not make one feel above the society that gave birth to him or her, shaped him or her, and developed him or her into a utilitarian human being who will service that same society. We South Africans are a dejected, semidepressed people who have let psychological trauma get the better of us. We need to discard this self-defeating paranoia and fear of the unknown and apply the social sciences in a practical, scientific, utilitarian way. Only in this way can we truly find one another.

We need to develop this mindset and let it envelop us to remake our fatherland.

Garibaldi, the soldier of Italian unification, offered his soldiers nothing but toil, hard work, and suffering to unite their country. I offer South Africans much of the same to unite South Africans. Italians today enjoy and are part of world-class football, with sopranos that grace the halls of our civilized world. This is what we are standing in the way of that would allow us to produce such musicians as Yanga, who was produced by *Idols* in 2018!

Like J. F. Kennedy, let us focus on what we can do for South Africa and not so much what we expect South Africa to do for us. Let us blow the horn of peace and reconciliation and together sing "God bless Africa, her sons and daughters" and together firmly stand and say that we shall live and we shall die for you, dear land, thus throwing our daggers of hatred, senseless vengeance, and apartheid blame games into the ocean. Do those words sound borrowed and paraphrased? Well, perhaps they are.

Considering how acidic our political situation is, with the poor and vulnerable exposed to politically toxic political parties, it is advisable to visualize a worse political scenario in our country to try to avoid it. This is a possibility with a questionable president whose every breath reeks of racial hatred! Truth be told, every South African, especially the poor, has to avoid this.

The poor are vulnerable to false promises by prophets of doom that are reflected in political rhetoric that gives the poor scapegoats for their poverty. This scapegoating tactic is one Hitler used to destroy his own people and the very country he loved. By blaming apartheid, the African National Congress has led South Africa into a messy, convoluted political conundrum with waves of one scandalous corruption after another. All the poor of South Africa need, as did the economically hard-hit Germans after the First World War, is an excuse for their poverty. Prophets of doom are providing this, and they are even not subject to laws that deny others the right to do their work as they manhandle journalists and assault them.

Blame whites as did Hitler the Jews, and this will lead to what we well know resulted in a human tragedy to beat all and sparked another international crisis.

History is our reflection of the past that we should draw lessons from. We do not have far to look. Just across our Beit Bridge border lies the economically hard-hit Zimbabwe, once the bread basket of Southern Africa. Queen Victoria Falls pouring out its immortal waters in a stupendous, spectacular fashion, attracting international tourists to Southern Africa, is a source of strength and hope that all will be well.

Young men can be misled into believing in impossible dreams. In his mind, Malema can be president, as he was so told by Winnie Madikizela Mandela, and his funeral oration—if you can call his rants at Winnie's funeral an oration—reflects this ambition. The possibility that the poor and unemployed could be fooled into giving him a nod is there, as it happened in Maluti-a-Phofung, where a political activist won a place in council on such a ticket. We therefore need to look into such a possibility and guard like hawks against its happening.

The ANC is caught up in its own false promises and now has to keep watch over irresponsible populist political agendas—especially those bordering around land issues. This is what causes the ANC president to be caught up in populist agendas to avoid the pulling of the rug from under his feet. We, as a nation, need to weigh such a possibility and educate ordinary South Africans against threats to democracy and economic advancement.

Journalists critically review some youth leaders in South Africa as bad news for the democratic revolution. According to them, as seen by the intellectual elite, they are a mixture of racial and authoritarian nationalism in the context of militarized beliefs in personality cults. They are all products of the ANC's authoritarian nationalism reflected in leaders who are unable to reconcile the nation. Such personalities offer the reason why they are being groomed to have the false belief that they are presidential material. Misleaders implanted in their minds that they are presidential material, while in reality the revolution no longer needs firebrands but needs statesmen to reconcile the people of South Africa and lead them towards a peaceful fourth industrial revolution. The time for firebrands is long over.

Some postapartheid South African nationalist leaders lack Nelson Mandela's spirit of Ubuntu (humanity), and their souls have died inside of them. In their view, Mandela was too conciliatory and not as politically aggressive as they wanted him to be. Rhetorical chants and rants to them are tools to move masses. Their burning racial hatred, whose intolerance does not augur well for South Africa, impresses radicals. Stompie, a child who recited some political rhetoric he hardly understood, reflects the kind of racial hatred such radicals nurture, and this must be discouraged to take South Africa forward.

Rhetoric today is a dangerous and popular decoy used by people to attack the wrong problems. Its aim is to cement its power, to weaken democracy, and to extract every ounce of power from the state. Rhetoric uses the anger of the unemployed to create radicalism.

Looking at this view against the background of how youth leaders impressed Robert Mugabe, who rolled out the red carpet each time such destructive youths visited Harare, begs serious consideration to resist the possibility of such a presidency with every ounce of our being. Robert Mugabe's own military officers saw the need to oust him in a smooth, bloodless revolutionary coup, meaning that to keep a clean slate of democratic practice in South Africa, the people should be enticed away from such a possibility.

There is only one way to do this, and that is to foreswear corruption and embrace good governance. At the very root of corruption is greed, which needs to be forked out with one of Gandhi's favourite quotes: "The world has enough for us all, but not enough for human greed."

Translated to our situation, our beloved country has enough for all and should be shared by all and sundry. We have to do away with tenders and let the municipality be the employer in all development projects. We need to take away power from mayors and make them ceremonial officers during occasions requiring political address as mouthpieces for presidents; they should not be delivering ill-conceived personal messages.

A mayor's speech must reflect government policy and be directed by the president at the head of national government. Government must wake up to the reality that tenders serve only to promote corruption and be situated against them.

This is the stance South African leaders should take. They should be discouraged from the obvious capture of state resources by a few for a few. I mean, for a president to place the interests of family above those of state simply because his son was catered for by a corrupt family to get president Jacob Zuma's hands into the people's treasury and proceed to tell the president how to run his country is a galloping disgrace. Where was the nationalism and patriotism which put such a man in prison and exile when he compromised his personal dignity, integrity, country, and its people when he succumbed to state capture?

Moses, the legendary Hebrew who was chosen and anointed to lead Israel out of bondage from Egypt, was such a person. He loved his people, deplored their suffering, and even killed to prove it. God's finger of choice pointed at him to take the lead because of these attributes, and I believe those who gave their lives to free this country from its comatose apartheid condition had these attributes. How did some suddenly deplete their consciences of such leadership attributes? If it be greed for sudden wealth, then the law must come into full swing to take its course.

We must compare and contrast the past and the present. By "the past", I am referring to the years up to 1994; and by "the present", I am referring to post-1994. Our past has Afrikaner leaders who had the plot to fight "die swart gevaar" (the black danger) since 1948, when Malan ascended to power. Afrikaner nationalism was the driving force of this plot, and it developed South Africa.

The Macmillan winds of change could not break this plot and could not discourage this nationalism. It was a solid nationalism blowing against the one blowing from the north of Africa down south. Its menacing force only strengthened apartheid as Verwoerd stood firm. It was broken by an African nationalism resistance that stood equally resolute on its back foot, assisted by a disgusted world after 1976. Various incidents herein explored weakened it until it fell flat on its face.

A new nationalism must now be developed to stand against corruption as a new threat to our freedoms, which we together as a country negotiated. If this new spirit of nationalism does not evolve, the youth misleaders will mislead the youth and we will forever regret we ever let that happen. South Africans must wake up, as they have nothing to lose but their racial hatred to fight a common threat to their hard-won democracy. It is as simple as that!

The changing faces of youth misleaders to those of constitutionalists make them lame ducks we should make a smear of on a wall. The ANC paints them as seasoned politicians, when in fact they thrive on racial hatred, past leadership weaknesses, and the corrupt, enabling weaknesses of the ANC leadership, especially in basic moral, fiscal, and behavioural disciplines. These things make an impression on youth misleaders and require us to cleanse public offices, instead electing men and women of integrity who respect human values.

The recalling of President Jacob Zuma by the ANC left youth misleaders with nothing to attack and they went out with political verbal venom and adopted a new hatred for white South Africans when they lost their punchbag in Parliament. They then found their new rhetorical rhythm and vitriol when they suddenly remembered the poor and unemployed and the land issue as a ticket to run with to retain their employment in Parliament.

Such youth misleaders are very loose semilearned cannons with points that make sense to the unemployed youth, whose predicament they are taking advantage of. They are simply running with ideas that they know very little of. They are disgruntled young men who will do anything to embarrass the organization that sought to destroy them with one stroke of a pen. The ANC must be blaming itself for not heeding Motlanthe's advice not to get rid of such loose cannons that misfire at every turn.

Having bettered their education but still talking like matriculants, they are still at the centre of the political scenario in the country—not because they care for the poor and downtrodden, but because they care for their own bellies and comforts. They identified another bone to run with, and an apparently meaty one—the land issue! They did this not because they want land for the poor but because they thrive on political rhetoric and racial hatred. Having played a major role in having President Jacob Zuma removed, they feel muscled up, if you know what I mean, and are flexing their muscles for their next target—what they have dubbed "white monopoly capital", which by now is tired and listless.

What is most disturbing is that "King" Ramaphosa is courting them instead of planning their capture! If in his own way his capture is contained in a strategy of a new dawn we do not see, then he is moving the wrong pieces to capture the misleading youth. The president has the formula but is playing right into the misleading leaders' web of deceit and could be caught up like a fly in a spider's web, its wriggling only adding to its misery and agony until the spider arrives.

Land in South Africa, as in Namibia—both of which were once apartheid-led Southern African colonies—has become so sensitized that it is very likely to seal a deal between the electorate and the party that makes it palatable and not bitter. In the wrong hands, land, like nuclear power and armaments of mass destruction, is a time bomb that will, when it explodes, hit our economy—and hard!

With load shedding owing to the shortage of coal, as energy analyst Ted Blom advises, we can brace ourselves for the worst economic hardships ever. Even basic foods will be a luxury. Eating out will remain a luxury for the well-heeled only.

Going into the 8 May 2019 general elections, when South Africans will be voting for the provincial and national leadership, the voters must think before casting their votes. Putting the interests of the country above those of even their own parties must be their goal. It is a known fact that the likes of Malema are Mugabe admirers and Zuma haters. This alone should keep the voters away from a promissory note (land capture) that will be cashed in only by youthful misleaders who will tie the economy in knots. Nelson Mandela is on record as saying that even the ANC must be targeted if the people feel that it has not delivered on its promises. He said that the people should do to it what they did to the apartheid government. The interests of South Africa, as J. B. M. Hertzog would say, must be above those of the individual, though he was referring to Smutsism, which put imperial interests above those of South Africa.

South Africans must avoid diving into their graves with their eyes wide open and breathing by heeding the wrong noise. As the people of South Africa, we have to embrace one another, strive, and be driven by a desire to remake our country by wrestling South Africa out of the grip of apartheid residuals. This will save us the indignity of our progeny spitting on every black and white progenitor's grave in the country with disgust!

The conflicting ideas and ideals South Africans have about their country can be resolved only when the people speak with one voice to eradicate the old apartheid racism and the new ANC racism. The people must redefine what they mean by the concept which the old apartheid government and its leaders referred to as "die mense" (the people) but must now evolve a new definition of what is meant by "the people". This is one concept Nelson Mandela was passionate about when he refused to be released from prison with conditions when "you the people" were still not free. He was referring to the African people, because white South Africans have always been free to exercise their freedom rights, whereas those of blacks were limited to impoverished homelands, which constituted 13 per cent of South Africa. Mandela's cordial relations with Matanzima were affected by his acceptance of independence for the Transkei. Admirably, he changed his tune after 1994 and tried the best he could to reconcile South Africans through sport. His was an attempt to redefine the concept of "people of South Africa", and that is what this generation of South Africans must do to move away from apartheid and a new black-defined practice of apartheid that ostracizes one group of people from another. Moses saw the children of Israel, and so should leaders in our country see the children of South Africa as one multicoloured race with a common heritage of a land that should be protected from radical rhetoric.

Chapter 14

JULIUS MALEMA IS OUR NATIONAL GRAVE—A PERILOUS MISLEADER

Do not get me wrong; I do not hate Julius Malema. No! What I dislike about him is his abusing his followers' trust, knowing fully well that he does not care a fig for them. Land-grabbing Zimbabwe style is his plan for self-enrichment. There is a new race—a rush for the best lifestyles in South Africa—as a new social mobility trend. Obtaining the best cars, designer clothes, expensive colognes, and the best suburbs whilst still young and in record time is the goal. Many have become multimillionaires within years of going into office, becoming filthy rich; and the poor are literally filthy poor, with raw sewage being a state of normalcy in their locations. As some became rich, the national treasury became depleted and the petrol prices shot up to finance the greed and corruption of ANC leaders. That this nauseating greed is stealing from the poor to nurture the rich and politically connected is my gripe!

Chapter 15

OPENING DEBATE ON OUR ECONOMIC FUTURE

Afrikaner opposition to the views presented by policies in favour of land redistribution presents a healthy political debate that helps find answers for sustainable land sharing or land redistribution policies. Our democratic dispensation calls for such debates in an attempt to move from apartheid to building the nation and to help define an ideological perception influencing and determining a national politicoeconomic and even a sociopolitical ideological life view.

AfriForum's attempt to redress the past by bettering the lives of the previously disadvantaged farmers in a sustainable way is admirable and appreciated. It is such debates that can and will generate public discussion on evolutionary economic policy debates to influence and impact positive economic practice changes. Yes, there are times when healthy debates and views are tainted by supporting Afrikaners in cases where they are legally guilty of human abuse on racial grounds in our times. This I chalk up to what can be defined as a human weakness, which should be handled by our courts. I keep my argument on what is good in the raging land redistribution debates, as well as on revealing what is bad.

The debates tabled and discussed have the potential to influence and fuel policy, positively shaping our economic policies to attack poverty challenges for a successful economic practice to grow a sustainable, growing economy.

In such debates, Kriel's argument is mind-numbing yet mind-opening. In rural Maluti-a-Phofung Local Municipality (M-a-P), where an agricultural experiment at Diatalwa is ongoing, much can be gained from his take. Not much is reported on progress here, but Diatalwa lies within a rural triangular farming area whose three points are Qwaqwa, Kestel, and Harrismith, where there are now thriving tracts of agricultural land belonging to previously disadvantaged farmers (PDF). These tracts of land have lain barren since being allotted to the PDF but are now lush green, showing a scientific agricultural practice.

I inquired why we suddenly have a thriving agricultural practice here and was informed it is a result of the **VRYSTAAT KOöPERASIE BEPERK** (VKB) interventions in developing the PDF by working with them. The VKB, whose head office is in Reitz, about ninety kilometres from M-a-P headquarters in Qwaqwa, offers previously disadvantaged farmers seeds, as well as planting and aftercare expertise, and in return they share in the proceeds on a 50/50 basis.

I leave this debate open to assess whether the intervention is a fair business practice or exploitative. If evaluated as fair, why can it not be translated into policy rather than a reckless expropriation without compensation? I am certain that this will develop emerging farmers sustainably without disturbing the rate and quality of agricultural production.

Do we honestly require the expropriation of prime agricultural land with or without compensation or the sharing of land resources and experienced farming expertise and proceeds after settling overheads, as the VKB does to grow our tertiary industry? It took the Land Bank one hundred years to build our tertiary industry, and it took one hundred years for the VKB, as seen in an advertisement in this book. It can either take another one hundred years to build agriculture and grow the economy, or it can take a reckless implementation of reversing the 1913 Land Act with one stroke of a pen, which will destroy what took one hundred years to build. We see silos that are preserving food for the people. We need to consider this view very seriously, because too many trial-and-error approaches may do more harm than good to the economy. For twenty-five years, South Africa has been on a trial-and-error path that has destroyed almost every fabric of the apartheid economy in a displaced psychohistorical political anger. Even discipline at schools, as places where responsible and utilitarian citizens should be nurtured and produced to build this country, is in a chaotic state.

To the little informed and easily excitable in economics and politics, the statement "expropriation without compensation" sounds nice to the ear, especially in Parliament, and looks beautiful on paper, just as the Reconstruction and Development Programme did in 1994, but in practice, it is a gorgon that still haunts service delivery today! Implementing expropriation without compensation has a likelihood of us facing the challenges Zimbabwe is currently facing, following Mugabe's errors, which the Mnangangwa administration is now reversing. The beauty of Victoria Falls and the stoic naming of the Zimbabwe Ruins as Great Zimbabwe do not flow with developments in the country today. Ecotourism in Zimbabwe has suffered just as its agriculture has. We do not want this. Indeed, we do not need this in our country.

Learning from this history would be wise, because "expropriation without compensation", to those seeking it, is a livelihood in the salaries and perks of MPs rather than what they honestly believe is a solution. It keeps them employed but achieves nothing to turn the economy around. It is thus advisable to look before leaping and clapping hands for parliamentary discussions and infighting, some of which is a farce and may have disastrous results and very negative economic side effects.

Some of today's opposition's focus, especially the Economic Freedom Front, is on settling old political scores rather than bettering the lives of the previously disadvantaged and marginalized. This, to our economy in a new political dispensation, is perilous. The multiple political parties we have for a population of 56 million is an ominous indication that politics' battlegrounds have become an end to a means for employment opportunities—a slumber South Africa should wake up from. These employment opportunities are created by gullible people who are "employers" through votes. As people vote for today's leaders, they employ them to pay them without their providing any gains to the people who vote for them. Let us wake and realize the importance and implications of casting a vote.

Kriel's media debates with Prince Mashele are indeed an awakening and ignition of a lively political debate that assists the influencing and laying the ground for a practical and sustainable beneficial economic policy in our lifetime. Such debates require sober minds free of psychological, attitudinal, and racial stereotypes. We must remember that whether we like it or not, we have to live together, and to do so, we need tolerance in abundance. Dr Martin Luther King Jr.'s prophetic words in his I Have a Dream" speech ring in my mind as I rest my case.

You can shoot a man down, but his idea will live on and keep pricking the human conscience, to be taken forward by posterity. This reflects the true value of journalism and its media. Without it, Martin Luther King Jr. would not have been recorded for posterity to influence and change lives in a positive truth- and justice-seeking way. Though King died for such an idea, his memory has survived time and will continue doing so for years to come where civil issues arise.

The media have interestingly echoed views on the take above, thus showing the true value of shared platforms in solution-seeking deliberations.

RADICAL YOUTH THRIVES
ON RACIAL HATRED

Chapter 16

Spats between rich Afrikaner farmers and youths who have openly challenged them on their views are of interest. The rich farmers have openly told them that they have all the qualities radicalized youth do not like. They have land and are businessmen who support the free market system and are of white origins. So to speak, they resent the misleading youths' views on nationalization, not because these farmers are selfish landowners, but because they can see the full import such policies will have on the economy.

Afrikaner landowners have expressed their feelings, wondering whether radical youths have a special hatred and whether incitements of murder supporting revolutionary rants and chants and many other racial threats are aimed at all white people.

They note that there are many people who are of the opinion, perhaps even rightfully so, that radical youths do not deserve the attention they get. A journalist recently expressed the opinion that they are not worthy of the attention they are getting and that people should not treat such radicalism seriously. Truthfully, some landowners do believe that radical youths are not worthy of attention but believe they should not be ignored either. We live in a democracy and everyone deserves attention, though they do not necessarily deserve to be heeded. This is because there are those who erred and made noisemakers like them rise to political prominence after ignoring or dismissing them. Not every noisemaker should be dismissed, but they also should not all be heeded, as they will surely escalate ruinous state-led corruption.

The emerging radical youths are portrayed as prominent role players on the South African political stage. They are seen as having revived a doctrine which focuses on and thrives on racial division, hatred, revenge and nationalization. This new doctrine deserves to be regarded as national suicide by every South African citizen. Furthermore, its deep resentment of whites is actually just a smokescreen aimed at scapegoating. The critics of radicalism believe, and rightfully so, that no person can reserve hatred for just a few, because human feelings cannot really be put on shelves, and similarly, no fountain can bring forth both good and bitter water. No person can hate selectively. Those who are now trusting people like the radical youths will only discover this when, in South Africa's worst-case scenario, the likes of such misleading youths fulfil their political ambitions and become presidents and cabinet ministers.

Radical youths are inventing evil and promoting a unique brand of evil to exploit the vulnerable situation South Africa is in. This cannot be allowed to happen.

South Africa is in a fierce battle for the soul of the country. Some want to make it a better place not only for themselves but also for others, irrespective of race and social class. Those are the ones who acknowledge that South Africans are custodians of their country for the benefit of future generations. On the opposite side, there are those who act only in self-interest. Race, economic status, and social status do not determine which category a person falls into. They believe that radical youths have positioned themselves on a destructive side, and those with evil intentions or who are being misled follow such misguided bigots. What people like the radical youths wish to achieve remains a stark reminder of what South Africa will look like if the people fail to find a better way to face the challenges the nation is facing—and this exhibits a need for reconciliation under a firm government's democratic "dictatorship." A leader has to emerge, and that leader will definitely not be from the ANC, because it governs as a collective, and once its president treads on the interests of others, he or she will be recalled like former president Thabo Mbeki, the second executive leader of the new democratic dispensation. Firmness is now required.

There is so much that needs to be done to make South Africa a better place. We have to talk to each other; we need to get to know and understand each other. Attitudes need to change on many issues for the love of the land.

According to the Biblical book of Isaiah, "Those who light fires ... will lie down in torment." This truth stands. However, "The righteous will inherit the land" is in stark contrast to this. Most see radicalized youths as having chosen a destructive path South Africans will regret if these radical youths are heeded and given credence.

The arguments made above highlight this book's main theme— bringing people together into a constructive critical discussion. Such deliberations, including the next one, illuminate the immense depths of land deliberations so that the reader can be given perspective and direction and factual cause regarding this deliberation to consider the best possible options to address present-day challenges—especially land redistribution.

Debates on land issues have stoked the fires of such heated views in various media. They started as deliberations which reflect nation-building perceptions for an informed economic policy regarding land redistribution going forward, and moving towards nation building. Such debates and views raise various issues among various antagonists and protagonists on the topic of land expropriation without compensation. Debating parties accuse some parties of sowing seeds of racial division and hatred. They point out that every time those representing white minority interests talk about protecting minority interests, they highlight AfriForum's idiosyncrasies. AfriForum's involvement in communal development speaks volumes and argues that its interventions far outweigh what they are being accused of in its quest to better the farming industry and the peoples' lives. I attest to this!

AFRIFORUM'S DEVELOPMENT
INITIATIVES

Chapter 17

Current debates show the role played by AfriForum in postapartheid South Africa. One objectively notes immediately that the organization is doing Local Economic Development municipal service delivery in road construction for economic rehabilitation. AfriForum is thus guarding the interests of safe travel and tertiary economic activity facilitation by tending to roads for expensive agricultural machinery and transportation of agricultural produce. This is actually the task of a government department.

A road full of potholes is a hazard to life and frustrates the transportation of agricultural products and implements in the form of huge, sophisticated commercial agricultural farming machinery. AfriForum, according to Kriel (its CEO), addressed this municipal neglect of its core function to smooth and facilitate agricultural practices.

Economic history studies show that the development of white monopoly capital, the current term for capitalism, was accompanied by roads, air travel, and sea transportation, as well as telephonic technology in a networked system of communication to facilitate economic development. To build a thriving economy, all these resources are necessary, as is, of course, water, to generate electricity. Capital is therefore a sine qua non!

America, because of ideological conflicts with Ghana during the Cold War, spited Nkrumah's application for a loan to construct a hydroelectric dam. In the long term, the superpower played behind

the scenes to trigger the fall of Kwame Nkrumah when he was on a distant flight abroad. In his absence, they plotted and executed a successful coup d'état that toppled Nkrumah from power.

This is the potential that roads and transport have to cripple not only an economy but also to overthrow a government. This explains why AfriForum identified road rehabilitation as a requirement, or sine qua non, for agricultural economic development.

The fixed potholes benefit all road users, and instead of casting stones and aspersions, we need to applaud and really appreciate the role AfriForum played under a questionable administration in local government service delivery.

Some political parties' councillors use their own resources to facilitate service delivery because municipalities have been run down and are bankrupt, with very few, if any, passing the general auditor's audits. At Maluti-a-Phofung Local Municipality, municipal property was confiscated by the sheriff of the court for auctioning to address municipal employees' grievances regarding the non-payment of their funeral and medical covers to service providers although these were deducted from their salaries. This is not merely an allegation, as this author and other onlookers witnessed the incident. Today the municipality has collapsed.

It is only fair to single out this positive element of AfriForum's involvement in local economic activity development, to demonstrate the strengths of the positive effects political reconstructive "surgery" can have, because whether we admit it or not, our relationships require reconstruction just as much as postapartheid local government does. There can be no denial about this.

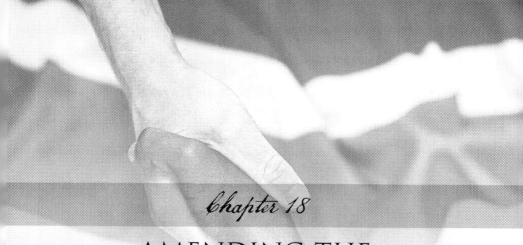

Chapter 18

AMENDING THE CONSTITUTION FOR LAND REDISTRIBUTION

There are views doing rounds that amending South Africa's Constitution to allow for land expropriation without compensation is not the solution to the country's problem. To be effective, land reform has to be overhauled through collaboration.

Such views are also aired by interested parties on this subject. Some are high-profile programme managers of government departments. The ANC in the Fifty-Fourth Elective Conference of December 2017 maintained that the issue of land has been a matter of great concern to our people whose land was taken from them. The organization felt the need to accelerate the programme of land reform, keeping in mind the 2019 general elections. The ANC's sudden land hunger and land anger made it pursue a radical transformative economic dispensation, obviously pushed by EFF rhetoric.

Many see this solution as a cure worse than the disease. They maintain that the Association for Rural Advancement (AFRA) has long held that land redistribution should address more basic pertinent questions, such as, Redistribution from whom, to whom, and for what purpose? Undoubtedly, a comprehensive overhaul of "land reform" is necessary if the real needs of the people, which include the necessity of equity, justice, and economic opportunity, are to be met with respect to the land redistribution question.

What is requisite here is a collaborative approach, and this relates to the ANC's own admission that mechanisms of implementing land reform must not compromise the economy and agricultural production. This, to responsible citizens with national interests at heart, requires that the obnoxious disease of corruption be guarded against in the interests of an equitable transformation that meaningfully engages all stakeholders.

Advisably, the land ownership audit should be speedily but carefully and efficiently done. All should be thoroughly engaged, and all stakeholders should be urged to uphold the values of the South African Constitution to collectively shape a new process of shared and equitable agricultural rebirth in which all are secure, protected, and prosperous. Past injustices and failures must be removed as impediments to our shared future. A land reform and agrarian transformation agenda that embraces change is vital for creating a solid foundation for our economic rebirth, to the advantage of our people and our environment.

Noteworthy is the fact that "our people" refers to all the people of South Africa and those residing within her who need plots and must eat to live, with land being the source of production to sustain and maintain human lives. Communal plots in the villages have to be created, and their locals must make them productive. Unoccupied land should be targeted for the settlement of people. Tampering with commercial land will be a national suicide the entire nation will regret as crime escalates to more alarming, distressing, and depressing proportions.

Chapter 19

THE POLITICS OF CONVENIENCE

At the centre of this storm is a restless and truculent youth whose patience is running out. Some have even developed public oratory confidence, and it is this that makes them vulnerable to rhetorical political persuasion. Adolf Hitler gave Germans a scapegoat for their misfortunes. Likewise, our youth want to make people to believe that their land misfortune is a result of white man's greed. However, not all are gullible, and there are those who see through rhetoric and denounce it contemptuously.

This brings to mind who, between the president of South Africa and fellow political party leaders, not only the Economic Freedom Front, should be wooing the other. Indeed, who should be wooing whom?

Much hype has been raised regarding the president pursuing a political relationship with the Economic Freedom Front as questionable bedfellows. This was triggered by the president's gravitation towards the party with an apparent aim of stopping it from making wrong noises with the potential to scare potential investors. At that stage he was preparing a team of selected people, including Trevor Manuel, to woo international investors in an ambitious drive to raise $100 billion over five years into the South African economy's mainstream. The Economic Freedom Front's land statements were upsetting this applecart.

Putting myself in the president's shoes, I would also approach small and big parties alike, to avoid scuppering sustainable economic development plans with job creation in mind—especially for first-time job seekers.

Those fresh from school have high expectations and qualifications from various schools of training. They have ambitions of a sustainable lifestyle that affords reasonable comforts in diverse social levels. Labourers also have hopes of a simple job for a reasonable income and a lifestyle affording them habitable housing and enough income to board a taxi. Ever noticed the long distances people walk because they do not have taxi or a bus fare?

That the president was wooing investors, whilst wooing all and sundry, was welcome news and would impact positively on local government revenue, where service delivery is offered, should the venture succeed. However, political stability is the rose that can make this succeed, and an expropriation-with-compensation land redistribution programme is a gorgon that has the potential to scare off rather than attract investors. The 51 per cent state ownership of investments policy in Zimbabwe has had negative results.

The labour unions' restlessness is another factor with a potential to scare off foreign investments. Work stoppages are not healthy for any economy and always have a negative effect on investor confidence.

That the Economic Freedom Front should be wooing the ANC but it is the other way round is not in the best interests of the country. This will not lay the groundwork for attracting the Presidential special envoy on foreign investments. The fact is that the expropriation-without-compensation policy is a scary reality in a country with a constitution such as ours.

A marriage of political convenience has since taken place, and collaboration between the African National Congress and Economic Freedom Front members of Parliament have had a successful coalition on the passing of the motion on land redistribution. However, care, diligence, and careful treading on the issue should be a watchword if we truly want to woo investors. With such a policy in place, not a single investor will be interested in doing business in South Africa. This should give Ramaphosa sleepless and traumatic nights as he wades through the economic meltdown, unemployment, and poverty. Reckless statements on land redistribution are a generator of self-induced economic ruin.

Investors want profits, and with this veiled threat of expropriation without compensation, one wonders how the economic malady will be addressed. It is the nation's hope to avoid a state of dependence on grants and develop a job-creating economic growth of 6 per cent. But the land issue makes this a mirage and a work in progress from one administration to the next over a period of another one hundred years to move from welfare state status. The past twenty-five years have miraculously created new black multimillionaires and billionaires in record time, and the next might see those gains dwindling—especially those that were ill gotten, because the gravy train has run dry. Sweat and one's own effort will be the sole requirements to make it, and this means proper planning along well-defined business plans reflecting sustainable profits over the years. There is nothing to steal from state coffers any more. The state coffers are depleted, and this is reflected in horrifying petrol hikes to fund the people's dependence on the economy.

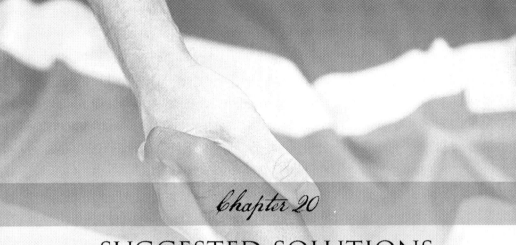

Chapter 20

SUGGESTED SOLUTIONS
TO OUR LAND ISSUES

Letters to the media address views on land issues sensitively and positively. Some papers, however, seem to fan the embers of the resolution adopted by Parliament that expropriation of land without compensation be carried out in a manner that does not affect the economy. Special emphasis is on food production, which has precipitated an inordinate volume of discussion and public discourse in the media.

This suggests that all in our constitutional democracy must be part of a positive solution seeking exercise, and not talk from the top manipulated by forces unknown to the public. If we fail to find lasting positive and sustainable solutions to postapartheid challenges, we shall together drown as fools.

Positivity is the only guiding light, offering a sense of reality and pragmatism for a paradigm shift. South Africans need to put their heads together and apply the knowledge gained from universal institutions of learning to good use. Scientific knowledge has made agricultural production what it is today, and the same scientific knowledge should be tapped to address today's forces and issues.

Indeed, what good is a song if it cannot inspire? Equally and conversely, what good is education if it fails to educate and inspire hope? Learned educationists need to come together like flowers, and all rival schools of thought must now contend, as Chairman Mao once taught. The many discords in our country must come into a uniform chorus to speak with one voice.

All political persuasions, despite their backgrounds and ideological foundations, must come to the realization that the rand is worth more to us than pride. In fact, our collective pride should be a national pride for the good of our common fatherland, South Africa, which we all so deeply and passionately love.

Let the affection we have for our common fatherland as today's custodians allow our patriotism to supersede all else.

Beyond Durban is a vast ocean—a mass of blue water. Beyond East London is an ocean—a mass of distant blue water. So is the case beyond Cape Town and Port Nolloth. All of us are terrestrial and have nowhere else to go, but we stand a reasonably good chance of being a gateway into Africa that former president De Klerk once referred to. And we should not lose sight of the fact that he crossed a Rubicon no nationalist apartheid leader dared to.

That, fellow countrymen, we must always remember, became the first step towards a liberated South Africa. As men and women of cultural values in our diversity and ethics, we must always keep that in mind as our radar and our compass in order to take South Africa forward towards a common destiny for a common legacy. To identify and to know our destination and for us to get there, we must know where we come from. This will allow us to grow into a responsible utilitarian adulthood. We are therefore called upon to put to test the function of history, and we must be mindful of the fact that we are children of the universe and children of South Africa; this is our common legacy and our destiny. If you destroy your land, you destroy yourself. We must be jealous and defensive of our democracy. We must develop our technocratic state towards capability and a compact competence.

Our common national anthem (which must forever stay with us) must relate us to our national symbols, our flora, our fauna, and our common heritage, and it must create a common new dawn for a common future. We must firmly clutch our hands as we hand in hand walk into the brotherhood and sisterhood of economic freedom with our eyes wide open.

For our progeny, let us bear common fruits. Let those who have ears listen and hear; and those with eyes to see debate the catastrophe of "expropriation of land without compensation" versus the "sharing of land" as the Freedom Charter advises. Sharing land means working it together as cooperatives do and proceeding to share the spoils with the Land Bank. This must be our guiding light for the next one hundred years of agricultural practice to successfully remove the current years of hunger and starvation. Failure to do so will doom us as naysayers, and our legacy will be destroyed. Should we fail, our forebears will not forgive us and our progeny will look back at us with disdain and disrespect. Together we should strive for the best, lead with honesty, and vote in matters of public interest with our hearts, not with our heads. Treading lightly and with care is advisable because negligence will hurt the very people whose lives we wish to better—the poorest of the poor!

Yes, land was forcibly expropriated from their native owners, but was it shipped abroad?

A resounding no! We are still walking on it but are threatening to destroy it by adopting evidently faulty policies born out of rhetoric. Let us sleep over this and rethink the views herein raised. Even though the idea has been adopted, let us tread lightly on its application. Yes, I know we know, and we are all-knowing, but let us tread with care.

Even the utterance "Now that I am a graduate and I know" should be buttressed by ongoing formal and informal research, because human nature is not static but is changed by factors beyond human manipulation man has no control over. Let us look at the means and find ways of harvesting water as it falls from the sky and reclaim it from the sea, because this is our next common challenge, which becomes our next eye-opening subject of interest. Let population growth inform our future plans and be not caught napping while managing by crisis. The development and heeding of scientific research will help us better our lives.

Academic research in master's and doctoral studies has highlighted the need to heed scientific research. Such research has the potential to increase the amount of usable water available to our country. Water right now is a commodity that is giving people sleepless nights, and we need academic research to address this with a view to purifying it using natural phenomena. Such studies will someday enable people collecting water from rivers to be able to use scientific materials to clean the water affected by industrial waste for human consumption.

What draws my attention to such research is that students are inspired to find scientific solutions to problems facing them and their nationals who lack clean drinking water in their native lands.

This inspires us to find scientific answers to problems besetting subsistence farmers in Maluti-a-Phofung and Thabo Mofutsanyana District, a land with vast potential. And I believe our answer lies in shifting the focus of Dipontsho Tsa Maluti from entertainment to showing scientific agricultural practices with a view to make people self-reliant and promote independence from state grants. Lethobane, a Wits student from Lesotho's scientific venture, whose focus is water purification, found her success to be a perfect example of addressing the small things that science has proved actually count. If we take care of pennies, as the English say, pounds automatically take care of themselves.

Once ready, recommendations should be forwarded to the executive mayors of local and district municipalities, the Small Enterprise Development Agency (SEDA), the Free State Development Corporation (FDC), the VKB, the Department of Trade and Industry (Dti), the Land Bank, the Development Bank of Southern Africa, and possible sponsors (multinational corporations). Coordination by the local municipality's Local Economic Development Department would make such an endeavour a heartening, eye-opening success.

Of course we love entertainment at Maluti-a-Phofung, and such a revisited venture would include entertaining events, just as the Easter show does annually. Cultural entertainment to espouse our culture in music and dance, such as *ditolobonya*, would incentivise the youth in their organizations led by communal mothers with a performance fee. Traditional music is gaining momentum in Qwaqwa, and the Fauriesburg event would be emulated and find expression in this envisaged change in Dipontsho. The Mangaung Cultural Festival, the Bloem Show, the Bethlehem Air Show, and Mieliebielie in Reitz are events that will develop locals.

The main aspects of some of these events or shows would display subsistence and commercial farmers' product specimens in the form of live animals: beef and dairy cattle of at least three types, bulls for breeding, and so forth. It would also display produce.

Soil tilling would also be demonstrated in the form best suited for the staple foods of the area, and organic farming would be encouraged. This would ensure food security affordably to a predominantly unemployed community.

In this way, those of us whose enemy sought to throw them under a bus in motion but who somehow made it on board to be passengers, navigate them towards a common desired destination—the rise of a real new dawn.

Even passengers in a bus talk freely and air their views. They do not necessarily become flies on the wall like researchers in participative research while observing a subject without disturbing it.

Passengers air their views in a constructive, collaborative, democratic way so that an ideal situation that benefits all can be realized. Implementation of the finest ideas is ensured in a collaborative fashion, as their suppression would not be beneficial.

If not, it would be a boring journey, depriving us of opportunities to see potholes and figure out ways of avoiding them. The potholes and road signs to heed twists and turns and to be careful of what other drivers may not see should be identified with care. Care and diligence will take us all to safety to reach our destination of becoming the gateway into Africa and becoming the economic powerhouse of Africa.

Some of the Zimbabwean commercial farmers whose farms were expropriated without compensation found their way to Nigeria and were offered land which has not been expropriated at the time of writing, and they are building a thriving tertiary industry. Some were swallowed up in what were parts of the USSR after its collapse. Do we in South Africa want this? I am sure even the most extreme radicals will give a resounding "No!" and agree that we cannot afford to lose our farming community. It would be a very expensive task to try to woo them back on their own terms that, no doubt, will turn the situation around to 87 per cent against 13 per cent when poverty makes those in power sign contracts that will force the wishes of the farmers on the government, allowing them to truly capture the state legally. There would be no other choice, because vultures would be feeding on corpses. Make no mistake about the fact that our farmers still have a choice that can still make them masters of our land. This I can clearly see in my mind's eye, and it is better avoided with a stoic love for our land and its people by sharing land and not expropriating it.

Chapter 21

COMMERCIAL FARMING SENSITIVITIES

What drives a commercial farmer to wake up at odd hours is the knowledge of the extent of his investment in his tilled, cultivated, and planted crop. He will want to see the investment yielding profits. This alone gives him sleepless nights.

The likelihood is that, under an emerging farmer's employ in a farm that once was his but that he is now manager of, he will not be as assertive as he was when self-employed in the farm. This will result in a fall in production. This fall will escalate, and the new, emerging owner will, of course, pick it up from the original bank statements given, as a buyer or allotted owner. You will notice the graphical representations on income and expenditure prior to and after purchase.

During the first three years, the figures will show consistencies, but the likelihood of a sudden drop is also possible. Yields will be suddenly displeasing, and with your investment threatened and the inability to service your Land Bank loan, as a new owner, you will have to reconsider your options.

Policy may then swing towards the reversal of expropriation policies, with former owners recalled as President Mnangangwa is doing in present-day Zimbabwe, and the investment will go down the drain. Some will be successful, but most surely will not be, because it takes years to acquire scientific agricultural farming expertise and mastery to optimize production and maximize profits.

We should not fool ourselves that now that we are free we can be successful in farming.

It is a tall order. The Esidimeni incident, in which the infirm died in the hands of NGOs unqualified in home-based care, must warn us that scientific expertise in human, plant, and four-legged animal life requires relevant expertise and experience; otherwise, production will die and the end result will be poor production, famine, disease, and death.

The Esidimeni incident has cost the state a jaw-dropping whopping R1.2 million for each of the 144 deaths caused by the unlawful discharging of mentally ill patients into ignorant, untrained NGOs, as retired judge advocate Dikgang Moseneke ruled. I leave this analogy to your trusted, able analysis regarding what ignorance in agricultural practice would cost the South African economy if the land issue were handled in a nonprogressive manner.

This eye-opening negative is realistically accentuated here to create a possible analogy of a positive assessment of human nature and production, to avoid disappointment and despondence, which have been reigning supreme since 1994. This despondence is reflected on the faces of many people today, both black and white.

South African democratic practice requires a reduction in number of our multiple political parties. The American political administration system is working like a charm—indeed a well-oiled democratic machine. In it we see clearly how Franklin Delano Roosevelt fought a diplomatic warfare when socialism thrived during the postwar period, coming up with a New Deal that saved America and the West from an ideological collapse that was considering socializing its economy.

The Roosevelt New Deal resonates perfectly well with the new South African dawn under Ramaphosa, and political sobriety will carry us through. We need to master the ability to be codified, beat the enemies of positive diversity, and swim across the ocean of diversity, together ducking the waves threatening our freedoms.

Yes, together we can! Sharks will not tear us to pieces and swallow us if we let dolphins guide us ashore. Yes, dolphins will happily dive deep around us in the ocean of despair, guiding us ashore towards hope and prosperity, keeping sharks at bay. Our sharks—yes, you have noted them—are prophets of doom trumpeting expropriation without compensation. We can instead guide them towards a future of togetherness, devoid of racial hatred.

Chapter 22

SPITE THE EFF BY DOING THE RIGHT THING

Many people believe that the EFF represents an obvious and urgent danger to democracy. Its leadership is similar to that of Yahya Jammeh, who is presently exiled in Equatorial Guinea after refusing to vacate office as president of the Gambia until ejected by military force. He robbed his country blind, leaving empty coffers when he, like a rat, scurried into exile.

The immature radical leadership excites concern as it participates in the elections, and it could force South Africa to declare a state of emergency. To avoid this, the ruling party has to lead the masses away from radical rhetoric by fighting corruption, genuinely stamping it out along with those associated with it. The National Prosecuting Authority (NPA) must be empowered to bring culprits to book. This is the only way of ensuring the restoration of the government's credibility of a new dawn. Doing the right thing now will turn heads away from the prophets of doom.

Radical youth are in the habit of assaulting journalists, and apparently they get away with it. Our justice system is too weak to arrest thugs like these and prosecute them. Democracy means a free press.

Chapter 23

DISCORD IN THE ANC

Discord in the African National Congress over the recall of Thabo Mbeki resulted in a Terror Lekota–run emotions-led Congress of the People, which failed to cope and lost political direction when Mbhazima Shilowa ran it down. He then disappeared into political silence as if his sole aim was to destabilise the organization. Other splits from the African National Congress seem to be a result of a leadership at war with itself going into the campaigning gear of cleaning locations undoubtedly being a canvassing strategy. Also, the call to address the concerns of the elderly in pension pay points is also a campaigning strategy, after which they shall be forgotten for the next five years. The effects of these internal discords have significantly weakened the ANC going into the 2019 general elections and beyond.

When former President Zuma dumped Julius Malema and, against Motlanthe's better judgement, expelled him from the ANC to become a persona non grata, this injured a rattlesnake, which turned the tide against the movement. This made Zuma Malema's major focus, and his Parliament assignment was to mark Zuma and make life unpleasant for him, and he saw to that! Does this make him a good prospect for South Africa? That I leave to your analysis.

However, proper governance fell off the rails, and corruption reigned supreme, calling for a strengthened National Prosecuting Authority (NPA) and the Hawks, which were seen as unable to arrest the mighty. Addressing this, Ramaphosa appointed Shamila Batohi to direct the NPA.

Noteworthy is the view that Shamila Batohi's appointment by President Cyril Ramaphosa gave many people the hope that corruption would be tackled head-on.

Batohi was congratulated by leaders and journalists who stated that she would require government support to rebuild the NPA and that she was certain to face a backlash in her attempts to rebuild the NPA into a credible crime- and corruption-fighting organization. She would also need the necessary legislative armoury to equip her in withstanding the backlash. Perhaps Thuli Madonsela should be considered to serve in some capacity in the NPA.

The role of civil society organizations is to act as guardians of a fearless prosecution service. The Council for the Advancement of South African Constitution, Corruption Watch, and Freedom Under Law consulted the Constitutional Court to halt Zuma's destruction of the NPA. The new director must have government support to give credence to its wish of resuscitating the power of the NPA in fighting corruption, which is undoubtedly eating the economy away. Proper, responsible governance must now be sought, at all costs.

My view is that the NPA must be beyond reproach and be seen to give every government official accused of misdemeanours his or her day in court as every citizen's democratic right. Every corruption charge must be heard in court to open prison doors to all found guilty beyond any shadow of reasonable doubt! The Zondo Commission is hearing disturbing corruption incidents, and all those that have tangible proof sustained by evidence must serve time.

This will strengthen our new democratic dispensation and ensure that citizens' rights are not trampled upon and that statutes are fairly interpreted. Shamila Batohi will surely face a backlash as she goes about cleansing and rebuilding the NPA. Our government institutions must be strengthened to avoid costly commissions of inquiry by arresting culprits and taking them to court. This is suggestive of a strongly government-supported National Prosecuting Authority under Batohi.

It is my hope that the government will do the right things in a proper way to keep our hopes up so we can see the new dawn unfolding. This will then steer the people away from political parties conceived out of hatred and nurtured by uncompromising rhetoric of populist racial hatred, concealing those who will be seen as having acquired ill-gotten wealth. A political rhetoric of fighting for the economic freedom of the poor is a destructive political distraction that allows corrupt politicians to gain from land expropriation without compensation. If we want to attract foreign investors, as Chief Gatsha Buthelezi maintains, let us place ourselves in the shoes of probable investors and consider investing in an economy that expropriates property without compensation. Indeed, should we proceed to invest under such an economic policy, then we shall need our heads examined.

Thabo Mbeki holds views that seek to correct the ANC's rot in governance. In international media, local as well, he is hobnobbing with people who seek to improve and discourage the wide ranging corruption in the ANC. His political aura stands out and he is known to be a strong protagonist of the Jacob Zuma years' administration. He sees the years of his administration as the years that entrenched corrupt governance leading to the capturing of the state and its administration to do the will of a Gupta family that served his interests. That a family took important decisions for government is seen as corruption beyond measure and this Zuma agreed with and this rocked the markets with the currency fluctuating. Joining the ANC in 1994 was seen by many as merely to have a hand at looting the economy and not so much that they sought to promote democracy.

Such views by Thabo Mbeki give people hope that something shall and can be done to change post-apartheid South Africa for the better. However, many are disgruntled and no longer participate in the new democracy as evidently demonstrated in the 2019 general elections. Steering towards good governance to inspire hope and instil a sense of national pride is a disappearing notion. The pride that we are one people and one nation is disturbingly at the lowest ebb and can only be rescusitated by men of conscience. We will together uproot corruption only when we agree as a nation and as a people with no racial overtones. This is our only hope!

Africa and South Africa in particular is a victim of money that flows illicitly from government coffers into personal pockets. These illicit flows are affecting African economic growth and promoting corruption. Since 1994, a lot of these illicit flows have drained national treasuries. In South Africa, they went into the Reconstruction and Development Programme projects, such as housing and the removal of toilet bucket systems. Some of these houses were not built, and their money was not refunded to government either.

The mirror never lies. When you look at yourself in it, it will be your reflection as you are, meaning we cannot lie to ourselves, because those who do so know how they have bled African national treasuries, with municipal coffers being their piggybanks. If their offshore accounts can be analysed, the truth can be excavated and brought to light.

Thabo Mbeki, as former president of the ANC and of government, mirrors the ANC and his candid criticism of government, credibly finding fault with the ANC is an inspiration of hope. The fact that a high-profile member of the ANC is vocal about the necessity for change inside the ANC is important and sustains our belief and hope that this change will happen. Importantly, it will happen as a process and not as an event, and this will occur in our lifetime, because we dare not hand this bad cheque over to our progeny. We must set the ball rolling for the next generation to keep the process and momentum going. This is the reality of the situation.

Enemies of progressive change inside the ANC are, like Caesar's enemies in the tragedy of *Julius Caesar*, already falling on their swords even before the ANC purges them to send them scurrying away as corrupt opportunistic self-enriching leaders.

The African National Congress has the ability to denounce corruption for clean governance. What we need to do to make this happen is to identify those who walked out of the ANC to form new political formations out of love for the ANC, and win them back during this ANC cleansing process. We must purify them and use their experiences. Some policies adopted have not entrenched democracy and nonracialism but have perpetrated racialism under a new guise of exclusive economic empowerment of those once marginalized. By and large it was an unavoidable policy, but the manner in which it was implemented was not pleasing and now needs to be reversed to include all South African youth. This, we need to realize, is not even an economic empowerment but merely a financial facilitation, because economic reconstruction and empowerment must be done in a sustainable way. Black companies that are "empowered" always wait for municipal financial years, when money from the national treasury is released into municipalities. This is usually followed by municipal budget meetings, and it is here that the spoils are shared. Towards the end of a financial year, the directors of these companies are in state of financial barrenness and wait for the next municipal financial year, and so it goes.

I remember seeing Tokyo Segwale sleeping in a shack overnight in a slum shanty township reeking with sweat and urine, and on leaving the next morning taking out a bulky wallet and paying for his night's sojourn. Surely that payment was enough for only one round of grocery shopping, and soon thereafter the family got back to its lifestyle of poverty, hunger, and starvation. This reflects financial facilitation and not economic empowerment. Economic empowerment refers to job-creation empowering policies, which allow families to buy groceries for themselves, rather than insulting and degrading them after a one-night sojourn.

This, in my view, was a kick in the teeth of the poor. He should not have bothered!

Stellenbosch University's Bureau of Economic Research has identified political reasons that the lack of investor confidence in our economy stood at 70 per cent in 2015, with no agreement from various institutions on how to correct the situation. The major reason for this is political incoherence, especially in matters pertaining to policy implementation, and this paralyzed the economy. With expropriation without compensation as a new political coherence (because whether we like it or not, land is the source and very stage of economic activity), the ways in which this will exacerbate the problem wait to be seen. It seems doubtful that an investor can risk his capital under such policy implementations.

Perhaps those who bled the economy must bleed the money back and reinvest it in ventures that will benefit employment with salaries people can live on. Our leaders, like Saki Macozoma, should agree with us on this one.

Finally, it is heartening to see that VKB is no longer just cooperative. Much has been said about it in agricultural development in our triangular Maluti-aPhofung Local Municipality to this point. The amazing VKB has grown beyond the status of being just a cooperative but now owns shares in a variety of companies, such as Free State Oil, Nu-Pro, and Grain Field Chickens, to mention but three of them, which now form part of the VKB Group.

VKB's outlets offer a diverse range of products to service the requirements of commercial and emerging farmers and the public. They help farmers producing grain to get the best prices. VKB handles, stores, dispatches, and markets grain, and this "remains one of the critical strengths of the value-added services VKB renders to grain producers and harvesters. The VKB Group has a seat on Safex to help grain producers to get the best prices." This the VKB does for the love of the land!

VKB manages the New Holland and Case dealerships in their various regions and has mechanization divisions in Reitz, Petrus Steyn, Warden, Vrede, and Frankfort and has an assortment of spare parts, more than 5,000, available in their sales outlets.

"VKB Insurance Brokers is one of the largest brokers in the VKB area. VKB offers the producer, as well as the public, suitable, cost-effective insurance products such as Asset insurance (commercial, agricultural and personal), Multi-risk for crops and hail insurance."

Its other strategic core function is to offer finance and provide credit as its primary part in the VKB Group. This function entails providing various finance products, such as seasonal production finance and monthly accounts. It is a service that makes a significant contribution to enable South African commercial and emerging farmers to be profitable and productive in the food chain. For this purpose, the VKB Group is presently exceeding R1.5 billion to finance agricultural producers.

"The VKB has prioritised the development of emerging farmers. It is focusing on financial support, mentorship and project management for the development of agriculture. The Developing Agriculture Division in its long-term development strategy therefore strives to attain the goals of Vision 2020 – Leadership in the Development Sustainable Commercial Farmers."

The company is making a contribution of 3 per cent of its net profit after tax to the development of emerging farmers, making "the company a Level 1 contributor to BEE in terms of enterprise development criteria. The VKB Group is interacting with 40 emerging farmers with a joint arable area of 3000ha in extent, which extends across the company's service area."

The VKB Group is also engaged in supporting communal educational projects, as well as training programmes in areas with scant resources, and skills development of the unemployed with a view to uplift the historically disadvantaged. It also provides a training programme for such communities as a key factor in the success of this programme.

"VKB is registered with the National Credit Regulator (NCR), as a well as the Financial Services Board (FSB)" (*EFS Issue* 4, February 2016).

Needless to say, the sudden change in local land owned by emerging farmers is evidence of this VKB involvement success story. Lamola who is an ANC national executive member has reaffirmed mixed ownership of the land (not nationalisation), that the land must be owned through the state for its use or lease to those who want to use it, and communal ownership and private ownership (individuals and juristic persons).

The said forms of ownership are in line with the mixed economy to create or facilitate the growth of the working class to a rural middle class with a view to grow a black middle class, forms of tenure must link the working class to the mainstream economy. Options considered are aimed at guaranteeing the security of tenure under communal land as recommended by a high-level panel. Once achieved, the banks should then be enabled to grant credit when the security of tenure is guaranteed on communal land. This will then unlock the economic potential of land held under communal systems as Lamola views it.

Lamola closed by saying that the ANC's development policies are in the interests of inclusive growth. Expropriation without compensation is aimed at defined areas. According to him this approach is central to the Freedom Charter, Ready to Govern, the Reconstruction and Development Programme, etc. Land redistribution requires that criteria and principles be established to achieve the objectives—the redress of past injustices, and economic development. In the process, some of the groups that could be prioritized are the rural and urban poor, women, farm dwellers, rural and urban entrepreneurs, and new commercial farmers.

If government, true to Lamola's word (which we shall hold it to) put into place such systems, the expertise and caring change of policy by big corporations in recent years should help government plan its land policy of expropriation without compensation, as passed by Parliament. "Diligence" has to be the watchword, and this must not be a partisan government relationship that favours a few on racial or political affiliation grounds, so that big corporations playing a role can also be beneficiaries and gain from their participation in tertiary economic development. Advisably, productive land must be left in the hands of those who know how to scientifically develop it. Land that is underutilized should be targeted for emerging farmers with government support.

In essence, government must appreciate that by playing a role, an enterprise is safeguarding its own interests as well. It must be a give-and-take type of sharing that benefits all participants. Together they must walk the tightrope, requiring careful treading and the involvement of enterprises and cooperatives, such as the VKB, and they must be trusted with providing experienced guidance to emerging farmers in a practical, hands-on way, safeguarding food security.

Such corporations should be trusted with Provincial Government Rural Development funds to help implement development initiatives in practically sustaining and directing the attainment of goals such as Vision 2020. Of course audited statements passing the auditor general's scrutiny shall be made to account for how such funds have been used for invested in farming skills development, lifting emerging farmers towards new heights. Such ideals, sounding lofty as they do, need to be acted upon to bring about a new lease on life aimed at economic recovery and the capacitation of previously disadvantaged individuals.

We should see such newly defined government policies and VKB's Vision 2020 as Stalinist-style structured five-year plans aimed at turning the economy around after our revolution, with a view to prioritize various areas of interest, such as quantity and quality of agricultural produce to meet the demands of various markets. This is how we envisioned Maite Nkoana-Mashabane's Agenda 2063.

The food chain retailer Woolworths is known to be quite choosy, while other supermarkets in Qwaqwa and Harrismith in Maluti-a-Phofung service the needs of not-so-choosy clientele. It is such requirements the Provincial Government Department of Rural Development should consider so that it can put its money where the people's mouths are. This, if practised, will make general and local elections a walk in the park.

Because the problem of the prevalence of poverty is national, not only provincial, ours can be regarded as a pilot project and emulated if experimentation is fruitful. Lamola's elucidation of ANC policy under consideration needs our ears on the ground to follow how this goes, because history has taught us to be sceptical of ANC government-led promises which are not met by implementation and end up resulting in letting sleeping dogs lie until the next round of five years. Each time we go into elections, many amazing mind-blowing promises are made, but after elections, when we open the promises package, we find it empty. We shall keep these promises on the radar and hope Lamola will keep us updated about developments. We unfortunately have heard nothing of Agenda 2063 since playing a role in its launch.

Meanwhile, we need to also appreciate the small efforts at development made by the Free State Rural Development Department and its MEC. The Provincial "Hlasela Tlala Ka Diratswana" (Attack Poverty with Communal Gardens) Project is a small-scale attempt at rural development. "Diratswana" means "home and communal plots". The department held such awards at Glenn College in Bloemfonte in January 2016 to encourage homegrown food security. The department often offers these awards to encourage organic agricultural practice to fight poverty (hlasela tlala) in Sesotho. Prizes in these awards range from R2,000 to R30,000 and winners are given trophies and certificates. (*EFS Issue* 4, February 2016).

This is a small-scale project and is subsistent in nature but needs encouragement. Produce from small-scale subsistence farming should be featured in the Dipontsho Tsa Maluti so people can take to this practice and also own Dipontsho Tsa Maluti to display big pumpkins, etc. Our economic rural condition should be showcased to impact positively in our lives in the long run. Poultry and animal husbandry practices with the VKB tent displaying animal production methods, medicines, and feeds should be showcased. These should be manned with personnel who can explain the usage of the featured products. People in the villages have quite big plots which they need to be encouraged to utilize for food security strategies. Communal plots have been neglected, and their communities must be helped with tractor services by the Department of Agriculture to plough, and locals must till and be given seeds to plant. Water harvesting in big JoJo tanks must also be showcased, and borehole companies must showcase their businesses.

The VKB and its group should also play a leading role so that its produce can be seen. Offering special prices for the event would assist in poverty alleviation, and the Dipontsho should be held for a week on days coinciding with old-age pension collection and children's grants. Traders will also buy in bulk to sell at pay points. Dipontsho can also be used by the Free State University's Faculty of Agriculture student marketing desk to encourage learner applications. Local schools should also be encouraged to introduce agriculture as a subject in their curricula. With the big yards they have, plots for agricultural practicals can be carried out, with vegetables being grown and sold to raise funds. As it is, rural school curricula in South Africa do not answer to the needs of the rural conditions of their municipalities and ecotourism. How do you justify a rural school without agriculture and tourism as subjects?

VKB holds an agricultural corporative event of its own, Bieliemielie, which I have had the honour of attending. It is a lesson to behold the place where the agriculture you see in the pages of Farmer's Weekly live!

Emerging farmers are well advised to attend this event, appreciating that commercial farming is a process that develops over many years. Advice is herein given to keep information from the media, as one may never know when it will come in handy. I cut and kept the clips on VKB from a well organized and managed freely circulated communal paper, *EFS Issue*, and kept them in one of my *Farmer's Weekly* magazines. From these clippings I gleaned important information on emerging farmers and the VKB's role.

LAND EXPROPRIATION WITHOUT COMPENSATION

Under pressure from the EFF, the ANC in its fifty-fourth Congress passed a resolution to radicalize land reform and rural development in South Africa. This triggered concerns in the print and electronic media. People in public arenas and transport expressed their views laudably. One said that he is unable to service his own backyard plot productively and wondered how government expects him to service a farm. However, the movement cautioned that it will ensure that mechanisms of implementation do not hurt food security by damaging production or cause harm to other sectors of the economy. According to the research of a PhD candidate studying constitutional property law, Dube, the ANC stated that it will target vacant, unused, and underutilized land for redistribution in an orderly manner, and that action will be taken against unlawful land grabs. There is no doubt this move is intended to prevent the negative detrimental effects such land grabs had on Zimbabwean food production and the economy at large. The ANC document stated that clear targets and time frames must guide the process along sound legal and economic principles. All this should be seen to happen within objectives that promote job creation and investment. Dube states that the government remains obliged to abide by the constitutional imperative for an orderly but robust land reform within the rule of law. This, the candidate indicates, is the ANC's ultimate acid test.

The document further states that reform measures like land tax support for emerging black farmers should be sensitized through training and related support measures. Spectators on the sides warn that implementation will be challenging with regard to addressing past injustices whilst keeping the economy going strong. Soon after this, the EFF came out with a strong campaign for an ultra-radical call for all land to be in the government's hands as custodian. This, in simple terms, refers to complete nationalization of land, but this is not ANC policy, as is made clear in the 1955 Freedom Charter, which indicates that land belongs to those who work it. A year later, the Constitution Review Committee recommended an amendment of section 25 of the Constitution to legitimize the land reform process.

Such expropriation without compensation is based on the discussed

Expropriation Bill of 2015. The updated bill will clarify instances in which property may be expropriated without compensation. Clause 12(3) provides for the expropriation of land occupied by labour tenants, land held solely for speculative purposes, abandoned land, and areas where direct state investment in the land is more than market value. The Property Valuation Act 17 of 2014, which determines the calculation of compensation for expropriation by the state, will also have to be amended to be aligned with the amended property clause.

With Parliament having approved the land expropriation bill, the government's main challenge becomes implementation, which will, either way, affect job creation, increase unemployment, and escalate crime whilst also affecting the currency and markets. This will not curb poverty and will make the plight of the poor and marginalized worse. The question will remain as to who will invest in such a climate of land policy. Following is some commentary on this policy and the ANC's tabled policy on the matter. The public appreciates the VKB's interventions in its VISION 2020 as an interventionist measure and assistance to immerging farmers. It must be noted that economic development is facilitated by good roads and related means of communication. Economic history shows that the South African infrastructure was developed to facilitate economic development. The construction of roads was part of economic development, implying that the current state of our roads should be cause for concern. Those constructed recently took a long while to complete, which has brought into question their planning and project management. Such concerns have to come up, because road transport is now the main means of transportation rather than the South African railway services. This heavy reliance on roads also hampers economic growth, because heavy trucks result in tar damage and accidents happen that affect road usage.

Commendable in this regard is AfriForum's intervention in road repairs to facilitate the transportation of heavy agricultural machinery. Without such interventions, the economy slows down and the servicing of emerging farmers becomes a challenge. These should be learning curves for policy-implementing government officials. The Mozambique economy slowed down and depreciated when FRELIMO took over, and today South African cruise tourists report disturbing levels of poverty in that country. This was the result of an emotional implementation of socialist policies that collapsed the state's economy under Machel. South African policy implementers should take a leaf from such failed policies and direct reconciliation towards calmer waters after our tumultuous past, learning from errors of past leaders in our front-line states. Botswana is enjoying political and, therefore, economic stability though its diamond industry and is being criticized for taking capital out of the country. Rwanda remains a shining example to be copied, even by South Africa. Her cleanliness puts her on the lips of international investors, and that is a good story to tell.

The commentary on land reform below should take cognisance of such developments in the southern tip of Africa, and Ronald Lamola and his team in the ANC National Executive Committee should take note, keeping in mind that positive criticism builds and nurtures growth. We are mindful of the fact that what is being corrected is the Land Bank's development "of an agricultural industry in which white commercial farmers were the sole recipients of exceptionally high levels of state support, both in terms of skills development and financial aid during difficult times such as drought" (Makhuras, 2013), with suppressed emotions.

Following is a reflection over Ronald Lamola's well-documented views on land redistribution. He is a known and well-met ANC cadre serving in the ANC National Executive Committee and sits on its economic transformation subcommittee. His take on land issues is as follows:

The ANC's development policies are in the interest of inclusive growth. Expropriation without compensation is aimed at defined areas. This approach is central to the Freedom Charter, Ready to Govern, the Reconstruction and Development Programme, etc. ... Land redistribution requires that criteria and principles be established, to achieve the objectives – the redress of the past injustices and economic development. In the process, some of the groups that could be prioritised could be rural and urban poor, women, farm dwellers, rural and urban entrepreneurs, and new commercial farmers.

The operative words here are "could be", not "shall be", thus indicating that further clarification on the matter is needed.

REFLECTIONS ON LAMOLA'S VIEWS

In Maluti-a-Phofung Local Municipality, there has been a sudden change in productivity in the lands owned by emerging farmers, and this pleasing change is credited to the **VRYSTAAT KOöPERASIE BEPERK** (VKB), which has grown into the VKB Group, whose headquarters are in Reitz, ninety kilometres from Phuthaditjhaba.

Lamola, who sits at the ANC's NEC economic transformation desk, has enlightening views that inspire hope. The newly reviewed ANC NEC policy is in good light, but the determination of whether or not it is in good faith is another matter altogether. The VKB's Vision 2020 is a programme designed to develop emerging farmers, and it is pleasing, heartening, and promising to hear what Lamola has presented in the light of what the VKB has already initiated.

However, given the ANC's promises in the past in our municipality, we are sceptical and despondent because problems inside the ANC are systemic, and this makes us cautious. Each time we go into an elections drive, the ANC, like dolphins circling a disoriented person at sea to direct him or her towards shore, directs us towards the ballot box. On getting the mandate, they leave us to our fate and devices, and emerge five years later.

This has developed into a rhythmic pattern, and we have now developed thick skins and learnt how to hustle to put bread on the table. If this plan can prove not to be one of the many empty promises made in the past, light at the end of the tunnel seems visible, and the ears of the investors are on the ground, intently listening. And so are ours, because the prevalence of poverty in our municipality has escalated into high levels of crime due to unemployment, making us feel ambivalent about the ANC's promises. We are prepared to listen but keep the ANC on the radar without blinking, because each time we go into an elections drive, many amazing mind-blowing promises are made, but soon after the elections we find the promises package empty!

I was part of a delegation invited for participation in shaping Agenda 2063 in Minister Nkoana-Mashabane's foreign office. Her reception address gave us hope as we tirelessly worked for three days and nights, booked in the luxurious Holiday Inn as her guests. But nothing came out of that, and we were not updated about progress made. Presently, the

VKB is piloting its Vision 2020 Programme, and it is already beginning to bear fruits.

The ANC's promise of reviewing its land policy as explained by Lamola is tempting, but we always pray not to be led into temptation—don't we? Lamola notes that the ANC's development policies are in the interest of inclusive growth, and that expropriation without compensation is aimed at certain defined areas. This approach is central to the Freedom Charter, Ready to Govern, the Reconstruction and Development Programme, and so on.

On the whole, this review is tempting and appetite whetting. We want to believe Lamola. But what choice do we have? The prevalence of crime triggers ambivalence towards ANC's promises, yet crime has escalated into unemployment. Maybe we should keep these promises on the radar and, if on mere suspicion we sense deception and inconsistency, we should disappear into other political parties to force the ANC into coalition in 2019, ensuring that it does not govern alone!

When people have on several occasions been duped and beaten, they become despondently shy. Usually just once beaten we become twice shy. We have been patient with the ANC—very patient, in fact! Well, it is now gone—depleted! A lot has to be done to win back the eoples' trust, and we are closely watching the ANC wooing us back into the fold. We want to believe, but then ambivalence persists because their campaigns are based on feeding them in rallies to "smash and grab that X" and then leaving them to their devices with SASSA grants and resurfacing five years later. This has become an obnoxious vicious circle that is extremely unpleasant and disgusting! I am not saying this lightly but with the deepest of feelings!

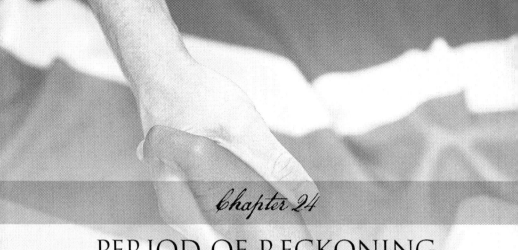

Chapter 24

PERIOD OF RECKONING AND RECONCILIATION FOR SOUTH AFRICANS

In the politics of Africa, one figure comparable to the current truculent youth is one Yahya Jammeh of the Gambia. This is how the likes of Mugabe developed to become political lunatics, and we need to nip the growing of such misleaders in the bud. Just as in apartheid South Africa under the oppressive heat of H. F. Verwoerd's interpretation and refinement of the apartheid policy, when his policies became controversial, Jammeh severed ties with the Commonwealth.

His full name, titles included, is former president Sheikh Professor Alhaji Abdul-Azziz Jemus Junkung Jammeh. It is a sentence of a name, and his political career and administration reflect the lunacy and insanity of that name, which is essentially an adolescent gesture that was poorly thought out. Some African thinkers, long sceptical about the British role and attitude of self-righteousness in the body, welcomed the news with alacrity and saluted the decision. They were soon to be extremely disappointed.

Jammeh described himself as a servant of the people in his address to his supporters in Banjul. Yet he was one of Africa's most ruthless and feared dictators. One wonders if a leader should be feared or respected by the people, and also what the cause of that fear could be. Could it be that the feared person regards himself as infallible and his subjects fallible?

As he puts it, "If you are a follower, you can never be a leader." This misses the point that leaders must lead with integrity because public office requires cleanliness, stoic nationalism, and patriotism, which we historically note among Afrikaners. Perhaps this is because they were a self-alienated minority from their motherland, Holland, and were flung far by fate to the southern tip of Africa by Jan Van Riebeeck to create a station of life between Holland and India for those much-valued spices the Indians are known masters of, and ivory. This is perhaps what drew them together, and they were cemented by their other two fates, viz., the Great Trek and the Anglo-Boer War, as history recorded it prior to 1994. And they were further strengthened by the Battle of Blood River, where an estimated 10,000–15,000 Zulus fell after entering into a covenant with God. Today this mishap is sealed as the Day of Reconciliation, changing it from the initially vengeful Dingane's Day, Day of the Covenant and Day of the Vow, to reconcile South Africans and let go of the bitter past encased in the very name Battle of the Blood River, to breathe a new hope.

That was a worthy digression, and now this is what Jammeh places his strength on!

On the entrance at the statehouse of the Gambian head of state under Yahya Jammeh was written in bold letters, "Behind every successful man, there is a successful woman."

Does this send the message that Jammeh put his strength in his beautiful wife, for whom he did everything to impress her? The ruthless raping of the poor Gambian economy became his target when he was under pressure to quit the presidency and go into exile. For this reason, Jammeh had to rip the Gambia off its pittance of wealth to ensure his comfortable sojourn in exile not only to satisfy his greed but also to prove his statement dubiously right. Otherwise, he would have failed his wife, who is the source of his strength if that statement is anything to go by.

The youthful Jammeh, who came to power via a ruthless coup d'état, is an example of why African states should carefully reconsider their constitutions and put restrictions on age to ensure mature leadership. This should be legislated for in stricter terms to avoid situations in which leaders come to power while still in their diapers. Thomas Sankara proves to be the only difference and only one worthy of emulation.

I know being led by youths in diapers is not possible, but I am sceptically referring to youths in political diapers. I experienced that "leadership" in my municipality and do not wish it upon any subjects. It is tasteless, lacks direction, and disgusts. This may sound dictatorial to the youth, but the Bill of Rights can allay their fears by ensuring that they are not victimized and oppressed.

Youth leadership is ruthless, despicable, and unwise because of its imbecility and uncaring arrogance. The youth do things to impress women because the youth themselves are by nature impressionable.

Major impressions are expensive colognes, top-of-the-range vehicles, and expensive beverages—especially blue label whiskies. This is their turf, and to get it they compromise municipal service delivery. We need experienced and mature leaders like the new north west premier to lead after the administration of the disastrous Mahumapelo, who took "early retirement". Does that induce laughter? No pity! This should show how sick the youths' minds are after our own youth leadership in Maluti-a-Phofung and elsewhere!

What demonizes black youth into a reckless radicalism is the very government that does not address their employment needs. If the economy were grown and the youth employed, there would be a general satisfaction. People's landlessness and homelessness constitute the reason behind development initiatives and visions. Today it is no longer only black people that have been impoverished. The problem has become one of all races. Agenda 2063's fifty-year term development initiative is not receiving the attention it deserves, and when assessed in 2063, it will be exposed as a sham, and this will escalate youth despondence, leading to another revolution. I last heard about it when launched, as I was part of Minister Nkoana-Mashabane's International Relations Department guests in Pretoria, but it is not receiving media attention to inform the public about its progress. This initiative apparently invited blacks only. In today's South Africa, such initiatives must be racially inclusive to be able to take the nation forward.

What goes on unabated are the few who enjoy tender-entrepreneurship and spend rather than invest their ill-gotten wealth. Connected family members spend tender income wastefully, recycling it within family and failing to spread it by empowering fellow youth in Agenda 2063–style job-creation opportunities. Municipality employment is bloated with youths whose roles and duties are not clear. This is applying the brakes on youth development.

In one incident in Maluti-a-Phofung, some youths were employed around Christmastime in 2017, and it is alleged their cellular phones registered payments of R7,500 the day after their employment. In another incident, a service provider based in Bethlehem was allegedly paid millions on 24 December, when municipal staff were already on Christmas leave.

Such irregular wasteful payments (in fact, sheer theft) from municipal coffers strangle and paralyze municipal service delivery and finances personal service delivery to offer a Christmas of a lifetime—probably in Dubai, the capital of splendour.

Looking back at the departure of Jammeh from the Commonwealth, I wonder to what extent capitals of democracy contribute to African despondence with their policies, leading to the justification of leaving bodies associated with them?

Let us look at America. When Barack Obama took office in 2009 as the American chief executive, a lot of hope and sheer political thrill was inspired. However, this was soon followed by a bitter disillusionment that engulfed the hopeful black world. His Nobel Peace Prize acceptance speech shocked black America and the world. To many people, Obama sounded very much like George Bush or Dick Cheney. It is a tradition among US presidents vacating the White House to leave a letter for its next occupant. This left me wondering what the letter left by an outgoing American president leaving the Oval Office for its next occupant contains. Have you ever wondered? Soon after reading this letter, Obama changed his tune from that of an evolutionary leader to that of an acceptance of the then reigning status quo, and he dispatched soldiers to Afghanistan and seemed to be politically paralyzed.

These letters, no doubt, affect an American chief executive's term of office and that of his administration. Former President Bill Clinton is ironically seen as the first "black" American president (I wonder what this says about Obama) because Obama did not become what he promised and because, compared to the Clinton administration, he did very little for African Americans. The African media have actually seen no gains from his administration. The letters between presidents are classified as top secret and can only be studied after a period of fifty years, and some members of our generation may never know what Bush wrote to Obama in that letter.

I am not absolving Barack Obama of not being himself after reading the contents of his predecessor's letter upon occupying the Oval Office, but no doubt, he seems to have been left with no choice but to continue with the Afghanistan invasion. This may have been the case more so because his predecessor was shaken and grieved after he was caught "napping", completely relaxed during a reading exercise at a junior school when he got the news that a second plane had hit the second tower. His grief was America's grief; indeed, it was international. 9/11 was horrific! America was under attack by some forces of destruction that were unknown until identified as Al Qaeda! George Bush, president of America, was visiting Emma E. Booker Elementary School when, on his entrance, he was briefed that an aeroplane had crashed into the World Trade Center. He imagined a small plane hitting the tower and being lost in a horrible tragedy.

After greeting the school principal and being led into a classroom full of second-grade learners with the teacher routinely going through a reading lesson, President Bush felt a presence behind him, and he obviously pricked up his ears to learn about a second plane hitting the second tower, effectively telling him that America was under attack. After this briefing, all hell broke loose, the result being the war in Afghanistan.

Obama's dispatching of 30,000 troops to Afghanistan must have been influenced by President Bush's letter to the next Oval Office occupant (President Obama), which former President Clinton says is an American traditional practice. This was a war Obama promised to end when wooing voters for the Democrats, but he saw things differently once in office, probably after reading that outgoing American president's traditional letter to his successor.

Bush Senior once whispered into his son's ear, "You've got to try everything you can to avoid war. But if the man won't comply, you don't have any other choice", thus implying that Obama must have had no other choice as well but to force compliance from those who had dared to make an enemy out of the United States, as an executive order. Those people were hidden somewhere in Afghanistan in the form of Al Qaeda and Bin Laden, and they had to pay with their lives. The US President and the CIA would not relax until the order was served and executed.

Yet President Bill Clinton, during the course of his administration, lived his dream of remembering a grandfather who taught him to look up to people others look down upon, because people are not so different after all. He never, ever overtly justified social inequality, as Michele Obama did. Neither did Hillary, his wife, ever do so.

Tracing Clinton's administration, we can see this view in every aspect of his life.

A tough-jawed firmness of purpose with an incredibly inspired intransigence of belief in his convictions proved to be the hallmark of his administration, and all his weaknesses and controversies far underweigh his credits and idiosyncrasies. He was a man of character! Looking at President Obama over two terms, can we truly say the same?

His wife, Michelle, justified American social imbalances during her husband's tenure and administration and blamed them on parental neglect, conveniently forgetting that parental roles are also determined by the depths of their pockets. Michelle, in her own words maintains that living "… in a poor neighbourhood, you will face challenges that somebody in a wealthy suburb does not have to face … but that's not the reason to get bad grades." That is rich but has some valid points. But does this justify the conditions of the poverty African Americans have to live with, having twice voted for change in the United States? In my view, the answer is a firm no.

Let us bring this assessment and analogy closer home to Africa, because the digression was meant to address this. Looking at our South African presidents since 1994, can we say they addressed our youth's socioeconomic challenges in inner cities? Does this question suggest understanding why our youths are so radical and seek to do things for themselves their own way? Yes, it shames me to respond affirmatively.

Our leadership has failed our youth by simply looking the other way—literally!

The other power, England, created social inequalities, sustained them, and justified them when an African delegation was sent to have the 1913 Land Act reviewed. They looked the other way, sacrificing them as gifts of reconciliation with the racist Afrikaners after "the stupidest war the English ever fought". But Harold Macmillan, fifty-seven years later, saw the need to conscientize colonial governments that the time was up for maintaining ruthless colonial policies. But Verwoerd's conscience was not moved. Like today's leaders, after toppling his ideology, Verwoerd looked the other way.

The two most powerful democracies, the United States and the United Kingdom, were stuck to a past they could not change. Remember that in our mines, companies that were profiting were Anglo-American. African mineral wealth silenced this voice of international conscience. The sufferings of black people were downplayed and were milked dry. Welkom and Virginia in the Free State have become ghost towns! America and England kept quiet—mum—until of course they could not any more, and then they imposed sanctions.

Our presidents since 1994 have lacked a vision for making our youth part of the national economic spectrum. Their need to put their potential to the test and their inclusivity in a Maslow hierarchy towards self-actualisation were overlooked. Our youth kept seeing things through the glass ceiling, and this became an unpleasant, intolerable experience, and justifying it is unjust! Many became addicted to mind-numbing states and trips of temporary forgetfulness. On being restored back to sobriety, they took one shot after another to maintain a drugged trance. Many have been buried, and the damage done has become our bane, because feeding the habit has generated a crime wave. The glass ceiling remained tightly closed to our youth, and this became frustrating and enraging at the same time.

You will at some point be driven to break that ceiling through unreasonable demands or through creative devices; you might leave the glass ceiling intact but figuratively broken through stealthy fair or devious means. Make no mistake; devious means like the VBS Mutual Bank debacle will surface, and perpetrators will find jail time. But fair ones will attract attention, respect, and facilitation for the beautiful ones not yet born, to be conceived and be born …

One youth in particular felt so badly used by former president Zuma that he put it in a most crude manner, insulting African traditional values and principles regarding how youths should address adults. I cannot bring myself to repeat his utterances. You know them well.

Is it therefore surprising that Yahya Jammeh felt badly used by the Commonwealth and was applauded when he left it as Verwoerd did? No, it is not! It was justifiable; but was his corrupt administration justifiable? No way! it was disgustingly deplorable!

Coming closer to home, are the youth making unfair, unjustifiable demands to be part of the new dispensation through economic empowerment? By all means no! But are they going about it the right way? Another resounding no!

If our youthful leadership were fighting for the rights of the poor and their needs, living among them, I would be the first to give them support, because they would be feeling the pinch of being without water, without electricity, without proper roads—generally without the satisfaction of their basic needs, as scientifically theorized by Maslow.

But how do you fight for the plight of the poor when you are living it up in the lap of luxury? There is no way you can! At some stage you will sound like the uncaring Austrian princess who said "Then let them eat cake!" when the French clamoured for bread, and who ended up under a guillotine with her husband when the Bastille was stormed.

You can use their poverty only for self-enrichment when you are in opulence and are used to it in the water- and electricity-fed Sandton, Johannesburg! So to speak, going into politics and forming political parties is a way of applying for a job through votes to gain a seat or seats in Parliament, breaking the glass ceiling and getting at the allowances and perks of being a member of Parliament. This, I suspect, is what Mohlaudi Motsoeneng and Manyi are presently doing. Remember that they are unemployed and could be decoys to be used in coalition, because Hlaudi and Manyi have ANC in their DNA system. Don't you ever forget!

We have no excuse not to give our youth economic freedom in their time and in our time to ensure a corruption-free economic practice. Most are unemployed but have employable skills. They are smart and well read. Some are qualified agriculturists but have no land on which to practise agriculture, no start-up capital, and no resources. Is this fair? No it is not! It needs to be addressed exactly the way former president Thabo Mbeki indicates in the video clip previously quoted. The ANC's self-cleansing and the review of the ANC's land policy should also be addressed, as stated by Ronald Lamola in the Sunday *Times*. But then the ANC is known to make breathtaking promises only to renege and emerge five years later with a mouthwatering manifesto of promises that will soon prove empty.

Michelle Obama's take above is ample evidence that those who succeed in breaking the glass ceiling justify social class imbalances, and this angers poverty-stricken African youth.

Those breaking the glass ceiling justify the socioeconomic repression of those who "fail" to. They fail not because they are stupid, but because doors of opportunity remain firmly shut for them!

As adults, we fail our youth in one way or another; we fail our youth, and we need to be accountable for this and put the matter right by encouraging our youth to establish cooperatives and to be monitored through financial statements and reports on progress at the end of every financial year. Receipts of payments and purchases made may be photographed; these include purchases of pens, paper, and furniture. Receipts of payments for offices rented (if applicable), payments to the landlord, and payments for vehicles (if applicable) must be relevant to cooperatives' business plans. These receipts should all be attached to financial statements.

Financing should be done in reasonable tranches that will help them address their needs for structural growth. We should also find ways in which our raw materials can be internally transformed into finished products to grow youth enterprises by way of the skills given to them by their schools and universities. This is the best way of creating jobs, because right now, our raw materials are creating jobs overseas, and this is what our youth is reacting against as it maintains the "proper" colonial relations between "master and servant". Africans of all hues are servants to their colonial masters, because as it stands, we are free slaves.

The closing recommendation is to retrain our youth through the Small Enterprise Development Agency (SEDA) to help identify their skills and establish companies assessed by SEDA as having potential for job creation.

There has to be a budget to finance such enterprises with a training support base in business and financial management, as well as marketing skills. These companies must be led by South Africans with no regard for race in whatever form, but business plans must be evaluated and accordingly financed to create jobs for the best qualified applicants. The time for oneness is nigh, and the time for race-defined classification is up!

The approval of the joint constitutional review committee recommending the amendment of Section 25 was greeted by scenes of jubilation by members of Parliament. They broke into song and chants of "Ma ba yeke umhlaba wethu" (let them [whites] leave our land alone) in news following the report. This is undoubtedly by no means a final say on the matter, as it has had divisive effects in the society and has unfortunately worsened race relations further. And these must be repaired.

The jubilation rubbished the 1994 accord that ushered in the new dispensation and declared it as having sold black people down the river, with leaders such as Nelson Mandela, seen as instrumental in negotiating its creation, dismissed as Uncle Toms or lackeys of white economic interests.

In his Reconciliation Day address to the nation in Umtata, President Cyril Ramaphosa stated that "land reform is central to eliminating inequalities in society" in the "land our forebears bequeathed to us." Yes, we agree, as this will close the chapter of "revenge and retribution" as he referred to it in his inspiring, uniting speech; but what remains is implementation such that it reflects ANC policy and grows the economy—rather than collapsing it, as the Nogqauze episode did. The government should pass legislation whose sting should be felt by all caught with their hands in the till and who are making government coffers their piggybanks! The law must deal harshly with them, saving us expensive, time-wasting, and unnecessary commissions of inquiry.

We are a new country with a new vision, whose economy should be for all South Africans, not only a few chosen connected youth as well as previously disadvantaged youth, according to definitions aimed at avoiding racial terms. All youth presently are "previously disadvantaged" because we have bred and added a twenty-five-year-old youth that has been disadvantaged since 1994. All our youth, irrespective of political affiliation, race, colour, or creed, must be given opportunity.

The national budget must be for all. Even food packages, where they have to be given, must be given to all—followers of the African National Congress, Democratic Alliance, and all other political parties—because we all pay the same taxes when we draw our salaries. And when buying from the business community that we pay VAT to and submit to SARS and these collected taxes, this must benefit every South African, without regard to political opinion or affiliation, race, colour or creed.

These taxes form part of the National Treasury's budgets deployed to local municipalities according to the number of citizens in a municipality. These figures are given as the number of citizens the municipality has to service, with no reference to race but to humanity.

Our numbers determine the size of the budget and the quality of our municipality for a mayor or executive mayor, the positions of which should now be ceremonial, with no political power or role in municipal administration, to enjoy the dignity that goes with a mayoral chain.

Hunger and poverty do not attack by natural selection, as Charles Darwin might have said; they attack all who cannot afford to put food in their stomachs—full stop!

Are the facilities pictured below in Maluti-a-Phofung lost to our youth, along with the possibility of transforming them into job-creating ventures through business plans that pass the scrutiny of SEDA, banks, and organizations like the Independent Development Corporation, National Empowerment Fund, Development Bank of Southern Africa, Provincial Development Corporations, and, in our case, the FDC?

The following pictures give you a scenario of what Dr T.K. Mopeli, pictured in academic regalia above, did for the people of Qwaqwa. Qwaqwa is now part of the triangular Maluti-a-Phofung Local Municipality in the Free State Province, South Africa.

Images 1 and 2 are of one of the many vandalised schools that Dr T.K. Mopeli built for locals in his vision of making education the instrument of development. Primary schools in this former homeland are within 5 km walking distance in local villages. This shows that Dr Mopeli sought to ensure that local children acquire reading and writing skills as a foundation of basic education. The name of the neglected school pictured above is Lesedi, meaning 'light' in English. You do not need a PhD thesis to show that Dr T.K. Mopeli equated education to light, meaning that his vision was that literacy is enlightenment.

The second image is where a classroom in which such enlightenment was sown at this school and children prepared for a future. The black rectangle you see on the wall is where a chalkboard used to be, spreading enlightenment to a generation of families before the entire school was invaded and its building material taken. In some villages you see slabs of cement where a school used to be, with the entire building material taken by locals. Many schools are vacant today and have fallen into disuse. Local out of school unemployed youth do not have places where they can engage in self-development initiatives assisted by youth development agencies. People are political and economic spectators and are not engaged in participatory democracy in the new democratic dispensation. Dr Mopeli's legacy is a barren desert with no oasis in sight. Image 3 below is an example of many such industrial sites that lie in waste, gates locked, hopefully awaiting unlocking by international investors reading this book of hope to delete the despair written in people's faces.

These sites are now under the Free State Development Corporation which can be googled on internet for further information to would be investors reading this heart rending revelation.

Image 4 is a place that can be used by locals for various Agri-Ecotourism economic activities but has also fallen into disuse under the new administration when many are unemployed. In the background of this picture is a magnificent natural view. It is one of the many tourism sites international tourists can view in Maluti-a-Phofung. This image forms part of the Basotho Cultural Village (image 5) that educates tourists on the Stone and Iron Age Basotho people's way of life within an area having various bird species. A must see to all tourists visiting the area!

CHANGING LIVES

Noteworthy is a developing political party that shows a pulse of conscience to better the people's socio-economics. This is the Afrikan Alliance of Social Democrats that emerged during the 2019 general elections. Its shortened name is AASD, (image 6) pictured below. Following the image are images 7 & 8 of AASD members building an informal home for a homeless family. It is a big hearted intervention whose voice and action of conscience was triggered by the plight of a homeless family in Botshabelo, Free State Province. There are many such families and they require urgent intervention to alleviate their poverty and state of political neglect.

Basically, the political problem in South Africa is a result of a lack of continuity from one administration to the next. Each administration since 1994 comes with its economic development plans and this has resulted in a lot of money going to waste with no successes gained. This has resulted in an economic bottle neck, resulting from administration bottle necks where unqualified people are occupying positions of authority. Those in such positions do not employ the youth with postgraduate qualifications in their departments fearing for their positions. The AASD is a glimmer of hope in the desire to change the lives of people within their area and if its wishes were to be fulfilled, poverty can be defeated by stopping corruption which it sees as stealing from the poor. The AASd's view is that the land question should be handled with care so that it can serve a purpose of changing the peoples' lives for the better.

A start in the Free State Province can be made by developing the legacy leaders like Dr T.K. Mopeli left for posterity and take it to the next level. The Department of Public Works in the Free State must consider developing eco-tourism by renovating places like Fika Patso Lodge to revive the local tourism industry. This lodge can be tendered to local tourism geared businesses like Bed & Breakfast companies. Our municipality is blessed by also being along the N3 main route from Durban to Johannesburg and an economic zone idea is already in place but needs to be taken to the next level to develop Harrismith and Tshiame Industrial Area. In reality, people in Maluti-a-

Phofung are starving in the midst of plenty because of politicians that are out of political and economic development focus. All they need to better the peoples' lives is to have a vision.

The reader should look at buildings that have been left derelict in their areas that our youth can change into job-creation businesses. They should conceptualize businesses and approach SEDA for business plans.

However, these plans must be convincing in their progressions, and there must be proper financial management systems in place to make financial reports at the end of every financial year. Importantly, the finances allotted must be loans, not grants, lest we end up grunting around like pigs, demanding more funds! Grants encourage dependency and do not develop business acumen.

If we live by grants, we are training our youth not to be entrepreneurial but rather to be dependent, and by and large, we are creating a state of dependence and not the economic emancipation our youth want. Assistance must come in the form of loans to be serviced at a rate determined by the borrower until fully paid. This will make our youth economically independent through well-structured business plans and not popular rhetoric.

Where we have wronged our youth, we need to acknowledge it, and this will restore youth–adult respect. Where our youth wrong us, they must also acknowledge it. As it is, we and the Mandela presidency generations wronged our youth by entering into agreements during negotiations that sold their economic freedom, and this must be put right.

Neglected buildings in our areas can be transformed into youth training centres by organizations that have acquired accreditation from relevant SETAs and the Department of Higher Education.

The driving force behind us should be to correct the first postapartheid administration's youth policies. We must keep in mind that the impressionable youth looked to Robert Mugabe for guidance, and his failed administration and the failure of his grandiose scheme should win our youth back. All that Mugabe sought was to undo Nelson Mandela's handiwork of being imprisoned by conscience and unmaking apartheid without crediting him, and he silently became hell-bent on not being outshined by Mandela in the perception of the West. After failing to realize this, he had to patronize the youthful Malema and roll out the red carpet for him, and what youth would not, at that tender age, be impressed by an elderly so-called statesman and African head of state rolling out the red carpet for him at Harare International Airport under the full glare of the international spotlight?

Mugabe did this to hit back at the West whilst misleading a generation of South African youth by catching one of them and misdirecting him in order to misdirect his following, infusing and channelling his hatred for the West into them to sow the seeds of irreconcilable racial hatred. Some names are unsuitable to those accordingly named! What kind of Gabriel is this—full of regret, vengeance, and impunity, and quick to severely punish those who cross him.

This was the case not only between nations (African ones on one side and Western ones on the other) but also between his own fellow nationals.

This meant our youth could do to their fellow nationals what he (Mugabe) did to his own people by sowing hatred.

However, Mugabe's plan badly backfired when his own army got rid of him, and Nelson Mandela's legacy still sits pretty because he humbly respected the constitution and the basic principles of democracy, as opposed to Mugabe's nauseating and disgusting thirty-year arrogance of a dictatorship and stance of "keep your Britain, I will keep my Zimbabwe!" To what end? A once healthy economy buckled at the knees because of the burning racial hatred of a man wronged by colonialism when it denied him the right to bury his loved ones during the time of a Unilateral Declaration of Independence government in Rhodesia, the present-day Zimbabwe.

Nelson Mandela suffered the same fate in the hands of his captors, but the man's pragmatism made him preach a heartfelt reconciliation sermon that none can deny, and all that is left of South Africans is to find it in their hearts to forgive. Reconciliation shall follow and shall form the base and foundation of an economic activity that will grow and feed the nation.

This man stands tall, and his legacy lives on because he fought for an idea that shall forever live—the freedom of all men and their equality to "live in harmony", having "… cherished the ideal of a free society in which people live together in harmony …" This is an ideal he lived for whilst prepared to die for it, but he lived to realize it. It is this ideal we must propagate and bequeath from one generation to the next, for the simple reason that there is no other in the minds of free and fair men and women to espouse and perpetuate.

But first, as former president Thabo Mbeki asserts, we must start with the ANC's self-cleansing. It delivered freedom, no doubt, and must proceed to lead us towards a democratically free and morally clean state from the moral bankruptcy of its past twenty-four years—especially of the nine years of the Jacob Zuma administration (9 March 2009–14 February 2018)! This requires a vacuum cleaner, a Hoover, to get into its every crevice and clean the mess out.

To Mugabe, Zimbabwe was his. He could not see himself under any other president except another Mugabe in the form of Grace, whom he would manipulate to neglect the nation, and who was questionable given a penchant for the good life and racial cruelty, while her people hustled for their next meal.

In South Africa, remember, she assaulted an innocent young woman, and apparently got away with it through diplomatic immunity (or was it really?). Given an unforgiving vengeance in her husband's heart, a once thriving bread basket economy has become a place where vultures are patiently circling, waiting to pounce on the next corpse to feed on, its supermarkets devoid of commodities to feed the nation.

South Africans should learn from this error of alarming proportions and would be best off avoiding it by walking a tightrope on land reform and not being directed by blind vengeance, throbbing hearts, and greed, but by clear minds and well-thinking calculating heads.

The beautiful ones are yet to be born to cleanse the Mugabe ruins of a once thriving economy. Mugabe's inspired renaming of Zimbabwe Ruins to Great Zimbabwe has been insulted by the economic ruins he engineered and brought about in Zimbabwe. Indeed, the beautiful ones are yet to be born, hopefully, in South Africa when the government-led ANC leads us towards greener national pastures through a land reform programme we are a part of. This will be the beginning of the breeding of the beautiful ones. The meddling with land matters at the moment seems to profit politicians. I hope this will be avoided at all costs, because our economy cannot afford corruption. People want to want to see the rising of a new sun; we long for it!

Greed and political corruption that mushroomed in newly independent African states has been exposed by journalists and African writers. Mugabe is the epitome of this exposition and makes his leadership as a senior statesman unexemplary—horrific in every sense. South African leaders have also had a hand in this; becoming multimillionaires and multibillionaires in just twenty-four years. Amazing! Just how this became possible is beyond reasoning. Can anyone explain the miracle? Maybe they became more equal than the others. Perhaps a deep-seated silent vengeance has a role in what we call "payback time!"

You see, when you are driven by vengeance, whatever you throw at your former enemy boomerangs—it hits right back, just as it has hit Mugabe flush in the face. He is virtually a prisoner under the comforts of his blue-roofed mansion in Harare. Is such a life enjoyable—being surrounded by material plenty, without the love of your people?

Maslow teaches that the basic human need is love and belonging, and

I leave this to your well-balanced and thinking mind so that it can be a lesson to those with ill-gotten and ill-acquired wealth. His people live in abject poverty, wondering where their next meal will come from, without the love Maslow says forms part of self-actualization.

A Zimbabwean I was discussing the "soft coup" in Zimbabwe with in Herschel Eastern Cape was not particularly impressed. He summed it up thusly: "The jockey has changed, but the horse is still the same." He is a young Zimbabwean for whom I had brought along a copy of a magazine with a report on the coup, believing I was bringing him the best news ever about his country. He did not even care to read the story!

This disillusionment found expression among Zimbabweans inside our country and within Zimbabwe when excitement about the coup soon died down.

Zimbabweans in neighbouring South Africa are well-educated but live in dire straits and abject poverty, with those employed earning far less than they are qualified to earn. Even ordinary Zimbabwean peasants speak impeccable English as they sell their wares in South African streets and from house to house. They are a reflection and expression of the excellence of their system of education.

But what kind of freedom is their freedom?

Nationals are free but church mouse poor because white farms were expropriated without compensation, with their owners being thrown into prison in a desperate show of political power to correct the Lancaster House settlement.

But was all this really necessary?

Do South Africans want farms they may never scientifically farm, and do they want to inherit Land Bank loans they may be unable to service because of poor yields? I guess not!

Now that the motion has been adopted, it will require a hands-on corruption-free government implementation, and those facilitating it should be reliable hands-on employees living on their excellent salaries and allowances. Municipal coffers should stop being used as the piggybanks of a select group of the corrupt elite, and corruption must be punishable by immediate Hawks intervention, working hand in glove with a government-supported NPA and the Department of Justice, with courts serving natural justice.

This will save time on commissions of inquiry as the accused with damning prima facie evidence have their day in court to face the full might of the law. This is a privilege and right of every citizen, contained in the supreme law of our land—the Constitution of the Republic of South Africa, with its Bill of Rights for the people.

REFORM, RECONCILE, AND REBUILD: PRELUDE TO IDENTIFYING POSITIVES

Photojournalism exposed the horrors of 16 June 1976 in grim pictures. The Hector Pieterson saga hogged international media and captured the brutality of the apartheid state and the lengths it could go to in maintaining firmness against those resisting the chains of oppression. Some "committed suicide", and others were pushed from the tenth floor of John Vorster Square. Steve Biko travelled from Port Elizabeth to Pretoria naked in the back of an apartheid police van, and his death as a result of this tragedy left a minister cold. His associate in their Eastern Cape exile, my homeboy Mapetla Mohapi (whose memorial proudly stands outside the Sterkspruit Public Library) "committed suicide" in a police cell, allegedly after writing on a piece of toilet paper.

The suicides referred to reflect the brutality of the apartheid state that Chris Hani referred to as a Terror Government in Pretoria. It is that probably made Pik Botha as Foreign Affairs minister in apartheid South Africa declared the possibility of a black head of state, as he could no longer stand the glare of international media. They extracted a truth out of him he could no longer suppress, and that statement made him the Afrikaner volk's pariah and polecat.

To foil the perpetuation of racial hatred, public debates on apartheid fanning racial hatred rather than reconciliation must not be heeded. We agree that apartheid's toll on black lives was deep. It claimed lives and depressed many people. Yes, apartheid was an atrocious system that made black lives miserable and cheap—so cheap that the putrid smell of burning human flesh blended with the aroma of braaied boerewors in the veld as Askaris laughed and sang drunkenly with the dead. Yes, the Nazis' Auschwitz and the apartheid prisons promoted the ideology of an inferior race whose inability to develop was blamed on them being "lesser" human beings, and they were disposed of without much thought. The plight of Palestinians in the hands of present-day Jews in Gaza, to which our foreign office appropriately reacts, cyclically replays racial atrocities. All these are sad reminders of where we come from together as South Africans. But we overcame all those things in 1994!

Some letter writers to editors of newspapers are fanning racial hatred rather than discouraging it, and if a letter is published, we believe it reflects the beliefs of the editor. He affirms what he publishes. Apartheid was an abhorrent cult system that should never have been that history has recorded. The atrocities of apartheid are unerasable from human memory and will forever stay with us. But is it really necessary to fan them into racial hatred?

How, then, do we find our way through it so we can together sing the Africa song during Africa Month? How do we together build a new brotherhood and sisterhood based on remaking a South Africa united in adversity and in diversity? How do we incinerate apartheid twenty-five years after its perishing and in its flames and smoke of incineration make it a fading memory? I believe that if you can read some letters to editors of papers, you will also ask antagonists to lead us in finding a way that will help us to heal our traumas.

Our wish is to realize a dream of brotherhood and sisterhood so we can see our children cross-culturally blending and embracing one another in transforming South Africa and making Africa a Tree of Life—a baobab tree planted on the great American Dream Martin Luther King Jr. shared with the world. To realize this dream, we must publish views that address the problem sensitively for redress in order to help us find closure.

The question is, How do we find one another if all we remember are negatives? Does reminding us of apartheid atrocities not stoke the embers of racial hatred and burn the hope for a nonracial brotherhood and sisterhood of love?

The civil war following Julius Caesar's assassination ended with Mark Antony looking for and finding Brutus's body and uttering words of reconciliation with his body lying across his arms, paying tribute to him, and giving him a state funeral. All was forgotten, and Rome found a new direction, a new dawn, through reconciliation.

From this simple act Shakespeare's creative literary genius, let us together find one another and try. It will not be easy, but if we try just hard enough, we shall together somehow find a way together—not for ourselves, but for South Africa and Africa, whose horn stands proud and whose "kreun van osse wa" (strained sounds of ox wagons) remind us that we truly belong to a common fatherland.

Right now we need messages of forgiveness and reconciliation, because forgiveness is vital to our emotional health and spiritual survival. Without forgiveness, our country becomes an arena of conflict and a fortress of evil. Forgiveness is the cleanliness of the soul and the purification of the spirit, and it liberates the heart. He who does not forgive does not have peace of mind and lacks in his soul communion with God. Keeping heartache in your heart is self-destructive. Those who do not forgive are physically, emotionally, and spiritually ill. As the saying goes, forgiveness brings joy where sorrow has brought sadness. Reconciliation is healthy for a nation that was once in conflict. It breeds a new generation, a new nation…

At this time of seeking ways and means of finding one another, we should together feel our feelings of forgiveness flowing through us, as a wronged mother who fought a system we all agree was subhuman was buried. With her burial should be buried racial hatred, which will be transformed into a seed that will develop a radicle of national reflection to grow interracial affection in our hearts. Winnie Madikizela-Mandela's burial should be seen as burying the hatchet by reliving her past and feeling it as she must have felt it. This will help us find closure. You cannot win a battle without casualties. She became one in her lifetime and never knew peace of mind. Tributes in her memory poured in because of her unifying influence. Her countrywide memorial services came with a void and a deep sense of loss. People cried inconsolably hardly able to cease sobbing. Her Methodist hymn "Nzulu Ye Mfihlakalo" (the depths of a hidden love) chorally sounded in people's minds. Members of the Methodist Young Men's Guild, lay preachers, and ministers made a plea that adherents of the movement she once served in with dignity, at times with questionable personal integrity in some of her decisions, should speak in unison, especially in public platforms.

We at times hear the ANC secretary general (SG) speaking at variance with the ideological stand of the president's movement, for which she laid down her life. Even the youth noted that they that the two are not talking in unison, seeming to contradict one another at every turn. There is no denying that after the Office of the Presidency, the Secretarial Office is the next most powerful. The SG is the spokesperson of any organization and should be beyond reproach regarding the ideological nuancing of the direction the ANC and the president chart.

At the hour of grief and sorrow, people sought to hear and see the president and his SG talking in ideological unison. The president's invitation to business to address the thorny land issue, and the SG emotionally wowing crowds by talking about land expropriation without compensation are at variance with the president's view and ideological statement.

Mama Winnie, political nurturer of Ace Magashule, among others, deserved a common platform that puts Cyril and Ace on the same ground and ideological footing. Winnie's passing should have embodied a turning unifying factor that defactionalizes the African National Congress. We heard instead, and still hear, differences between leaders of an organization Winnie gave her life to.

I say to Mama Winnie's family, the Mandelas, Amampondo, and Abathembu, the Eastern Cape and the nation at large, let us make Winnie a unifying icon that bore, and still bears, the title of Mother of the Nation—deservedly so. We remain truly and deeply indebted to her and what she went through. Her life signifies the hard work ahead to liberate this country and its people economically in a diplomatic way, which we shall not regret.

People were bleeding inside, and the tears that fell dressed a wound deep inside their souls, helping them to find closure. When a tear falls, it takes out a pain from deep inside that nothing else is able to remove. Her funeral became an expression of mixed feelings as it turned into be a political battlefield of political adversaries.

Below is an admonishing eulogy—a tribute to a woman wronged by her society and her children growing used to their mother's political ill treatment and emotional abuse by a brutal state ideology. The eulogy, if you can call it that, should help you to heal and to find it in your heart to feel her pain. I hope your humanity will help you face the truth without flinching and heal, whether you loved her or loved to hate her. Remember that forgiveness brings joy where sorrow has brought sadness and offers grounds for a meaningful reconciliation. A reconciling nation is a loving nation full of brotherhood and sisterhood to take the nation forward.

MAMA WINNIE'S FUNERAL

Funerals are not occasions for casting aspersions and settling scores, but solemn holy occasions during which the departed are respected and fondly remembered. Statements, therefore, should rather be uttered in a diplomatic, aspersion-concealing way that will make the targeted listeners hear and revisit their inner persons and consciences for a positive change. Attacking a person could make him or her more rebellious and hard-hearted, and it is unjustifiable to attack someone during a funeral occasion. Even Antony, in one of the greatest funeral orations ever recorded, did not find fault with Caesar's murderers overtly. He praised them to destroy them.

Ordinary mortals whom we pay our last respects to are respectfully remembered and all human follies are forgotten, but it is different for famous public persons. All speakers address the bereaved family with a veiled sense of respect and spiritual empathy when a famous person is departed. That is why there are men and women of the cloth at the end of the programme, after all others have spoken. After they read from the Holy Book, offering an interpretation of the holy message and pronouncement of extracts from the Bible in front of the departed soul's coffin, mourners are led towards the hearse with preachers reciting holy verses. The leading preacher leads the cortege to the grave site.

To turn funerals into political battlegrounds is a sorry sight, as happened during Mama Winnie's funeral, where political point-scoring became the order of the day. Talking about Mama's denigration on the occasion when we were supposed to be mourning with the bereaved family, close relatives, the women's league, and indeed the entire nation was unsightly.

We hoped to hear soothing words to heal our afflicted souls, but alas, it was not to be.

Mama's funeral became a political battleground that could have turned into the chaos of Julius Caesar's funeral when his namesake, Julius Malema, spat venom. Attacking mourners the way he did was completely un-African. This, however, proved beyond words that Mama belonged to the people, as his funeral turned out to be the parliament of the people.

It is not only Malema who did this, of course, but he was the noisiest, perhaps proving that the multiplicity of political parties we have are self-serving, as De Lille noted in a telephone conversation with Mama. They are not really serving the interests of the people but rather using the seats earned to settle vendettas against antagonists.

What prevented possible chaos following the volatile speeches was probably the invisible hand of God, in the form of a statement made famous by Maradona, justifying a controversial goal.

Mama's funeral deserved to be peaceful, tranquil, and typical, as with the funerals of ordinary mortals who have lived their lives away from the public spotlight. Be that as it may, the opening up of old wounds at her funeral spurred the creation of a clinic to heal them. It is God's way that foes are brought together, just as Pilate and Herod, the chaotic drunk, were brought together by an act of God. Maybe it was God's way of letting people bleed for the last time to nurture, soothe, and dress their reconciliation in a spirit of goodwill.

The tirade and tsunamis that flew at Mama's funeral must be a uniting factor that rids us of the racial stereotypes she overturned—prejudices as well as attitudes—to bring South Africans together.

The now defunct National Party's leadership was made conspicuous by its absence, and this should not be taken advantage of negatively but as an atonement of a deeply felt sorrow for tearing a God-fearing family apart, and a mother from her children, at times at ungodly hours. I say this because Bishop Desmond Mpilo Tutu told me once through the media during the tough P. W. Botha years that "the Afrikaners are a God fearing nation". And I believe him.

Their absence should be interpreted as an expression of a deeply felt remorse and regret and of asking for pardon, and Mama's passing should be the glue that brings Africans of all hues together to bury the past.

Your spirit, Mama, which still lives on among us, should convey our gratitude to our ancestry to have been given you for our country, our nation, and our people. Christ died to heal sinners. Your passing should heal divisions. You are not the woman who gave the world a saviour, but you became that saviour in your deep faith. Your parting brought multitudes from far and wide—even foes—together, not to watch a football game at a football stadium, but to give you a deserved fond farewell. Adieu, Mama. Adieu, beautiful Mama from within, ethereal jewel and pearl of Africa.

There is no doubt that had you been treated fairly, you could have lived your life differently. You never were like a candle flame flickering in the wind, but your profession became your calling and grounded you, giving you a definite purpose in life—changing your people's lives for the better. You became a strong and solid pillar of strength to the nation, and posthumously, you are even the mightiest baobab tree. We are branches and leaves fluttering in your afterlife to realize what you truly stood for—an assignment and task we uphold with resolute pride and a deep sense of sadness as we send you. Fare thee well, dearest Mama. Adieu, Mama.

Epilogue

ACCENTUATE THE POSITIVE

Building a new nation the above oration also reflects "the burial of apartheid" and necessitates a need to wear new spectacles of accentuating positive perceptions by identifying similarities among a once divided people and downplaying their differences. This means we need to accentuate what is good in one another and downplay the negatives to change attitudes, stereotypes, and prejudices. Pride and prejudice are central to the South African's problems, and we need to melt both pride and prejudice to remake ourselves.

Gaining new perceptions simply requires finding new ways of looking at one another. Vicky Momberg's prejudices have earned her a three-year stretch in prison, with one year suspended, which in our post-1994 era of judicial discipline is a first, and a lesson to all of us.

The incident and case tell how deeply etched racial prejudice is in the minds of some of our people—and their hearts as well. Vicky vocalized what many say in their hearts and minds, and this stands against the vein of accentuating the positive.

To be able to develop this mindset, positive thinking must dig out our mental negatives and expose their roots to the scorching sun. We must loose positive purity from the heart, the seat of all emotions. Our minds must be reflected in our behaviour, and our utterances must be truly what we feel rather than keeping our negative utterances to ourselves.

Perceptions such as these will help us become a new nation with a new ideology.

I once said "*je taime*" to one lady in a group of French tourists en route from Durban to Lesotho via Qwaqwa who were genuinely consumed by the beauty of the amphitheatre (which is a must-see, like the Garden Route across the two Capes). Her reaction was a heartfelt smile. I could see the positive reaction from the depths of the lady's heart. She was quite a beauty, and I will never know whether she was reacting to true feelings of affection, because I was only demonstrating my limited knowledge of French to her when the rest of her party were listening.

To the uninitiated, "je taime" means "I love you", and having said this, following the lady's reaction, I could see the effects of accentuating the positive. The lady saw me for what I am—human—from the depths of her mind, with no obvious prejudicial reactions. Now, one might wonder how a woman like Vicky Momberg would have reacted to such a statement from a native African male! She could have torn me apart, repeating Anna Steenkamp's prejudices, attitudes, and stereotypes in no uncertain terms!

When we look at positives, we make people feel made. Histography has this effect. The making of a nation makes a nation feel made by this accentuation. The opposite of this would be the destruction of a nation which obviously injects a negative feeling of destruction, thus making a nation feel destroyed. History well served makes a nation and builds it, no matter how bitter its political developments have been.

That is why we need a nurturing, building historiography written by postapartheid academics to remake our people and our country.

NATION-BUILDING PERCEPTIONS FOR A NEW NATION

Each one of the seven words above, like those on the cross, is aimed at encouraging positives and derailing us from condemning one another. They are words that induce us to find it in our hearts to influence positive change. Instead of condemning Vicky, for example, we should positively use the experience as a lesson to not let the incident replay itself.

Music remains human food for thought, and it is song that accentuates the positive. We should be induced into liking to look at the bright side of life and accentuating it. In our interactions, we should focus on a positive assessment of one another as human beings until that assessment is proven otherwise. Even after the initial disappointment, we should hope for a change, because man is amenable to change.

Accentuating the positive side of a human being and human nature is a risky shift, because people are by nature more guarded towards the self than towards togetherness. A study of human nature through the social sciences reveals personality as being egocentric, but in a sociological setting this self includes others selves. It thus becomes imperative for a person to view himself and his existence in the light of others. When a self is within other selves, it becomes necessary to undergo an introspective self-analysis of that self within other selves.

This is when accentuating positives becomes necessary, primarily to avoid uncalled for and unnecessary conflicts. One is more likely to maintain sound human relations with others if he has a positive image of others. Negatives will always be there; after all, we are human. But these should, however, be guarded over and controlled.

We need songs of joy that keep us in contact with love and spiritual reawakening to accentuate our positives and downplay negatives. We need songs that preach understanding and peace. Looking at history-makers like Nelson Mandela and Alan Paton, in the accentuation of the positive, one readily understands how easily they practised the sermon of forgiveness and reconciliation. Nelson even overlooked Mahatma Gandhi's one-sided political strife and struggle in South Africa and accentuated his positive side. He marvelled at his rich statements as we do, including statements like "The world has enough for us all, but not enough for human greed" and many others.

Mandela has left us quite a rich anthology of his own statements, which we seem to forget immediately after uttering, thus giving credence to the notion that man's folly is to be excited by the views of great men and women, whose magnitude they lose sight of as ordinary mortals. Men, and even women, with Nelson's qualities are iconic because they fully understand human nature. Their stoicism accentuates their positive assessment of others, and that is what makes them leaders like Mother Theresa.

For us to live together in harmony intra-culturally and cross-culturally, we need in our diversity to cross-pollinate the positive aspects of our own cultures to breed the poetic Archbishop Emeritus Desmond Mpilo Tutu's rainbow nation and, like colours of the rainbow, harmonize South Africa through song, the arts, and sports to impact positively on world politics. It is this that rehabilitates economies, basically because it is people who drive the economy, and they need to be harmonized like the chords of a jazz song for a smooth transition aimed at making a sustainable economy work. Our harmony as a people will harmonize economic development. The Tower of Babel was abandoned because men became lingually deharmonized. This shows that racism disharmonizes us, and this affects economic development. We can avoid this by tenaciously clinging to racial harmony by accentuating interracial positives, and this starts with forgiveness and then reconciliation.

Practise right now how to forgive whoever wronged you in the past, and prepare yourself to greet them when you meet them, keeping in mind that a sour heart wrinkles the face and wraps one in regrets and hatred. A sour heart carries a baggage that makes one bitter and forever consumed by hatred.

Accentuating and highlighting human positivity is an art of forgiveness and reconciliation. It is the first step towards a brighter, happier life, which will have a positive influence on our current generations, helping them to carry the legacy forward towards a brighter future.

At the time of this writing, two women's (one African the other Afrikaner) natural natures are in our media. On the eve of the passing of Winifred "Winnie" Nomzamo Madikizela-Mandela, Vicky Momberg hogged our media with rants about a past South Africans find themselves still entrenched in twenty-four years after apartheid. Vicky's racial slurs and rants brought to mind the historical Afrikaner woman Anna Steenkamp, whose views during the eve of the Great Trek reflected the spirit of her times, which encouraged "die kreun van osse wa" (the strained sounds of ox wagons), which was the mode of transportation of the times. This was the 1834 Great Trek.

Anna Steenkamp's well-known statement "Were these people not meant to serve us?" refers to blacks the British were freeing from slavery, whose owners wanted to collect compensation from England. Piet Retief's manifesto published the causes of this trek in the *Grahamstown Journal* in

1836, which in our matric we recited from memory as "We complain of the unjustifiable ordinance that has been cast upon us by interested and dishonest persons whose testimony is believed in London. We are resolved to uphold the just principles of liberty and to maintain proper relations between master and servant." This was the pride of our matriculation times in our history classroom. Little did we know we were celebrating our oppression.

Anna Steenkamp expressed Afrikaners' views of the times, which made nonsense of the views of the then prevailing philanthropic spirit of benevolence and human liberation, declaring slavery a barbaric practice.

Slavery cannot be justified even now, and neither can the views of a woman who believes in white supremacy in our times. Momberg, after a period of twenty-three years, which removed a system that both locals and the world condemned as a pariah and an international polecat, dared the courts. She justified her racism against officers of the law who sought to come to her rescue.

She insubordinately drew a line between black and white with the most arrogant and defiant belief in white supremacy she could muster. No sensible person could breathe a word of advice to her, not even her attorney, to show remorse, and she went on to win the first sentence of crimen injuria in our time—a three-year stretch in prison, with one year suspended for the use of a derogatory denigrating word.

She called to mind Anna Steenkamp's piercing words of 1834, 184 years ago, in 2018! She made her shocking utterances at a time when our police system has been revolutionized from a force to a service to the people of South Africa—a service to help rather than enforce the laws of the land, which apartheid South Africa did, envying what the Gestapo had been able to do to the Jews.

Vicky Momberg became an instant insult to present-day South Africa, and all media denigrated her distasteful words, which were satiated with racial venom and hatred. This negative should serve to draw races together.

In the time of her racial slurs against South Africans, on a gloomy Monday, we were struck by the chilling breaking news of Winnie Madikizela-Mandela's passing.

Here were two women: one who had seen the bad side of apartheid South Africa but had formed the ideology of appreciating her fellow

South African, whose recital regarding a dead past nauseated members of the public of all hues. And yet, even though Momberg's words seem to sound irrational and lack frankness, we should accentuate the positive flip side of such mishaps and see in them a period of reawakening—a renaissance necessitating forgiveness and reconciliation. These opposing forces, represented by two vastly different women, should be expunged to produce a new positive-minded society. The lessons therefrom derived should show us just how much we need one another as South Africans.

Our history, like all others, is a story of cause and effect, and as the saying goes, everything happens for a reason. That so callous a statement was uttered on the eve of the Mother of the Nation's death, after the formation of the Truth and Reconciliation Commission—chaired by a man of the cloth, Archbishop Emeritus Desmond Tutu, a Nobel Peace Prize laureate—shows the challenging task lying ahead of us. His statement "They (Afrikaners) are a God fearing nation" stayed with me and found a permanent place in my heart, and nothing will pluck it out, because this could be the beginning of the wisdom that will save and serve South Africa.

This is how we should read the accentuation of the positive, and we should see in it negatives that can be turned into positives with strengths to bring South Africans together. Everything happens for a reason, even unfortunate incidents like Vicky's, and this could be one of the reasons that this happened—to reconcile a people through forgiveness and glue them together as one nation.

What induces reconciliation is the coherence of the media in condemning Vicky Momberg's utterances and also a coherence of the expressions of sorrow, ambivalence, and empathy with the Madikizela and Mandela families, their clans, Amampondo and Abathembu respectively, and their children, grandchildren, and great-grandchildren.

South Africans' togetherness brings to mind the passing of an English Princess, Princess Diana. Buckingham Palace became piled high with flowers as the English expressed their sorrow and condolences with the Royal Family in a melancholic rendition of "Candle in the Wind." This occurred during a time when the hunter (Diana) had been turned into the hunted, which the paparazzi flew after with powerful telephoto lenses, to take even the most private of pictures to sell to the world media in exchange for the breath of life called earning a living.

It was indeed the worst of times, as it was the saddest moment in South African history when an icon died at a time when we were licking wounds inflicted by a negative utterance by an unrepentant racist in the person of Vicky Momberg. She was being frank, candid, and honest, as Mama Winnie was in her stance against a vile, vicious system that came between people—a system that brutalized a mother when it ripped her from her young children for stretches in prison while she was fighting a vile system.

Indeed, ours is a system we justifiably can refer to as one that is capable of taking a woman's milk for gall. The system ripped forgiveness out of her heart, and in her own words in 2010, she stated that the name, Mandela, is an albatross around the necks of her family. Winnie stated that Mandela was not the only man who suffered and that many others did, hundreds who languished in prisons and died. She referred to many unsung heroes of the struggle, and others in the leadership too, like Steve Biko who died of the beatings, horribly alone. She states that Mandela did go to prison, and he went in there as a burning young revolutionary but came out meek and humble. Winnie stated that she could not forgive Mandela for accepting the Nobel (Peace Prize in 1993) with his jailer F.W. De Klerk and thus either intentionally or unwisely missed this as a diplomatic statesmanlike way of harmonising reconciliation among South Africans. Winnie Mandela's bitterness echoed in her words when she said that: Hand in hand they went. Do you think De Klerk released him from the goodness of his heart? He had to. The times dictated it, the world had changed.

We know that the acceptance of the prize was diplomatically aimed at healing a politically bruised divided nation, and that it was done without justifying or compromising the people's economic freedom. At the the time political freedom was key and now yes, economic freedom is nigh. However, this should be done wisely without compromising food production by expropriating land without compensation as Zimbabwe did and now regretting it. This would be most unwise and actually expropriation itself is an unadviseable path or route to walk to address economic freedom.

Momberg's self-imposed imprisonment calls to mind Winnie's imposed one, in which it can be said that her motherly milk was taken from her mammary glands and replaced with gall. Yes, the evil spirits Lady Macbeth prayed to "unsexed" her and made her a man in maternal dress and form.

It is in such events and happenings that we should accentuate the positives and keep soldiering on courageously. Yes, some are bitter, but then it is this bitterness that must be sweetened and positively accentuated to remake a people.

When Giuseppe Garibaldi took over the reins of military leadership in a divided Italy under Cammilo de Cavour's diplomatic leadership, he frankly told his soldiers when leading them to wars of unification that he had nothing to offer them but blood, toil, and suffering, after which he took home only a sack of wheat after unifying his beloved Italy. This is reminiscent of J. F. Kennedy's patriotic statement "Ask not what your country can do for you, but ask what you can do for your country." This, in my view, is accentuating the positive and overlooking the negative, with a view to remaking South Africa—a country whose past is murky with the waters of racism.

We must find it in our hearts to understand how a woman could be hardened as Winnie was.

We should enter our souls and consciences and find it in our hearts not to be judgmental and conclude that as a society, we failed her, and that we may not understand why she became, as Dr Nkosazana Dlamini-Zuma described her, "ungovernable."

Even Nelson Mandela, as a man by birth and by tradition, may have failed to really understand why she could no longer share a bedroom with him while he was still awake after the day he walked out of prison. He may have failed to accept that during the twenty-seven years of his forced absence, she became mother and father and could not submit to the role of motherhood and wifehood. She had been used to playing the roles of matriarch and patriarch.

Secondly, if we replay the tape, we shall see that at one point she flew in the Ghanaian presidential plane during the administration of Flight Lieutenant Rawlings, who was a pan-Africanist—which Winnie became over the years. This is something that Nelson Mandela lost, and maybe never had, as he did not see eye-to-eye with Robert Sobukwe, the renowned pan-Africanist in heart and spirit.

Implanted in her heart was a deep-seated pan-Africanism she could not compromise on, but Nelson compromised in the name of reconciliation. Yet, in truth, pan-Africanism simply would not work in a diverse country such as ours, beloved Mzantsi—South Africa. We wanted it, because I know I wanted it and hoped it would work, but we were and are still too diverse to pursue pan-Africanism. Pragmatists like Nelson could see that as much as it was an ideology based on nationalism, nationalism as a broad concept could be pursued from another angle that respects cultural diversity—especially one planted and nurtured by apartheid policies. Our races were too far apart to be pan-Africanists, and they still are.

Nelson's inability to pass Winnie's scrutiny and his one-sided reconciliation estranged her from him. They were worlds apart because the Nelson Mandela that came out of prison was no longer the same Nelson Mandela that went into prison. He had changed dramatically.

This put Nelson and Winnie on ideologically opposed sides, and therefore at political loggerheads, because the apartheid system had brutalized her, plucking out even the barest seeds of reconciliation from her heart.

Yes, she sought reconciliation, but she did so on her own terms with her calling the shots. She had become used to that kind of life and felt her political soul mate gone in Nelson Mandela. He no longer was a "black man in a white court." To Winnie, Mandela had let black South Africans down by accepting bad deals for them in the negotiations, which are historically recorded as talks.

But did this bad deal for blacks emanate from these talks, or did they come about long before he left his prison home? This begs for answers, but we will never know. The man suffered years of apartheid imprisonment suffocation and sought a breath of fresh air out of prison cells, yet his intransigence for an unconditional release to pursue the struggle for freedom is well documented.

That they would separate and ultimately end their romance stood in the logic of history. But even their divorce should be seen from a perspective that accentuates the positive—this being that everything that happens, happens for a reason.

This allows us to look at ourselves and see what happens to a woman when she is treated like a man. This must help to educate today's men to be their partners' soul mates and to be protective rather than abusive. Not that Winnie's husband abused her. No, she was abused by men in a system that sought to keep her silent, only to succeed in making her even more resolute and perhaps even brutal in her stance.

Our societies have become breeding grounds for such women through various methods of brutal emotional and physical abuse, and the slogan "Wa thinth 'abafazi, wa thinth 'imbogodo" (You strike a woman, you strike a rock) should not be taken lightly when looking at what the system of apartheid did to scar Winnie's mind and womanhood. The apartheid "*imbhokotho*" struck her too many times, and she developed a thick skin and a rock for a heart. Nothing could change that—not even her husband's freedom. President Thabo Mbeki failed to see and understand that, hence their live television spat. Many found it hard to forgive him, and they must find it in their hearts to forgive him, because those were tightrope-walking times!

Winnie, as she is affectionately known, became a human rock of ages to many a South African woman. She has become a rock of ages for the South African people; in the cleft of that rock many can hide to wait and prepare for the hereafter.

In her struggles, Winnie also spoke openly against patriarchy, which she described as keeping women in a state of subjugation. "The overwhelming majority of women accept patriarchy unquestioningly … and even protect it, working out the resultant frustrations not against men but against themselves in their competition for men as sons, lovers, and husbands. Traditionally, the violated wife bides her time and off-loads her built-in aggression on her daughter-in-law. So men dominate women through the agency of women themselves."

This statement reveals her own built-in frustrations and makes clear that manhood had solidified inside her during the many years in which she mothered and "fathered" her homestead. Yet her feminine beauty, natural and cosmetic, made her a woman still, and she was expected by society to do her husband's bidding. But she could not. Apartheid had made her man and woman in one body.

Her ethereal natural youthful beauty captured in still photographs resonated in her elderly years, causing us to recall that before the system of apartheid treated her poorly, beauty resonated from deep within her soul and spiralled out for all to see.

The nation realizes that it is Winnie who made Nelson Mandela the icon that he became. Her black-and-white pictures taken by professionals make modern coloured pictures a mockery of professional photography. They simply defy the word "beauty"! They perhaps best explain the most beautiful diamond ever dug out of South Africa, christened "the Star of Africa". She indeed was one.

Her beauty also found expression in making her profession, social work, a calling in a country of social contrasts defined by extremes of poverty, just as her husband made his law profession a calling when he advised his coaccused to put apartheid on trial at Revonia—a black man in a white court! When we accentuate the positives in our history, we are not poets that see beauty where there is none, but in our minds' construction, we simply seek that hidden quality of beauty that makes a people a people.

Overt beauty we appreciate, but covert beauty, the beauty you seek before seeing it first-hand at a glance, we even appreciate more. Her covert beauty found expression in her ebony skin and in her looks, but she was courted by controversy at almost every turn.

Pouring out a tribute from the heart, a close friend to Winnie related that they met during the most turbulent and violent times in South Africa's history. It was in 1990, and although Mandela had been released from prison and exiles were returning in large numbers, no one knew what the future held.

Her visits to Mandela on Roben Island, when they were not allowed to hug or touch, were most painful. These were the trials that really built rather than broke her character. She had to sacrifice her family, and she experienced the worst things. That is why she was so fearless. She understood the need for reconciliation.

She understood that once the apartheid state and its system were destroyed, the highest challenge would have been dealt with. She had a good sense of self-reflection and her own environment. She had wonderful ideas about South Africa's future and helped lay a solid foundation for its democracy.

The Bill of Rights was crafted to prevent the kinds of human rights abuses that Winnie went through, such as detention without trial and solitary confinement. And our constitution is built on the tears of women who wept for their children, the blood of those who paid the ultimate price, and the sweat of the women and men who laboured for freedom for future generations.

Winnie was demonized during and after the struggle as part of a character assassination that was started by the apartheid regime. It became clear that it was a deliberate effort to discredit her because she had a big following, and the aim was to discourage her supporters. But before her death, she became optimistic about her country's future, and there are very encouraging signs that the next phase of building South Africa has begun.

Her memory and sacrifices can be honoured by our ensuring that we improve on the South Africa that we are entrusted with. In 2010 she described herself and her destiny when she said she was the product of the masses of her country and the product of her enemies and that she was courted by controversy at every turn. Driven by forces against her, she defiantly made inflammatory statements that encouraged brutal violence. She said that the people would liberate South Africa with their matches and necklaces, referring to the live torching of controversial councillors in Soweto and those considered to be sellouts to the liberation cause. They would have tyres put round their necks, be doused with petrol, and be set alight with matches in a lethal blaze. In 1987 she stated that the years of imprisonment had hardened her. She said that if one is given a moment to hold back, waiting for the next blow, his or her emotions would not be blunted. When it happens every day of one's life—that is, when pain becomes a way of life—one no longer has the emotion of fear; there is no longer anything one can fear. In Winnie's case, there was no pain the government had not inflicted on her.

But it was the 1960s that set the foundation for what was to become a defiant Winnie Madikizela-Mandela in later years, and she defied the system that confined her husband to an island, hoping he would be forgotten. But the harder they tried to silence him, the louder she would become. She refused to allow the selfless efforts of her husband and his friends to be abandoned. She continued struggling for a free and equal South Africa.

In 1976, encouraging the riots that were ravaging the townships, Winnie became vocal: "It is only when all black groups join hands and speak with one voice that we shall be a bargaining force which will decide our destiny." In closing she said that to free oneself, one has to break the chains of oppression. Only then can one express one's dignity, and only when we have liberated ourselves can we cooperate with other groups. Any acceptance of humiliation, indignity, or insult is acceptance of inferiority.

Clearly, Winnie's inspiring and encouraging expressions of faith in the struggle endeared her to the masses, and there is no doubt that her 1960s defiance had the support of the nation and freedom fighters in prison and armed struggle in exile.

As *aluta continua* gained momentum and strength in the 1950s and the 1970s to the mid-1980s, so did the government's resistance against all efforts until 1989, when government resistance felt the strain of economic sanctions. This triggered clandestine negotiations behind prison walls that were not in accord with developments outside prison walls.

Nelson Mandela had become the target of government negotiations to ease the pressure of economic sanctions and cultural boycotts against apartheid. Something had to give on one of the opposing sides, and apparently the suspension of the armed struggle without a broad-based consultation displeased some leaders—especially those who were at the heart and forefront of the armed struggle, who bore the brunt of the battle against apartheid like Chris Hani who was Winnie Madhikizela-Mandela's political soulmate.

But they had to show discipline as soldiers and take heed of diplomatic interventions by leaders such as Nelson Mandela and Oliver Tambo. A dream for freedom after years of strife manifested itself, and compromises had to be made. Such compromises continue to be made to rebuild South Africa and make her a beacon of internal and international hope. Many in Europe love the Southern African sunshine, as I learnt from one English lady, who said that people count the number of times they see the sun in a year in London. Such women want to invest in our country, and our reconciliation and politics of conciliation will encourage that, allowing us to give all our youth jobs to better their lives and build the ideal future they dare to dream about.

While some wanted total freedom and a positive dream for a future from the sufferings and sacrifices of women like Rosa Parks and Winnie Mdikizela-Mandela, they can make women like these their pillows and realize their lives' ambitions.

Dr Martin Luther King Jr. had such a dream—a positive dream that became reality thanks to the experiences of a woman like Winnie named Rosa Parks, an American activist whom the US Congress christened "the first lady of civil rights" and "the mother of the freedom movement", who defied a bus driver in refusing to relinquish her seat for a white passenger in a segregated bus on 1 December 1955. This led to the Montgomery bus boycott, which lasted over a year. She was born in 1913 and died in 2005 at ninety-two, but her spirit lives on. Such people never die, because what they stood for keeps them in human memory; they fight for ideals that live on.

Minor though it was, this 1955 incident was to incite civil unrest that would torpedo white domination in the United States. This was to be accentuated by film actors in an educative form of passive resistance through the arts. Dr Luther's great sermon is necessary reading to inspire our youth to accentuate the positive and sing songs that help them to hold on to their dreams and believe in them.

We held on to our dreams, dim though they were. They twinkled like a little star in the dungeons of a dark despair, growing brighter and brighter over the years to become a shining bright reality. But then they were dimmed by economic ruin, unemployment, poverty, and crime escalation as our trauma tremored through every fabric of society. We refuse to listen to reason and denounce corruption.

But still we dream, and still we rise from the ashes of despair to make the worst of times the best of times by seeking a common interracial thread of brotherhood and sisterhood.

Dr Martin Luther King Jr.'s dream generates feelings of hope that a new nation can be born from positive writing. He gave this speech years ago, and it planted a hope that today is a reality. We cannot wait for it to happen but must work towards it! Americans did until an African American man, woman, and their two daughters occupied the White House over two terms. The closing lines of King's great sermon inspire such hope:

> My country 'tis of thee, sweet land of liberty, of thee I sing.
> Land where my fathers died, land of the Pilgrim's pride,
>
> from every mountainside, let freedom ring!

> And when this happens, and when we allow freedom ring,
> when we let it ring from every village and every hamlet,

from every state and every city, we will be able to speed up that day when all of God's children, black men and white men, Jews and Gentiles, Protestants and Catholics, will be able to join hands and sing in the words of the old Negro spiritual":

Free at last! Free at last! Thank God Almighty, we are free at last!

Yes, thank God Almighty, we are free at last! Free from perceptions of inferiority and superiority, and on to perceptions of human equality. Free from the dungeons of racial superiority, and on to perceptions of racial equality. Free from perceptions of racial demographic zoning, and on to interracial demographic zoning. Free from perceptions of male superiority and female inferiority, but all liberated in gender equality and equal abilities.

PRAYER CHANGES THINGS

Prayer: Thank You, Lord

Thank you, Lord, for the beauty of my mind. Without you I could have been an empty vessel. Without you my sun could have long set. But you keep me from falling. You grace the dungeons of my life with your mighty physical presence, which I feel even in sleep! You taught me to protect my enemy. You hold from me my enemy's hand. You have set my mind to great things without malice, without hatred, without revenge, and without jealousy!

Thank you, Lord, for my eyes, the beauty of my mind.

Thank you, Lord, for the use of my limbs and the use of my senses.

Thank you, Lord, for the genuine love you implanted in my heart, which allows me to do well when man does badly

I fear and respect your mighty hand. Make me abhor violence, but use my discretion wisely when faced with a situation. Let the power of negotiation reign supreme in my mind. I should exhaust my head and my tongue before lifting my hand in self-defence. Even then, help me remember always the sixth commandment.

The teaching profession, no doubt, is the centre of human production. Unfortunately, as we are involved in the production process, we have products and by-products. Products are those learners we shape and who are amenable to the production process. This process is triangular and involves the teacher, the learner, and the subject matter. As we together work, our team is incomplete without the parent. Parents are the biological catalyst of the teaching process, as they are the teacher's helper in his or her in loco parentis status. The community also plays a prominent role in this process by being the teachers' and the parents' eyes when neither is there. Our product, the learner, is a future adult citizen of our country for whom the product is prepared.

As a future citizen, the learner will play the role that we are playing as a productive utilitarian citizen. Experience has taught me that as we guide the learner, we shape the learner in various roles, especially presently in our dynamic society. Its dynamism is determined by an environment without negative attitudes, stereotypes, and prejudices in all their various forms. The learner must grow into a God-fearing individual, which is the essence of wisdom. To be able to grow in this way, the learner must be orientated towards life after school and be guided towards a career that will shape citizenship and parental roles. Importantly, the learner must be conscious of the fact that a career is where one spends most of one's precious time. For this reason, it must be the right career choice determined by our psychological being to derive what we want most in life—happiness!

This refers to choosing the right career for a personality type. For example, the love for children is a prerequisite for a career in teaching and for any career in which the person is likely to be with children most of the time. That is a key requirement. Career development is a central continuous process in a person's lifespan, and it requires career choice and adjustment to that career.

Career choice can start at lower school levels and develop throughout a person's lifespan. Career burnout is possible in a person's lifespan and needs to be monitored through a variety of practices via formal and informal research. A teacher using the same methods of teaching throughout a practical career lifespan is likely to suffer burnout. Such a person cannot boast of twenty years' teaching experience if his approach to teaching does not vary and is the same year in and year out.

This means that a teacher and the school a learner attends must be creative, especially in keeping mentally gifted children interested in the learning process. In one grade-twelve class history class, I had three such learners. The prescribed school history handbook could not keep them concentrating. A quick think resulted in my visiting the local university library and registering, at personal cost, to be able to borrow five books at a time. I would then borrow three books on the same subject by various authors and give them to the trio, asking them to circulate them among themselves whilst I focused on the average slow learners. The results at the end of the year were startling! Those three students received Bs, and 100 per cent of the class passed with no grade being lower than a D.

A loving, caring teacher can inspire hope in a class of learners who conceive of themselves as developmentally disabled as they have been made to believe that they are. A resolved teacher can turn the learners around and teach them that they were capable of success like any other learners at any school. Such learners can be amenable to change and respond positively. All it takes is an ability to inspire and an ability to be inspired.

What a teacher tells learners comes to pass. A teacher can become a learner's friend or be a learner's worst enemy. In present-day South Africa, school and classroom management has completely changed. Our situation has become much like what a South African teacher experienced in the UK, where a parent came to school to reprimand a teacher in front of her class about disciplining a child. This was unheard of before 1994 but is prevalent in today's schools in the country.

Be that as it may, firmness of purpose is still necessary to train disciplined learners by disciplining them. It is not necessary to use physical punishment to discipline a learner. A practiced verbal treatment can turn a learner around! It is this that makes me admire the Vygotskian philosophy of educational psychology and the Piagetian philosophy as complements of each other. In the Vygotskian approach, we see the child as a social being, and in the Pigetian philosophy, a child is a biological being in a pychosocial setting. Vygotsky gives the social aspect of a child and explains how to deal with it, because in his view, a child is a social being and socialisation processes are realizable in child teaching and minding.

Today's teacher therefore needs a strong daily prayer to maintain sanity when dealing with children. Prayer is a human creation. When out of ideas on how to pray, I simply pronounce The Lord's Prayer as taught by St Matthew and St Luke. Following is a prayer I created that has seen me through my teaching career even before I formally wrote it in 1989. I came to realize that the expressions in the prayer I wrote are exactly how I dealt with my classes. I never cease to be amazed by this prayer's power in shaping my ability to understand children. My second school principal even appointed me as a school psychologist and referred problematic children to me—something I relished doing.

SPIRITUALITY AND TEACHING

The teaching of children has to be based on traditional spiritual values, without which no utilitarian citizens can be produced. Teaching is a meaningful, deliberate activity whose aim is to mould. It is for this reason that this starts with a conscientizing prayer by the one involved in the teaching activity or process. Following this prayer, I will discuss the teaching of African children based on the Piagetian and Vygotskian (in that order) psychosocial educational theories.

The Teacher's Prayer

Dear Lord,

Grant me, Lord, the lion's ferocity in labour. Gant me, Lord, the patience of a vulture.

Grant me, Lord, the memory of an elephant.

Let me be aware of my shortcomings. Let me forgive but be alert all the time.

Help me be with my colleagues but not understand.

Help me learn from them as much as they learn from me.

Help me guide the educand towards self-reliance.

Bless me; do not make me vault in ambition.

Bless me; do not make me jealous of my colleagues.

Bless me; allow me to help those I can without malice.

Above all, let me always abide by thy commandments

So I can love my institution of learning

So I can be exemplary in deed and word.

Grant me David's and Solomon's wisdom, fused with the serpent's

In dealing with the child entrusted in my care.

As he enters my care, help me enrich him. As he is with me, help me build his self-image.

As he exits, add my efforts to build his self-esteem. Wherever he shall serve, help him be a spark of light.

Wherever he shall serve, instil a sense of pride in him. Help him be Socratic in method.

Help him be cooperative but assertive. Help him spread his motto. Help him spread science.

Let me give you a practical guidance situation involving a learner in one of my classes at one of my schools. The boy was always at school and never missed a day, yet he failed my monthly tests and other subjects' monthly tests, passing only in the class of his mother tongue, Sesotho. During one recess period at school, I summoned him to an empty classroom and began talking to him, asking him why he failed not only my monthly tests but other monthly tests as well, though he always was at school.

What came after a lengthy period of silence and thinking, which I allowed without rushing him, surprised me. First he cried inconsolably, and I let him spend himself as he drifted into sobs. We had thirty minutes at our disposal. Then he started talking. He had a domestic problem of parental abuse in which the abused party was his mother, because of paternal alcohol abuse. Having listened to him relate the sad story, I asked him one question: "Do you want to add to your mother's misery by failing at the end of the year?" We left it at that, and he went to sit out the remaining few minutes of the school break.

He was in grade twelve (standard ten then). The next month, while marking tests, I missed his book because all learners had passed that month! I went back to look for his book and found that he had passed. My history essay marking was done in three categories: facts (60), language, (20) and insight (20)—total 100. He had got a healthy 65 per cent, and at the end of the year, he passed in all other subjects and got certified for university entrance!

The other one was a mentally gifted boy who today is one of our local millionaires. He came from a very poor background and was in the natural sciences. During recess I conversed with him on what his post–grade twelve (then standard ten) plans were, and he said he was going to study towards a teaching profession. I impressed on him that he would not make a good teacher because he would not understand why a learner fails to understand a simple mathematics or physics problem. He told me he had no choice because his home was church mouse poor. I proceeded to give him addresses for Fort Hare University and its bursar, which had helped me through my studies as well. He was admitted, and he sailed through his bachelor of science in mathematics and physics and got a bursary to study in England, where he completed his master's degree in mathematics. He is a Cambridge University Mathematics master's graduate.

By then I had forgotten about him. Years later I met him in a church service at a local college of education. It was, of course, a Sunday, and I asked him what he had done, and he related all that I had already related above. I felt a deep sense of gratification. I then asked him what he was doing, and he told me he was a lecturer at our local university. I laughed and asked him how he was doing, and he poured out his frustrations about teaching. Reminding him about what I had told him years ago, I advised him to register for an MBA degree in financial management. He again sailed through his courses and received an MBA in business management, and he left teaching and got a job in Johannesburg. Today he is a successful self-employed businessman in the millionaire bracket.

This proves that teaching, of all professions, is a calling!

One writer dedicated his book on education and development in Africa "to the teachers in Africa in sympathy and faith." It is not difficult to guess that he did so because African teachers are faced with several challenges. A Ghanaian doctor friend once told me that during his medical school training in Ghana, his mentor told them he was going to train them such that they could become an expensive instrument the medical school did not have and could not afford. This is the problem many a teacher in Africa is faced with—especially in laboratories. They are expected to perform miracles. What is left is to be expected to carry learners across flooded rivers to and from school because municipal finances do not go into municipal budgets to build footbridges between villages and schools. It is this that earns us the sympathy of admirers of our thankless profession in African schools.

What drives African teachers, I believe are our school mottoes. The one below, religious in nature, is my Fort Hare University alma mater's motto, which has become part of my DNA.

"IN LUMINE TUO VIDEBIMUS LUMEN – IN THY LIGHT SHALL WE SEE LIGHT"

School mottoes are small statements that contain big lessons. Do not take them lightly. One in particular taught me a lot in a local district school (Retief Hoer Skool [High School] in Kestel, Thabo Mofutsanyana

District, Free State Province, South Africa) when I was already a teacher: "Oorwen Jou Self En Wen!" (Defeat yourself and win!).

I once received a very misleading social media message that said, "Christianity left Israel as a family, came to Rome as a religion, went to England as politics and ended up in Africa as a business." If this makes sense, Dr David Livingstone (the modern St. Luke) must have been a very lousy businessman. The truth is that there is a power above man; enquiring as to how that power came to be is not the point. The point is, and this is a blessing, realizing that it came at all. Dr David Livingstone's heart lies buried in Zambia. My heart and soul are there with his heart, for his transmitting Christianity to Africa. Like pollen transmitted by bees, it was transmitted from England and distributed throughout Africa as an agent of political and sociopolitical change.

Archbishop Desmond Mpilo Tutu, Nobel Prize laureate, saw Afrikaners as a God-fearing people. An analytic assessment of Potcheftroom University, former president F. W. De Klerk's alma mater, shows that it is based on *Kristelike Hoer Onderwys* (Christian higher education). This makes Christianity the healing clinic and the very rock of human transformation. This is our common identity for our common destiny, and it can sustain every South African and help him find and redefine his wandering, beaten-up soul for a spiritual dressing and healing.

Mahatma Gandhi's assertions are eye-opening and mind-blowing. He once stated that the world has enough for all, but its insufficiency is satisfying human greed. This must remind us that we came naked into this world with nothing, and yonder shall we depart, still with nothing! This should guide us away from earthly desires and prompt us to seek divine desires, whose bedrock is forgiveness and reconciliation.

The inability to forgive burdens the nonforgiver with baggage, and forgiving relieves one of baggage, allowing one to live a fulfilling life. This calls to mind the sinner who found Paradise at the last minute on Calvary while dangling on the cross. Emulate him to find your wandering lost soul, and find it in your heart to let bygones be and turn over a new page in life.

Pardon me; I did not mean to preach. I merely wanted to make a point.

THE EDUCATION OF AFRICAN CHILDREN

Nelson Mandela (1918–2013)

His legacy to all children is that

education is the future!

Education is a formal and informal process aimed at grooming the young for future adult roles as responsible citizens. African adults should therefore conceive of involvement in the grooming of African children by starting communal projects to address common challenges. Crime is a communal challenge that should be addressed by citizens with government support through relevant departments, especially the Social Development Department. Poverty affects every aspect of life, especially for children. African traditional belief holds that it takes a community to raise a child. This by implication challenges parents to think of organizations with a defined community development purpose, such as the Qwaqwa Jazz Moods Club (QJMC), whose defined purpose is showing that jazz is spiritual—and so is their mission's Thuto - Lesedi La Setjhaba (Education – the light of the community) Communal Project, which addresses teenage pregnancy and related youth challenges. Interventions are creating Youth against Crime communal groups, identifying youth skills, encouraging income generation, and supporting sports, chess, and fundraising to "walk children towards education."

> Jazz arists call jazz a "noble sound." We invite ladies and gentlemen of this "noble art form" to form part of the core membership of Qwaqwa Jazz Moods Club. Sounding a mournful horn in memory of jazz greats' untimely passing, we mourn losing our children to substance abuse. Our children walk to school barefooted in winter. We invite you to adopt a needy child with a pair of shoes to walk them towards 'Thuto - Lesedi La Setjhaba' (Education – Light of the Nation). This invitation for membership in our Jazz Club requests you to keep children at school. Traditionally we are communal. These are our children. Join us in empathy. Like Joseph from Arimathea, who jumps into action asking for Jesus' body, we implore you to jump into action. The disciples loved Jesus but after His crucifixion they go back to their old ways – but Joseph asks for Jesus' body …

> *Join us in m*ainstream and related jazz appreciation. Call 064 525 6807 OR send an email to: qqjazzmoodsclub@ gmail.com for membership information.

> *On this note we invite membership for QJMC jazz appreciation:* Mainstream; Fusion; Acid, Afro & Popular-Jazz. Age groups 30 years+. For inquiries, please call MB 'Oupa' Seitisho: 064 525 6807. Also write to qqjazzmoods@gmail.com for membership information.

The education of African children should not only be a family responsibility, but a communal responsibility, and organizations like the one above must mushroom to address drug abuse and crime prevention, and to assist children to be career oriented. We must accompany our children to adulthood in every way conceivable in participatory democratic practice.

To encourage communal involvement in educating children we now address the education of African children. Putting this in perspective, African children are not defined by pigmentation. All children born in Africa are African children and can serve their countries in any field—even government departments, Parliament, and the cabinet—by virtue of their birth. Take the example of former US president Barack Obama, whose presidency set this precedent. Let me digress a bit to highlight a point on the teaching of African children.

Barack Obama is an American of African parentage. His paternal progenitor originates from Kenya in Africa. By implication, children born in Africa by so-called foreign nationals can also be what Obama became to the United States of America.

The African National Congress fought racism for eighty-two years (1912–1994) while being racist against its own cadres. Gill Marcus, the first woman to be the governor of the Reserve Bank; Trevor Manuel, former minister of finance; Dr Frene Ginwala of Parsi-Indian origins of Western India, a journalist and a South African politician who became the speaker of the national assembly (1994–2004); and Ronnie Kasrils, an ANC cadre of impeccable character and also a member of the South African Communist Party Central Committee (1986–2007) and minister of intelligence (2004–2008) are all presidential material for the ANC and government. They are corruption free and are disciplined members of this respectable organization and movement. Despite their virtuous standing and credentials, they have never been considered for the presidency of the ANC by a leadership fighting racism. Trevor's name was once tossed around but was dumped because of his pigmentation. He was considered too light to be black. Does this make sense?

This digression is meant to address the teaching of African children, and without a doubt, the mentioned ANC cadres are self-taught children of Africa who, after winning the battle against racism, were subjected to racist analyses during the consideration of potential ANC presidents. They no doubt qualified in every area but their pigmentation. They were self-taught in the sense that they firmly stood against a racist ideology and that despite their pigmentation they were subjected to the same state of misrule their black counterparts were subjected to. Their humanity made them African through and through. How did this come about? A white Afrikaner woman once lived in Soweto, married to a Zulu policeman in the 1970s, and behaved in every way as African women do. These people saw themselves as Africans, implying that every child born in Africa can be taught and brought up the way African children are raised. Children born of foreign nationals lack African physical features but speak fluent African languages according to the areas they are born in. In Qwaqwa, a predominantly Sesotho-speaking area, they speak fluent Sesotho.

Cognitive development among African children should be a topic of academic interest, because as educational psychologist Mwamuenda advises, Africa is a dynamic part of the international community. It is through education that the continent can develop technologically and otherwise. Africans not only cling to their cultural heritage but also share an international heritage of knowledge. Piagetian theory with its inherent principles of science in all its forms, which African children should master to be in step with the rest of the civilized world, is relevant to their education. However, Vygotsky's theories are equally relevant in the socialization of all children, especially those born in Africa. African children are in need of the zone of proximal development (ZPD) for their socialization. Children all over the world need this, as it refers to children needing parental interactions in their processes of socialization. The ZPD is a level of development attained when children engage in social behaviour. Children in Africa need this most because their environment of socialization is more challenging than those of children elsewhere in the world.

In South African educational studies African children's educational budget is far less than that of children in the developed world Piaget is readily acceptable in. Their environment of socialization is rich. They have playgrounds, their streets are tarred, and their homes are paved and have lawns and trees. Their home environments also have television sets, radios, computers, and, lately, smartphones. Not many African homes have such luxuries for their children. On the contrary, their homes are full of stones, shrubs, and snake-infested forests. The luxuries mentioned are ZPDs that facilitate and support children undergoing socialization processes even in the absence of parents. The rich home environments are very relevant to Piagetian theory, whilst the scantily resourced African environments some children grow in suit Vygotsky's theory, which is based on the sociocultural theory of literacy acting as scaffolding in the learning of children. Whilst children of the developed world have toys that teach language and counting at an early age, very few African children have such luxuries and therefore require parental scaffolding most of the time.

A scaffold is a support structure used by workers for climbing in construction sites, and Vygotsky's theory sees adults as scaffold structures children climb on during learning. The African environment requires the presence of adults who act as scaffolding in the absence of the learning aid resources well-resourced children have as scaffolds.

When current Zimbabwean president Mnangangwa arrived in an expensive presidential jet in Europe recently, he was rebuked by international leaders because he left a volatile political situation back home. In the midst of the poverty he left behind, he was in a luxury jet, justifying why Zimbabweans saw his ousting of Robert Mugabe as the jockey having changed but the horse flogged being the same. The literal flogging of people protesting against a huge petrol price hike that accompanied the protests made this opinion even more poignant and tangible. Pictures shared on social media showed the baton-scarred bodies of Zimbabwean nationals, proving that democracy in Zimbabwe is no more than an impractical word.

African children should thus be taught the finer points of improvising (e.g. devising means of creating things that can help them learn even in laboratories requiring test tubes and microscopes). They have to see stomata in leaves with their naked eyes, because microscopes are a luxury few African schools can afford (but ministries of education have luxuries they do not really need). In South Africa, local municipality executive mayors in rural areas drive in Range Rovers whilst administering over areas with bad roads requiring 4×4 Land Rovers to reach areas for first-hand observation to be conversant with people's challenges. The neglect of roads also hampers job creation and education because school managers are either unable to reach these places or are able to do so only with much difficulty.

Because of its biological nature, Piagetian theory makes "conservation and concept formation" important aspects of learning and prepares a teacher-to-be for the task ahead. Fused with Vygotsky's theory of socialization, it prepares children for life after school. Both social and psychology theorists' views are instructive in shaping children's learning. Piaget perceives the child as a biological being, whilst Vygotsky's perception is more towards socialization processes. Vygotsky's theory sees children as social beings and their cognitive development as being led by social interactions, whilst Piaget sees children as more independent and their development as being guided by self-centred focused activities.

Piaget's view requires "independent" learning in concept formation; meaning it requires no scaffold. In Vygotsky's theory, on the other hand, learning is an interactive social activity that requires support structures (i.e. scaffolds) like parents in a teaching–learning environment. This makes parental involvement in education key, and many educationists have contributed instructive articles on this subject in accredited international journals. So to speak, Piaget's theory makes learning an individual cognitive activity in which the child can quantify something, such as by cognitively realizing that despite an object's shape, its volume can be the same as another object. Vygotsky bases his theory on sociocultural interactive processes or activities which are more African-environment-based than in the developed world.

The African child requires a learning environment that prepares him for a tough life ahead. His teaching should be like the training of a soldier to adjust to very cold environments because his mission requires him to adjust even in extremely hot environments. One soldier, on a particularly cold night, clad in a sleeveless shirt, told me that he was not feeling the cold because he had been trained not to dwell on such weather. So should the African child be taught. He must be taught to withstand extreme and very challenging life conditions. The African child's socialization to be educative must be reflected in the school curricula. Rural children are most likely to need agricultural training to master food security skills, and urban children's curricula should be more technological than agricultural. Vygotskian theory seems most likely to teach such endurance and survival skills, which should be, in essence, the focus of learning. During Shaka

Zulu's years, children were socialized to be physically fit and learn the art of surviving in a harsh environment, requiring military expertise.

The African education system must also inculcate a practical application of scientifically gained knowledge. Of interest is Rwanda's turnaround in central Africa after a civil war human memory will not forget. The cleanliness taught scientifically in schools in South Africa is seen in Rwandan streets. The Democratic Republic of the Congo also has a video that reflects the evolution of some African states towards cleanliness. One European tourist in Rwanda confesses that he could not throw a toothpick in a Kigali (the capital of Rwanda) street because of the cleanliness of its streets.

A French tourist once wrote in *New African Magazine* that "Africa is beautiful without Africans." And indeed, when looking at a map of Africa, one sees nothing but beauty. This beauty has to be practically turned into cleanliness by strictly applying by-laws. To do this, African children should biologically, through Piagetian theory, be socialized into cleanliness through Vygotskian theory. Socialization means training a child to learn to behave in a way that is socially acceptable. This means that officials holding public office must be virtuous men and women who lead lives that are exemplary to children. African children with African features are daily seen socializing with children born of foreign nationals with physical features clearly foreign to Africa that anthropometry clearly recognizes, and these children, brought up in African environments, can be future leaders in government departments, cabinets, and even, like Barack Obama, African heads of state. This is what Africa must take cognisance of and take note of, especially when looking at the Zambian deputy president today.

Africa therefore needs to use what we can refer to as Piagetian–Vygotskian theories of learning in making learning tangible in classrooms. Elkind and Flavell pose a very instructive question in a book they are editors of: "How does one honour a great man?" which they answer by saying "In the scientific community, it has long been recognised that perhaps the highest honour students can bestow upon their teacher is to continue the work he has begun."

Our African world view—our philosophy, so to speak—should change with the times, and we should practise what we preach. Such sermons must start in our classrooms, where we should socialize our children into seeing themselves for who they are—all African despite physical features that may be different.

This means that the books we choose, especially in the genre of literature, should be free of stereotypes, attitudes, and prejudices of a racial nature; instead they should promote human values bordering on cleanliness in all its forms. They must reflect humanity with its inborn human-nature weaknesses, with a view to discourage them. Such literature is contained in the creative works of one literary genius—William Shakespeare, whom Benson sees as not being of an era but of all times.

Think of any African literary genius. They all bear Shakespearean influences, and if the beautiful ones are to be born in Africa, African educationists must have an educational plan that will teach African children that they are one and that their education is preparing them for future roles they all have equal opportunities to play, if they put their minds to them. The South African struggle, as Nelson Mandela reiterated, was a struggle for equal opportunities; and if the views herein expressed do not reflect this notion, then they are not worth the paper written on. We have to move from a world of contrasts, in which the poor are extremely poor and the rich filthy rich, to a world of equal opportunities, in which an Afrikaner can be head of state and head of government business. This is what the struggle has been all about—not to replace racism with a new form of racism. And until that equality is attained, no country in Africa is a free country.

In conclusion, the socialization of African children should develop a work ethic as well as proficiency in sports and recreation. As far back as 1967, Dr Julius Nyerere conceived of a theory of "Education for self-reliance" ("Ujamaa" in Swahili), aimed at equipping learners with knowledge, skills, and attitudes for tackling societal problems and preparing youth for work in a predominantly agricultural society. Tanzania's mission is to enable learners to know, appreciate, and develop a culture of Tanzania. Its aim is to transmit knowledge and skills to encourage independence and self-reliance.

According to Tanzanians who are in South Africa, the Tanzanian education system, despite its well-defined aims, amongst other challenges, lacks teaching and learning materials, as well as in-service training. Dr

Nyerere, through this system of education, himself a former teacher, sought to encourage an enquiring mind and encourage learners to learn from what others do, reject or adapt what they learn to their own needs, and develop a basic confidence in their own positions as free and equal members of the society who values others and is valued by them for what they does. Analysing this education system may well be said to be like South Africa's apartheid education system, which inculcated self-reliance in the white education sector and dependence on whites for black education. However, whilst apartheid education for white self-reliance succeeded in producing self-reliant people, the Tanzanian system failed dismally, and the reason for this is what it lacked and what white education in South Africa had because of unequal educational budgets.

Africa has become a continent rife with beggars across all walks of life. This is a result of failing education systems. Upheavals in the Maghreb, specifically Tunisia, have parallels to South Africa, where challenges caused by the questionable character of leaders with audits failing the scrutiny of the auditor general, related bad governance, and a poor education system, among other things, will bring the government to its knees and force the ruling party out. The collapsing education system is affecting development and needs to be addressed as a matter of urgency!

This problem of failing to make education an important human development resource is prevalent today in postapartheid South Africa owing to poor planning. Whilst teachers are given in-service training, teaching and learning materials are a challenge. Secondly, in-service training is provided during times when teachers should be at school teaching, rather than during holidays with adequate compensation. The result is the passing of children who should repeat classes, resulting in them being unable to make it in grade twelve when nationally assessed. Thirdly, the South African education system is book-oriented, and the practical aspects of education curricula are downplayed, viz., gardening, sports and recreation, and sociocultural activities.

As a result, South Africa's world-class stadiums designed for the 2010 FIFA World Cup are white elephants largely because development in football skills at school has been neglected. In the past, famous skilful players, such as Jomo Sono, Kaiser Motaung, and, later, Teenage Dladla and many others, were spotted at schools and grew to become legends, with football becoming their chosen profession and livelihood. Today they are living their dream. This was during the time when Wednesday afternoons and Saturdays in schools were set aside for sports and recreation. Athletics also found expression in school curricula. Morning assemblies fed learners spiritually and helped produce well-behaved utilitarian citizens.

Today's schoolchildren are confined in classrooms, and their natural talents are not exploited for development, and the result is that they have too much time at their disposal. Some of those being "overfed" pocket money experiment with drugs which consume them, and those who become caught up and addicted find criminal ways of feeding the habit by breaking into homes and becoming young criminals. Some are used by adults to commit crime, taking advantage of an act of Parliament (the Child Justice Act 75 of 2008) stating that children below seventeen years of age do not have the capacity to commit crime. This poses a challenge to communities to develop crime diversion services to divert children from crime using practical accredited programmes

Our education system should inform our approach to education in South Africa. If we fail to apply and adapt Piagetian-Vygotskian theories in positively socializing our young, they will be negatively socialized into lives of crime. Perhaps authorities should consider appointing South African educationists who are in the diaspora as well in key positions to influence education policy practically. One such educationist is Professor Jansen, former vice chancellor of the University of the Free State. If as South Africans we do not wake up to this reality and cease politicizing everything and blaming it on apartheid, we shall remain static and unproductive. We need new mindsets—even that of redefining who Africans are as a new set of Africans emerges in a South Africa that is home to all who live in her. The emerging Africans are not only in South Africa, but the rest of Africa as well.

About the Author

Moikwatlhai Benjamin Seitisho has never been exiled and has studied, lived, and taught History & English in formerly racially oppressive state schools in South Africa since 1980. He views the struggle for political freedom in South Africa over the years as haing inevitably disintegrated into a struggle against corruption. In his view, Solomon Mahlangu, Chris Hani and many others gave their lives only to water the tree of corruption that has destroyed the South African economy and has set in a struggle for economic freedom. This book chronicles the history of a nation torn asunder by a political theory (apartheid) that diversified an otherwise unitary state. Unlike other Southern African countries Lesotho, Swaziland and Botswana, South Africa is a multi-cultural state that needs an honest and truthful forgiveness and reconciliation to take its people forward into an economic freedom enjoyed by all and sundry. The book's synoptic nature is focused on that *vision*. It is a *vision* aimed at seeing corruption, which steals from the poor, disintegrating and a journey beginning to unite the people and build a corruption free economy.

Journey with the author through this book, share his thoughts and together build a new South African rainbow nation...

Printed in the United States
By Bookmasters